ROUTLEDGE LIBRARY EDITIONS: LEISURE STUDIES

Volume 11

LEISURE AND THE FUTURE

A. J. (Tony) Veal is Adjunct Professor in the Business School, University of Technology, Sydney. He is past president of the UK Leisure Studies Association and of the Australian and New Zealand Association for Leisure Studies. His latest book, *Whatever Happened to the Leisure Society?* was published by Routledge in 2018.

LEISURE AND THE FUTURE

A. J. VEAL

LONDON AND NEW YORK

First published in 1987 by Allen & Unwin (Publishers) Ltd

This edition first published in 2019
by Routledge
2 Park Square, Milton Park, Abingdon, Oxon OX14 4RN

and by Routledge
52 Vanderbilt Avenue, New York, NY 10017

Routledge is an imprint of the Taylor & Francis Group, an informa business

© 1987 A. J. Veal

All rights reserved. No part of this book may be reprinted or reproduced or utilised in any form or by any electronic, mechanical, or other means, now known or hereafter invented, including photocopying and recording, or in any information storage or retrieval system, without permission in writing from the publishers.

Trademark notice: Product or corporate names may be trademarks or registered trademarks, and are used only for identification and explanation without intent to infringe.

British Library Cataloguing in Publication Data
A catalogue record for this book is available from the British Library

ISBN: 978-0-367-11036-9 (Set)
ISBN: 978-0-429-24268-7 (Set) (ebk)
ISBN: 978-0-367-13737-3 (Volume 11) (hbk)
ISBN: 978-0-367-13738-0 (Volume 11) (pbk)
ISBN: 978-0-429-02837-3 (Volume 11) (ebk)

Publisher's Note
The publisher has gone to great lengths to ensure the quality of this reprint but points out that some imperfections in the original copies may be apparent.

Disclaimer
The publisher has made every effort to trace copyright holders and would welcome correspondence from those they have been unable to trace.

Leisure and the Future

A. J. Veal

London
ALLEN & UNWIN
Boston   Sydney   Wellington

© A. J. Veal, 1987
This book is copyright under the Berne Convention.
No reproduction without permission. All rights reserved.

Allen & Unwin (Publishers) Ltd,
40 Museum Street, London, WC1A 1LU, UK

Allen & Unwin (Publishers) Ltd,
Park Lane, Hemel Hempstead, Herts, HP2 4TE, UK

Allen & Unwin, Inc.,
8 Winchester Place, Winchester, Mass. 01890, USA

Allen & Unwin (Australia) Ltd,
8 Napier Street, North Sydney, NSW 2060, Australia

Allen & Unwin NZ Ltd,
60 Cambridge Terrace, Wellington, NZ

First published in 1987

British Library Cataloguing in Publication Data

Veal, A. J.
  Leisure and the future.
(Leisure and recreation studies; 4)
1. Leisure – Social aspects – Great Britain
I. Title II. Series
306'.48'0941   GV75
ISBN 0-04-790006-7
ISBN 0-04-790007-5 Pbk

Library of Congress Cataloging-in-Publication Data

Veal, Anthony James.
  Leisure and the future.
(Leisure and recreation studies; 4)
Bibliography: p.
Includes index.
1. Leisure – Great Britain. 2. Social prediction –
Great Britain. I. Title. II. Series
GV75.V398   1987   790'.0941   86-22191
ISBN 0-04-790006-7 (alk. paper)
ISBN 0-04-790007-5 (pbk.)

Set in 10 on 11 point Bembo by Computape (Pickering) Ltd.
and printed in Great Britain by Billings and Sons Ltd.
London and Worcester

Contents

	Preface	*page* ix
1	Questions of Leisure, Values and Economics	1
2	Back to the Future: Philosophers, Visionaries and Utopians	22
3	The Post-Industrial Society: An Appraisal	46
4	The Shortage of Work I: Changing Attitudes	63
5	The Shortage of Work II: Sharing the Work Around	85
6	Political Dimensions	111
7	The Leisure Forecasting Tradition	125
8	Leisure Providers and their Futures	157
9	Concluding Thoughts	176
	Bibliography	180
	Author Index	193
	Subject Index	197

Preface

The origins of this book lie in a small grant awarded to me in the early 1970s by the then Social Science Research Council (SSRC) to conduct a fairly mechanical 'number crunching' exercise to see if I could produce forecasts of leisure participation for Britain (Veal, 1976, 1979, 1980). Having ventured into 'leisure forecasting' I soon discovered two things; first that there is a great deal more to forecasting than number crunching, and secondly that a concern for and interest in the potential role of leisure in future society is by no means novel. So in addition to conducting the promised quantitative work for the SSRC project I also found myself exploring the history of ideas about the future of leisure. The initial research was started in the context of growth in the UK economy and population, but as the 1970s drew to a close recession and unemployment and the 'micro-electronics revolution' pushed to the fore a very different set of concerns about the future, all of which had to be taken into account in writing a book on leisure and the future. So great has been the task of monitoring and keeping up with the deluge of written material on work, leisure and the future which has appeared in the last five years, that I have often thought that there was a danger of the future arriving before the book was finished.

The aim of the book is not to advocate one particular point of view. I have attempted to review and reflect the state of the art and to illustrate that whenever there is a firmly held, even dogmatic, view about the way the future will develop a contrary view can be found which is believed just as firmly and can be argued just as convincingly. The aim of the book is therefore to be a guide and a source rather than a polemic. If there is a message in the book it is that although we cannot know what the future will be we should at least be actively concerned about it.

I should like to acknowledge the support of the Social Science Research Council for the initial grant which launched my interest in the field of futures research and the Countryside Recreation Research Advisory Group and the Office of Population Censuses and Surveys Social Survey Division who afforded me access to the General Household Survey data. I am grateful to my colleagues, initially at the Centre for Urban and Regional Studies at Birmingham University and later at the Polytechnic of North London, and more widely in the Leisure Studies Association, for providing the intellectual companionship and support which is necessary if one is to survive the potentially lonely activity of research. Finally I would like to thank Stanley Parker and Sarah Gregory who have provided the vital encouragement and gentle harassment necessary to ensure that I completed the book.

AJV
London
February 1986

1
Questions of Leisure, Values and Economics

For the vast majority of the world's inhabitants leisure has not been a significant phenomenon, let alone a problem, in any age except the present one. Minorities such as members of royal or aristocratic families and the merely wealthy have frequently enjoyed lives of leisure; they have been faced with decisions about what to do with their leisure time. For the mass of the people it might be said that religious observances have provided a form of leisure, designating certain periods, such as the sabbath and saints' days, as non-working time and providing spectacle and entertainment and, incidentally, channelling and controlling potentially disruptive leisure-time energies. Anthropological research suggests that some primitive societies, particularly those in favourable climates such as the Pacific, have enjoyed substantial leisure time and there is the historical quirk of certain periods in the history of Rome when its citizens are said to have enjoyed no less than 175 days' holiday a year (Mercer, 1980, p. 182). But this has not been the general pattern in Western society. When periods of peace, good harvests and benevolent rulers coincided life may have been less of a struggle, but for most of the people for most of the time their lot has been one of unremitting toil. It is no coincidence that the most numerous group in any society is referred to as the working class.

A Leisure Society?

In the latter part of the twentieth century this has begun to change. Nevertheless it is no longer fashionable to speak of the dawning of a 'leisure society'. Some have referred to such a notion as a 'chimera', a 'nonsense' and a 'mega-fantasy' (Ecology Party, 1981, p. 18; Porritt, 1984, p. 68) and writers who acknowledged such a possibility in the early 1970s now take a very different view (Roberts, 1971, 1978, p. 148). But compared with the lives of some of our forebears the lives we lead now could be described as lives of leisure.

In the nineteenth century retirement as it is experienced today was virtually unknown, given the low level of life-expectancy. Paid holidays were certainly unknown. Working weeks of seventy hours or more were common, whereas many full-time workers today work hardly more than half that number of hours. In Blaenavon in South Wales early steelworks dating from the eighteenth and early nineteenth centuries are being restored as a tourist attraction. A guide to the site published by the local Museum Trust reports that in 1841 the manager of the works, in evidence to the Children's Employment Commission, stated that he employed thirty-seven children aged from 7 to 14 at the furnaces; the boys worked seventy-two hours a week, 'in some heat in the summertime, and sometimes get burned, but not very bad'. The working week in the UK has declined by over 20 per cent since the beginning of the century (Young and Willmott, 1973, p. 132); annual holiday entitlements have increased from one week to at least four weeks since the 1950s; young people spend longer in full-time education which means that they have more leisure time than they would if they were at work; retirement pensions have been introduced and the life-span has increased, giving a considerable period of leisure time at the end of most people's lives. All these factors and others have resulted in an increase of some 70 per cent since the beginning of the century in the amount of non-work time available to the average male worker during his lifetime. Women who go out to work are the group with the least leisure time in contemporary society, and since the bulk of domestic and child-care work still falls to them, such leisure as they have is less clear-cut than that of most men. Nevertheless, changes in child-bearing patterns, labour-saving household appliances and materials and increased life-expectancy have dramatically increased women's leisure time compared with that of women three-quarters of a century ago. As demonstrated later in this chapter, some 30 per cent of a man's total lifetime can be described as leisure time and some 27 per cent of a woman's.

The leisure phenomenon can be measured not only in terms of time availability but also in terms of activities engaged in, that is, how people spend their leisure time. It can also be measured in terms of consumer expenditure, that is, the extent to which people spend their money on leisure goods and services. The trends are unmistakable. Growth in participation in virtually all leisure activities since the Second World War has been dramatic, despite some notable exceptions such as the decline in cinema attendances. While leisure expenditure has not grown substantially as a proportion of consumer expenditure in Britain, it is nevertheless estimated to account for almost 30 per cent of all consumer expenditure (Martin and Mason, 1979). It is estimated that more than a million people work directly in the leisure industries in Britain (Corley, 1982; Chairmen's Policy Group, 1982, p. 83) and that this is growing at 50,000 a year (Morrel, 1982). In short, while work and 'bread and butter' issues dominate politics and public life, leisure has become a highly significant element of people's lives and of the economies of advanced industrial nations. In comparison with previous ages, we live in what is virtually a 'society of leisure'.

Should we Study Leisure?

Viewing society in these terms and celebrating the trend towards a leisure society might be open to criticism on a number of counts. First, it could be argued that it is premature to place increasing emphasis on leisure in a society with inadequate health and welfare services, decaying inner cities and substantial minorities living in relative poverty. Secondly, on a world scale, it is surely immoral for the advanced economies to be producing leisure goods and services on an increasing scale while a substantial proportion of the world's population is desperately short of food and basic goods and services. Thirdly, it could be argued that, while it may be morally justifiable to be exhausting the earth's natural resources to produce 'necessities', it is surely indefensible to do so to sustain a mass-consumption 'leisure society'. Finally, the 'leisure society' perspective appears to ignore the economic crisis of the 1980s and the consequent mass unemployment currently being experienced in many of the advanced industrial economies.

Such criticisms seem entirely reasonable. But even if they were accepted politically in the advanced industrial societies and if measures were put in hand to meet them, leisure would not go away. If anything it could become even more significant. Before looking at these arguments in detail we should look more closely at the relationship between leisure, work and economic growth.

Leisure, Work and Economic Growth

At the heart of the modern leisure phenomenon is the increased productivity of the worker. In order to consider possibilities for the future it is necessary to understand the relationships between work, productivity, economic output, prosperity and leisure and to understand that such relationships are dynamic, not static. As a result of technological change and the accumulation of capital in advanced industrial societies, one worker today, in a shorter working day, produces many times the quantity of goods, and in many cases services, that workers of fifty or a hundred years ago produced in a working day. If productivity – output per hour worked – increases by only 2 per cent a year then the amount of goods and services which can be produced increases by 50 per cent after twenty years and doubles after thirty-five years. If the rate of increase in productivity is as much as 4 per cent a year then these periods fall to ten and seventeen years respectively. Such increases in productivity and output, and the resultant increase in material prosperity, have been a feature of the advanced industrial economies over the last 200 years and particularly over the last forty. In Britain (and to some extent the USA) the growth in productivity in the post-Second World War period has been slower than in many other industrial countries. The general despondency which this has produced among economic and political commentators has tended to eclipse the fact that the period up until the early 1980s was a period of unprecedented growth in prosperity.

As well as bringing increased material prosperity, increased productivity has also facilitated increases in leisure time. All the increase in productivity has not been used to increase production of material goods and services. Some of it has been used to:

(1) reduce the length of the working week,
(2) increase holiday entitlements,
(3) raise the school-leaving age and increase further and higher education opportunities,
(4) introduce retirement pensions and opportunities for earlier retirement.

It has been estimated that one-fifth of the fruits of increased productivity since the beginning of the twentieth century have been absorbed by reductions in working hours while four-fifths have been devoted to increasing production (Myerscough, 1974, p. 9). This can however vary: Levitan and Belous (1977, p. 21) point out that in the 1970s, in a period of high inflation, in America less than one-tenth of the fruits of increased productivity were being allocated to reducing working hours. But Best and his colleagues (1979) found from a survey, that American workers' preferences were moving in favour of more free time, especially if this was in the form of extended periods away from work, such as longer weekends or holidays (see also Zuzanek, 1974).

The quantity of leisure time currently available can therefore be seen as the result of the technological and economic changes of the last 200 years. But the balance between work, leisure and output could have been different: we could have been working longer hours and have been materially more wealthy; or we could have been working fewer hours, enjoying more leisure, but with less material wealth. How or why the particular situation we now experience came about is not clear. The extent to which reductions in working hours and increases in holiday entitlements arise from a conscious preference of workers for more leisure and home life rather than more pay, or are simply an almost accidental by-product of the collective bargaining process, is debatable. Legislation played a small part in reducing working hours for some groups in the nineteenth century and in introducing holidays with pay, but has not played a prominent role in these matters in Britain in the twentieth century. The results of this process could have been very different: there is after all considerable variation among developed countries in the length of the working week and the amount of holiday entitlement. For example Americans tend to have less holiday time than the British while the Germans have a longer working week (Clemitson and Rodgers, 1981, p. 69). The important point to bear in mind is that there is a trade-off between work-time, income and leisure. In periods of economic growth it is possible to enjoy increased leisure and increased real incomes.

Leisure and Poverty

To return to the criticisms advanced earlier: the first was that it is wrong for the bulk of the community to be increasing leisure time and leisure consumption while social services are neglected and while substantial minorities remain in poverty. The second criticism made a similar point on a world scale: that rich countries should not be developing leisure and leisure industries while the rest of the world starves or lives in poverty. There are two alternative political and economic views on how poverty should be eliminated in the modern, capitalist, world, whether it be the poverty of individuals within the wealthy nations or the poverty of whole nations. One view is that the rich should aid the poor in cash or kind – that there should be a direct transfer of resources. The alternative view is that such transfers are not of lasting value and undermine the morale of the recipients, and that the better strategy is for the rich to concentrate their efforts on becoming even more prosperous, so that the poor will benefit from the general prosperity and demand for goods and work which they generate: the 'trickle down' effect. This approach can of course be seen as an excuse for doing nothing.

Our purpose here is not to consider the merits of the opposing views but to examine their implications for leisure. In the first scenario, money raised in taxes from the well-off would be transferred to the poor who would buy the goods and services they are short of, or those goods and services would be bought on their behalf. Thus there would be a change in the rich economy from producing the luxury, including leisure, goods and services demanded by the well-off towards production of the more basic requirements of the poor. This, of course, already happens to a certain extent, both within and between countries: the argument is that it should be increased. We have already noted that leisure expenditure accounts for nearly 30 per cent of all consumer expenditure in the advanced industrial economies. If the effect of the measures to transfer incomes were only to reduce this to 25 per cent some £15 billion per annum would be released in Britain for redistribution, roughly doubling the current social welfare budget or, alternatively, multiplying the foreign aid budget many times over. In other words leisure is now such big business that even a substantial shift in resources in absolute terms would not make a great deal of difference to its relative position in the economy: in the above scenario leisure would still constitute a quarter of consumer expenditure. And, of course, if economic growth were to be maintained at a modest say 2 per cent per annum, then the resultant general increase in production would restore the position of leisure to its former absolute state in about three or four years.

The second view – that the rich should concentrate on getting richer – is based on the belief that the sort of taxation and transfer of resources from rich to poor discussed above distorts the working of the market economy and produces disincentives to work and therefore reduces potential wealth production for both the rich and the poor. Much better, it is argued, for the economy to be left to develop and expand of its own accord so that higher paid jobs are created for the unemployed or less well-off and expanded markets are created for the products of the Third World. In this scenario leisure continues to play a significant and growing role. Many of the growth industries in the advanced industrial economies are, and will continue to be, in the leisure sector, including such industries as tourism and home audio-visual entertainment equipment. Such a view is associated with the right in politics and it is perhaps significant in this context that the British Prime Minister recently drew attention to the growing importance of the leisure industries as a source of economic growth (Thatcher, 1983).

Resources and Values

In the case of the 'planet earth' criticism – that consuming the earth's resources for leisure purposes is unjustified – making changes in any of the industrial economies to meet this criticism could increase the significance of leisure rather than reduce it. One implication of the argument is that material production should not expand beyond current levels – except for the production of 'necessities'. A consequence of this is that much of any increase in productivity brought about by technological change or more efficient working practices should in future be entirely devoted to reducing working time rather than increasing output – a move which seems most unlikely in capitalist economies whose whole basis is the accumulation and expansion of wealth. Nevertheless if this were to happen it would increase the significance of leisure, not as a sector of the economy but in terms of time available to the individual.

A further implication of this position is that consumption of non-renewable resources, particularly energy, should be reduced, either by substituting renewable resources such as solar or wave power, or by substituting human energy and becoming more self-sufficient. In the case of the use of more renewable energy resources there is no reason to suppose that this would have any noticeable effects on the balance between work and leisure. In the case of self-sufficiency it is likely that there would be more work and less leisure, but this is by no means certain. The life-styles which people might choose to adopt in conditions of greater autonomy and self-sufficiency could well involve a greater sense of leisure than is currently enjoyed by the average industrial or service worker. In fact the blurring of the distinction between work and leisure which is said to have characterized pre-industrial societies could return.

The 'Green' perspective raises a fundamental issue concerning industrial societies, and capitalist ones in particular. The question is, do people have an insatiable appetite for material goods or will they at some stage say 'enough is enough'? Is the goal of increasing material prosperity one which will always be there or is there some point at which success will be judged to have been achieved? As Stafan Linder (1970) put it: 'will we reach a consumption maximum?' If such a point were to be reached then either all of any further increases in productivity could be transformed into increased leisure time, or the economic system could turn its attention to expanding production of services, many of which would be leisure services, since this would be the only way to expand. Some would argue that capitalism would never allow this situation to arise, that it will always find new products or new versions of old products to keep the workers working, the consumers consuming and the profits flowing. The experience of the United States as the most materially prosperous nation would suggest either that this strategy can be successfully pursued, or that people's appetite for material goods is indeed virtually insatiable.

Leisure and Unemployment

But what of the recession and mass unemployment? Surely this must place in doubt any prospect of a truly leisured society. One of the difficulties in addressing this issue is that there is no agreement on the nature of the problem, let alone its solution. One view is that high unemployment is a temporary result of an, admittedly severe, economic recession coupled with some structural change, but that appropriate economic management will restore full employment and economic growth. Although they disagree about the nature of the 'appropriate economic management' measures, this is the position of the major political parties in Britain, and most of the governments of the West. An opposing view, put forward by an increasing number of commentators, is that even if economic growth could be restored to the levels of the 1960s unemployment would remain a chronic problem because new technology, structural changes in industry and world-wide shifts in manufacturing activity are displacing jobs in the Western economies faster than new jobs can be created, and therefore exceptional measures are needed to deal directly with the problem of surplus labour.

Again our purpose here is not to determine which position is correct but to consider their respective implications for leisure. If the 'business as usual' view is correct then there can be no doubt about the continued importance of leisure. Leisure is a £55 billion a year industry in Britain and in the context of general economic growth would be one of the fastest growing sectors. Workers would continue to trade-off some of their potential increased income for reduced working hours and increased holidays. While all reductions in work time are not automatically translated into leisure activity, this process would nevertheless lead to some increase in leisure time, as has been seen in past periods of economic growth. In this rosy scenario the newly employed would also boost the leisure industries with their enhanced incomes and would be able to participate in leisure activities from which they were previously excluded through lack of resources.

Those who believe that the second view is correct, that high unemployment is, or is threatening to become, endemic, have put forward a wide range of proposals to counteract this tendency. These include action to shorten the working week, increase holiday entitlements, provide sabbaticals and extended education for all, and lower the retirement age. All these measures, which are fully discussed in Chapter 5, are designed to share the available work more equitably, thereby reducing or eliminating unemployment. Far from leisure being irrelevant in this situation, nearly all the proposals have significant leisure implications of one sort or another. In fact some have suggested that it is society's failure to take leisure seriously, its failure to educate for leisure and its tendency to cling to an outmoded 'work ethic' which is contributing to the failure to accept and implement these measures.

The British trade unionists Clive Jenkins and Barrie Sherman were among the first, and the most forceful, to advance the thesis that unless something was done to avoid it unemployment would climb inexorably upwards, regardless of the level of economic growth. But in their view leisure is a key element in any solution to the problem. In their book, *The Collapse of Work*, they say:

> It is time for action, not words: a time for policy implementation, not electoral promises. The action must cover two separate things: preparations for the ever-increasing unemployment levels and the setting up of mechanisms to ensure that the collapse of work is transmuted into a policy for leisure.
> (Jenkins and Sherman, 1979, p. 174)

Thus to focus on leisure and its future at this particular point in time is by no means to ignore the serious problems of unemployment and economic disruption currently being faced across the world. In fact, it is hoped that an in-depth look at this facet of the problem, which is often discussed in a very shallow and ill-informed manner, will aid discussion of these serious problems.

Inevitably many of the futures explored in this book are generally optimistic. No one can deny that the possibility exists that the debate about leisure could be rendered irrelevant by crises and catastrophes, by stagnation and decline brought about by economic mismanagement or misfortune, or by natural disasters, or war. But these possibilities should not preclude discussion of other possibilities: indeed it could be argued that it is only by discussing the full range of possible futures that mechanisms to avoid some of the disasters might be found.

The Context

This book has been written in the context of a debate about the changing nature of industrial society and the place of work and leisure in society. In recent years there has been a spate of publications discussing these issues, including Jenkins and Sherman's *Collapse of Work*, already referred to, and their follow-up work *The Leisure Shock* (1981). Others include Clemitson and Rodgers's *A Life to Live* (1981), *The Shattered Dream*, based on a television series (Allen et al., 1981), *World Out of Work* by Merritt (1982), *Work in Crisis* by Clarke (1982), Martin and Mason's *Leisure and Work – the Choices for 1991 and 2001* (1981), a number of conference reports from the Leisure Studies Association (Cherry and Travis, 1980; TRRU, 1982; Veal et al., 1982; Glyptis, 1983), a contribution from Australia in the form of Barry Jones's *Sleepers Wake!* (1982), Stonier's *The Wealth of Information* (1983), Handy's

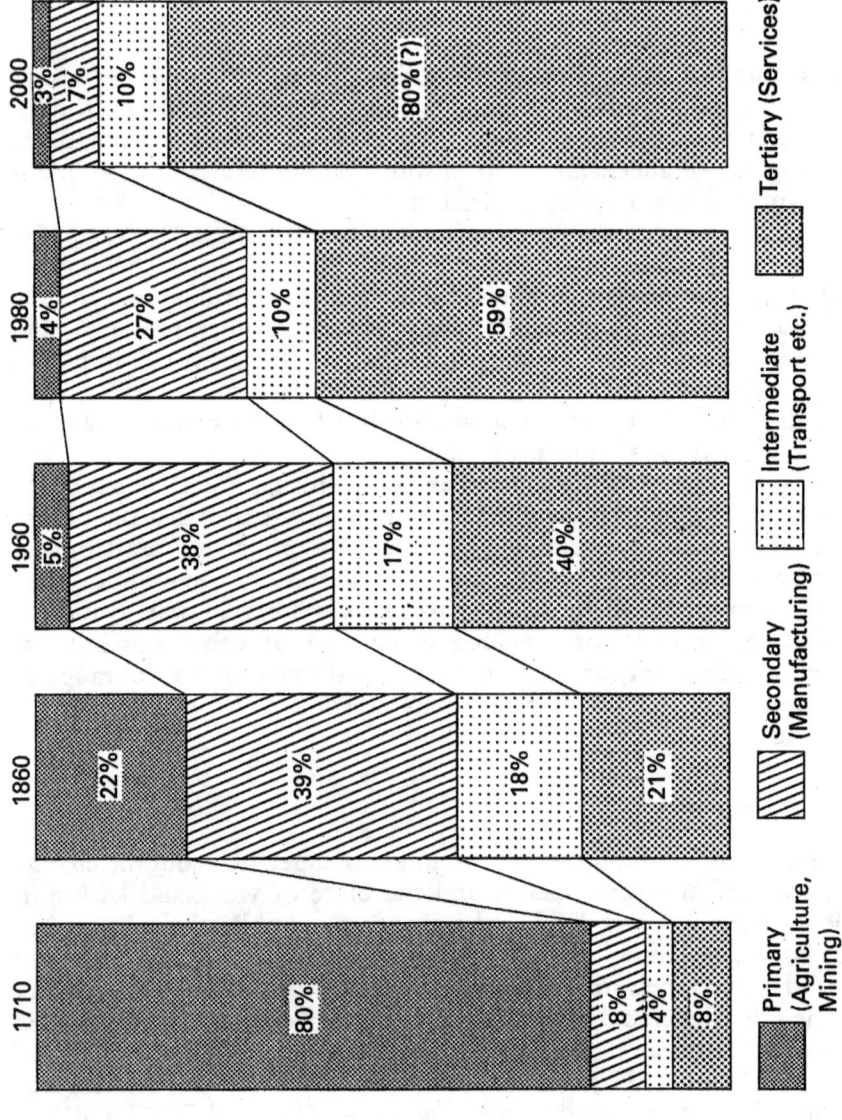

Figure 1.1 The changing structure of the workforce in Britain.

The Future of Work (1984) and *Future Work* by Robertson (1985). Curiously, no American title appears in this list – either this is not an issue in the United States or the relevant publications have not reached European shores. America's latest 'futures' bestseller, *Megatrends* by John Naisbitt (1984) virtually ignores the subject of leisure. This plethora of literature on work and leisure is supplemented by an even greater volume of material on microelectronic technology, which deals to varying extents with the social, including the leisure, consequences (e.g. Barron and Curnow, 1979; Forester, 1980; Large, 1980; Laurie, 1980; Nora and Minc, 1980).

One thing which most of these works have in common is the view that the advanced industrial economies are facing significant economic change and that the 'business as usual' perspective is inadequate. In particular, the demand for labour per unit of output is falling rapidly. Until recently it was primarily manufacturing industry which was affected, but since the 1950s it has been the service industries which have been absorbing labour displaced from the increasingly mechanized and automated agricultural and manufacturing sectors of the economy. The decline in manufacturing employment is, it is believed, comparable to the decline in agricultural employment which accompanies the process of industrialization. Figure 1.1 charts the changing sectoral structure of employment in Britain since the eighteenth century when 80 per cent of the workforce was in agriculture. At present only 3 per cent work in agriculture and still provide half of the country's food needs. In the United States a similar proportion not only provides all the country's food needs but a substantial surplus for export as well. It appears that manufacturing is moving in this direction. Stonier (1983, p. 122) estimates that early in the next century 10 per cent of the workforce will be capable of providing all our material needs. Figure 1.1 therefore illustrates the dilemma: assuming that a certain proportion of the workforce continues to work in intermediate sectors like public utilities, how will the remaining 80 per cent be occupied? Given that large sections of service employment are also under threat from automation, are the service industries, including leisure, capable of expanding to create this scale of employment? If not, will there be a permanent and increasing pool of unemployed? Or will the solution be to reduce the workforce by various means to fit the work available?

The purpose of this book is to explore the implications for leisure of these various scenarios, particularly the last. But first it is appropriate to give some consideration to the scale and nature of the leisure phenomenon as it exists at present.

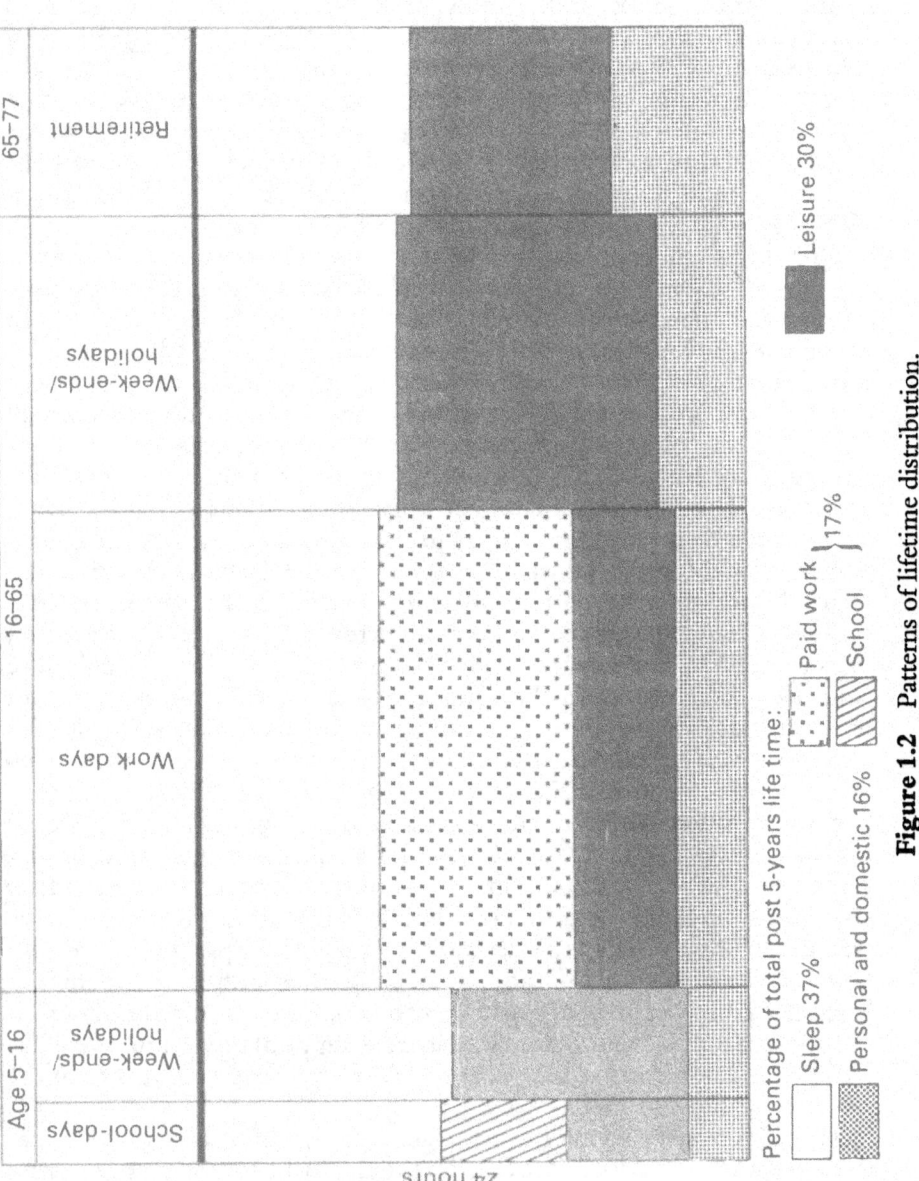

Figure 1.2 Patterns of lifetime distribution. Case A: Male manual worker pattern.

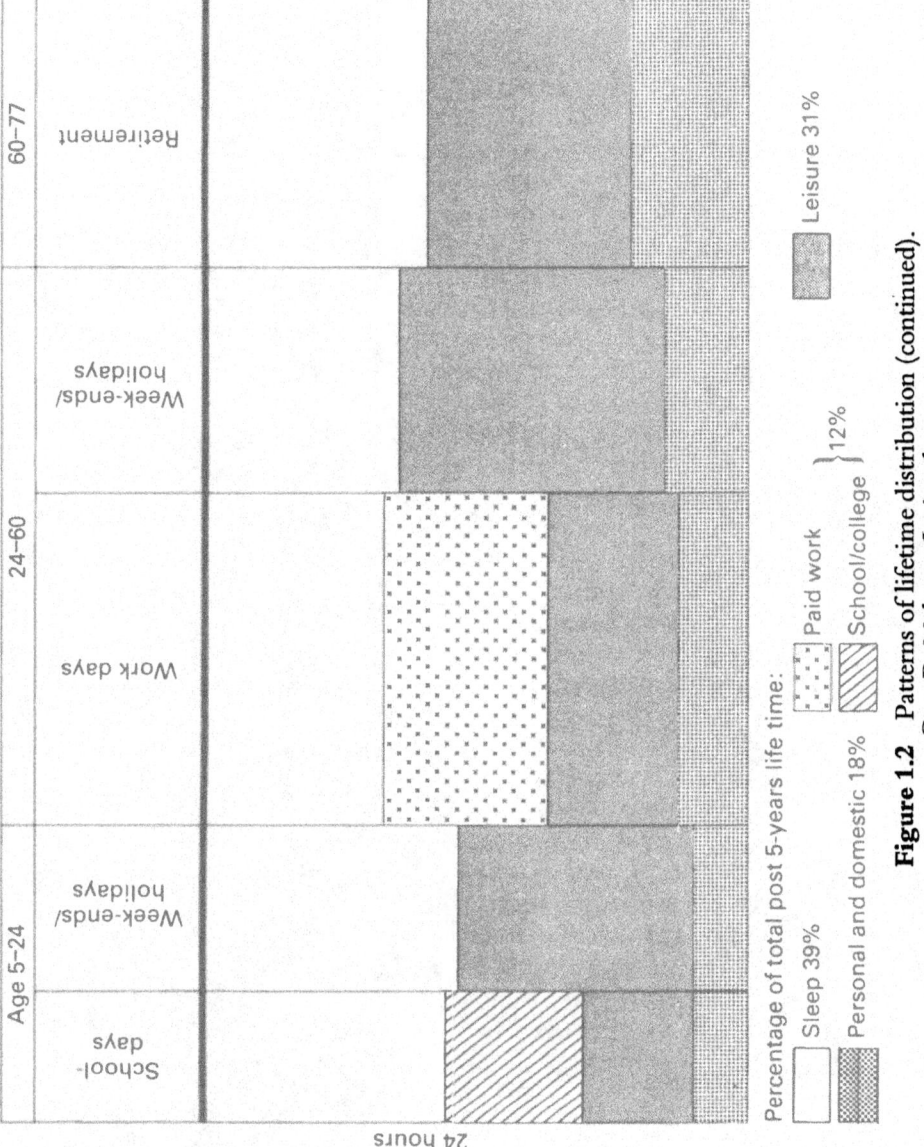

Figure 1.2 Patterns of lifetime distribution (continued). Case B: Male professional pattern.

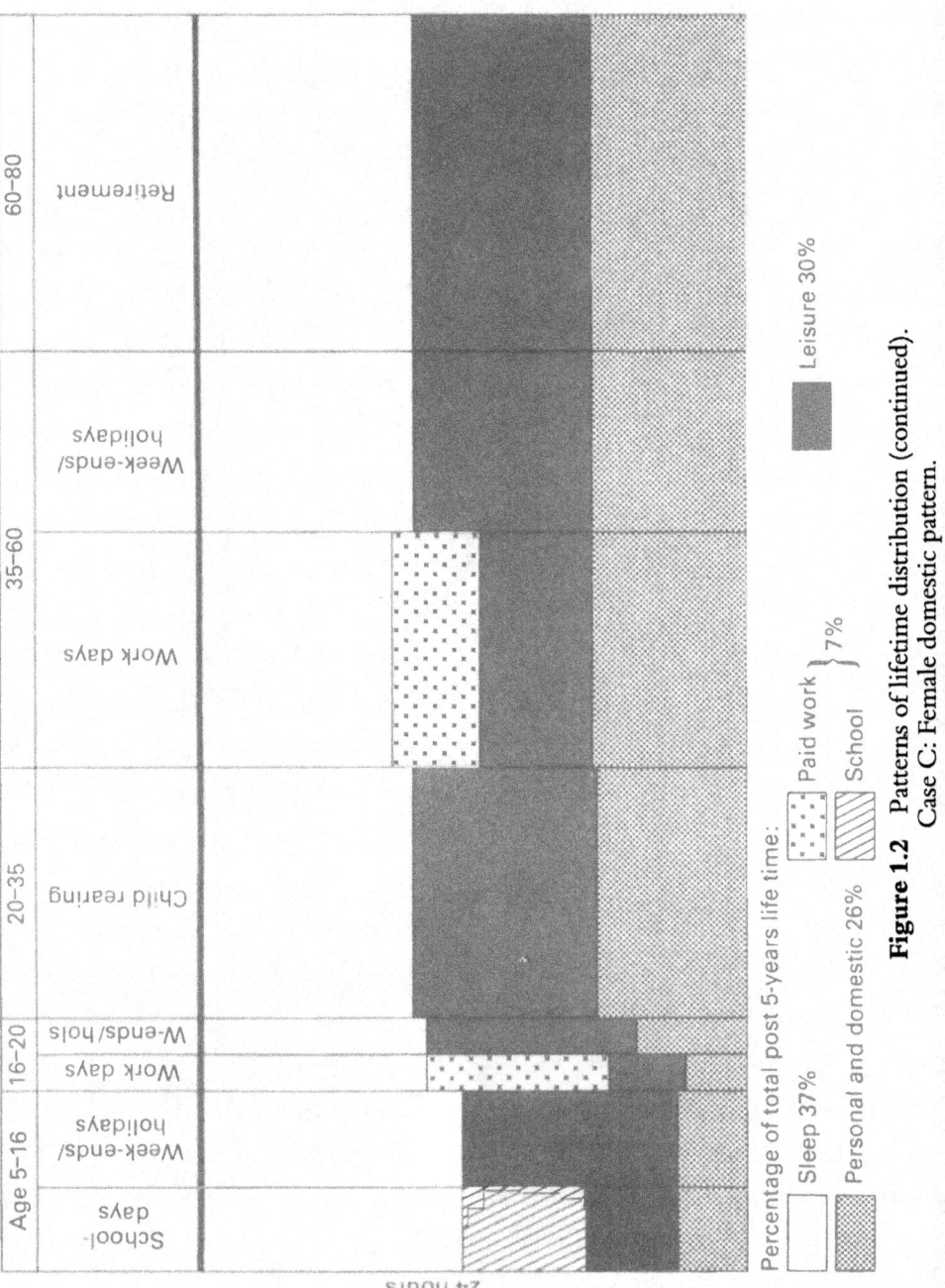

Figure 1.2 Patterns of lifetime distribution (continued). Case C: Female domestic pattern.

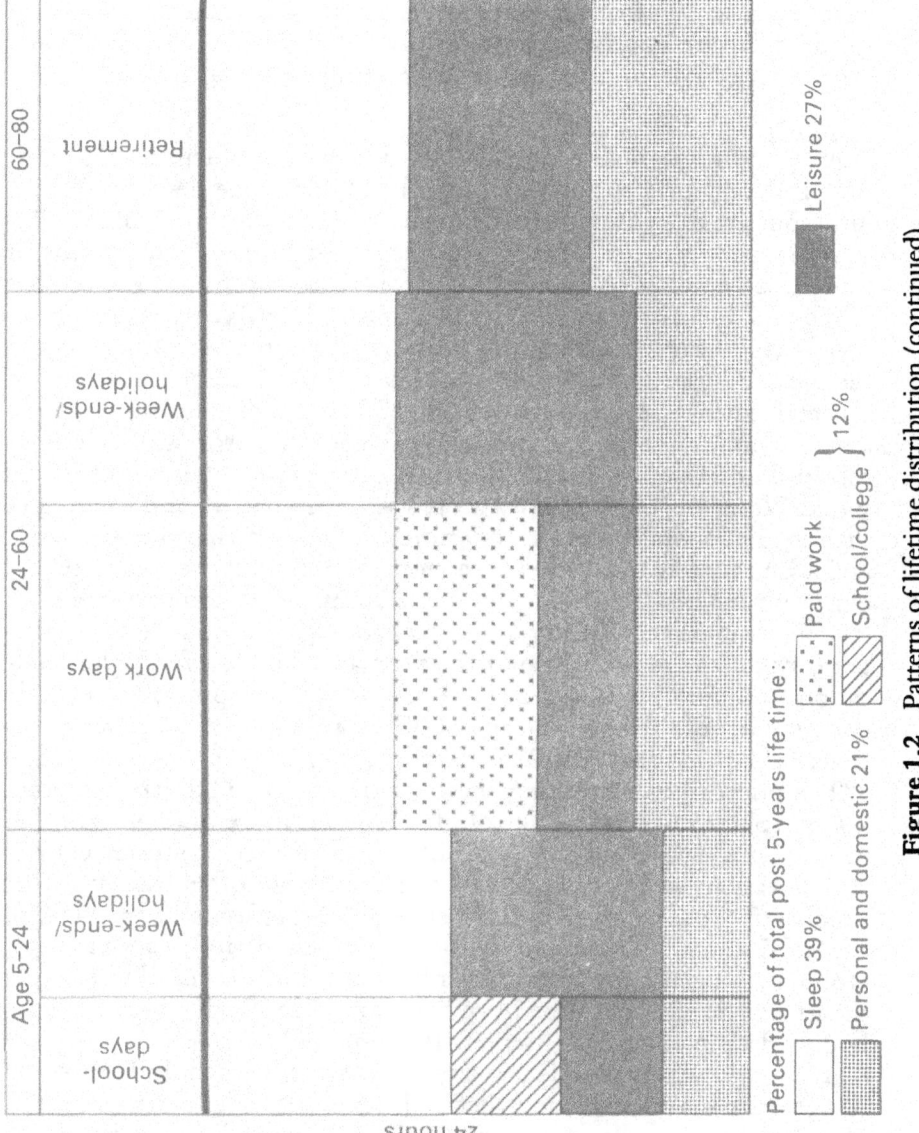

Figure 1.2 Patterns of lifetime distribution (continued). Case D: Female professional pattern.

Leisure Today

It has already been suggested that the scale of leisure can be considered in three ways: the amount of leisure time available, the activities engaged in during that time, and the amount or distribution of money spent on leisure goods and services. In this section we consider these three perspectives in turn, focusing on the situation in Britain.

Leisure Time

Figure 1.2 shows the life-time distribution pattern of leisure and work time for four different types of individual. They are developed from 'time-budget diary' research conducted in Britain for the BBC (1978), in which people recorded their activities in diaries for a fixed period of time. Case A refers to a man who leaves school at the age of 16, goes into manual work, works an eight-hour day, five-day week and forty-seven-week year throughout his working life, retires at 65 and lives to the age of 77. From the age of five years until death some 15 per cent of his total time is spent in paid work and 30 per cent in leisure. Case B is a man who receives higher education, works in a profession and lives to 77; some 31 per cent of his time is leisure and only 9 per cent is paid work. Women typically have a more varied life-pattern and live longer than men. Generally they spend more of their time in domestic work and less in paid work. Case C is a woman who leaves school at 16 and experiences periods of full-time and part-time work and periods out of the labour market, resulting in 30 per cent of her time as leisure and 5 per cent as paid work. Case D is a woman who receives higher education and follows a similar life-pattern to her professional male counterpart, but lives to the age of 80, as a result she has 27% leisure time, 12% paid work and 21% domestic work.

The purpose of presenting these diagrams is to illustrate the point that people from many walks of life spend far more of their total lifetime at leisure than in paid work. Even personal and domestic chores, such as eating, washing, child care and housework often takes up more time than paid work, for both sexes. A significant proportion of leisure time is concentrated in the retirement period, especially for women who generally retire earlier than men in Britain and live longer than men. Similar patterns have been found by Ruthven from time-budget data in Australia (Mercer, 1980, p. 186).

In a world where people identify themselves by the job they do and where there is a widespread belief in the existence of a 'work ethic', the idea that work time is only a small part of a typical life seems incongruous. In fact many might take issue with the implied 'residual' definition of leisure which assumes that all time not taken up in sleep, domestic work or paid work can be called 'leisure'. Much of this so-called leisure time is available only in small blocks, which limits its usefulness. Or it comes at times of the day or week or at times in people's lives when, because of tiredness from paid or domestic work or the infirmity of old age, they are not able to make great use of it. This may help to explain why much of the increase in leisure time achieved over the last twenty-five years by working people, has been in the form of increased holiday entitlements rather than reductions in the working week. A large block of leisure time is clearly viewed as more attractive than the equivalent in small packets. A 2 per cent reduction in the working year gives a whole week's holiday in a year, whereas a similar reduction in working time taken in the form of a reduction in the working week yields only forty-eight minutes per week.

What is clear from the figures is that some dramatic changes would be necessary to make any fundamental difference to the patterns illustrated. The professional man in Case B stays in full-time education some eight years longer than his manual counterpart, works an hour a day less and retires five years earlier and yet the proportion of his time spent on leisure is only 1 per cent higher. This is because all the reduction in work time does not get converted into leisure. The retired and those in full-time education tend to use some of their additional non-working time in extra sleep and, in the case of the retired, in additional domestic work. Nevertheless all the trends are tending to reduce the proportion of people's life-time spent at work and this will continue to have the effect of increasing leisure time.

The trend is being given an added spur by the concerted efforts of European trade unions, as a response to the high level of unemployment. The British Trades Union Congress (TUC) has launched a 'Campaign for Reduced Working Time' involving:

- a thirty-five-hour basic working week,
- six weeks annual holiday,
- choice of early retirement on adequate pensions,
- cuts in overtime working.

(Trades Union Congress, 1982)

Some successes are already claimed, with two-thirds of TUC members covered by agreements to reduce working hours below forty per week, and a number of 'pace-setting' agreements bringing working hours down to thirty-seven and thirty-five. Overtime working, however, tends to be endemic in Britain with those involved working an average ten hours overtime per week (Ardill, 1982).

Activity
Leisure activity in contemporary society is characterized largely by home-based activities such as watching television or gardening, and

Table 1.1 *Leisure Participation in England and Wales (% participation in four weeks prior to interview, 1980)*

Activities	Adults aged 16+
Outdoor physical activities	38.0
Including: Walking (2 miles +)	22.8
Swimming in sea	6.1
Golf	3.1
Fishing	3.1
Soccer	2.9
Tennis	2.3
Indoor activities	23.0
Including: Darts	7.9
Swimming in pools	7.9
Snooker/billiards	7.2
Squash	2.7
Badminton	2.5
Table tennis	2.4
Watching sport (live)	10.0
Including: Soccer	5.0
Cricket	1.5
Motor sports	1.3
Horse events	1.3
Visiting the seaside	15.5
Visiting the countryside (not for any of above activities)	6.7
Visiting historic buildings	17.0
Visiting museums and galleries	5.2
Visiting exhibitions	3.5
Visiting zoos	3.1
Going to cinema	10.8
Going to theatre	5.2
Dancing	15.1
Going out for drink or meal	68.2
Bingo	8.3
Home-based: Gardening	59.1
Do-it-yourself	39.9
Watching TV	98.1
Reading book	57.4
Visiting friends/relatives	92.1

Source: General Household Survey, conducted by the Office of Population Censuses and Surveys (see Veal, 1984). The survey covers over 100 separate activities; the above list is an illustrative selection of the most popular.

social activities such as visiting friends and relatives in their homes, or going out to the pub or for a meal. This pattern is illustrated in Table 1.1 which reproduces some results from the government General Household Survey. The table demonstrates that home and family are the focus of most people's leisure, rather than publicly or commercially provided leisure activities outside the home. In particular, sport and the arts, those important planks of publicly provided and supported leisure, are minority activities. This pattern of leisure participation is the base from which forecasts of leisure activity, of the sort discussed in Chapter 7, have to be considered. It means that some activities, such as individual sports, can grow rapidly over a period of years and still only involve 1 or 2 per cent of the population. On the other hand, even 1 per cent of the adult population of England and Wales amounts to almost 400,000 people.

Expenditure and Employment
The third way of looking at the scope and dimensions of leisure is through the patterns of consumer expenditure on leisure goods and services. We have already noted that leisure accounts for between a quarter and a third of all consumer expenditure in Britain, making it an industry worth some £55 billion a year. These figures are detailed in Table 1.2. The major item is alcoholic drink, which represents 7p in the pound of all consumer expenditure and almost a quarter of the 'leisure pound'. While some items in the table, such as books or DIY, may include non-leisure items there are also leisure expenditure items which are not included, such as transport costs and leisure clothing. Short-term and medium-term forecasts of these expenditure items are produced regularly for the industry by such organizations as Leisure Consultants and the Henley Centre for Forecasting, and their activities are described in more detail in Chapter 7.

A further way of viewing leisure as an industry or economic activity is in terms of the employment which it generates, details of which are presented in Table 1.3. As with the expenditure figures these data are incomplete. The figure of 1.2 million employees excludes those employed in the manufacture of leisure goods and in leisure transport. As we have already noted, it has been estimated that employment in the leisure and tourism industries will grow at around 50,000 jobs per annum during the 1980s (Morrel, 1982).

So we can see that leisure is currently a significant element of people's lives, in terms of time, activity and expenditure and is a significant industry in terms of turnover and employment. The question is whether, and how, the scale and importance of this phenomenon will change in future.

Table 1.2 *Consumer Expenditure on Leisure in Britain*

Consumer item	£ million 1983–84	% share of all consumer expenditure	Share of 'leisure pound'
Alcoholic drink	14,547	7.43	24p
Arts and crafts	450	0.23	1p
Audio	1,128	0.58	2p
Books	640	0.33	1p
Cinema	123	0.06	—
DIY	2,400	1.23	4p
Eating out	8,064	4.13	14p
Foreign visitors	4,318	2.21	8p
Gambling (net)	2,097	1.07	4p
Gardening	758	0.39	1p
Holidays abroad	5,380	2.75	10p
Holidays in UK	2,819	1.44	5p
Home computers	501	0.26	1p
Magazines	454	0.23	1p
Musical instruments	229	0.12	—
Newspapers	1,561	0.80	3p
Pets	1,237	0.63	2p
Photography	363	0.19	1p
Records and tapes	675	0.35	1p
Sports	2,481	1.27	4p
Television	2,160	1.10	4p
Toys and games	1,029	0.53	2p
Video	1,440	0.74	3p
Total	54,854	28.37	100p

Table 1.3 *Employment in Leisure Industries in Britain*

Industry	Employees '000s 1980
Public houses	268
Sport and recreation	111
Betting and gambling	94
Clubs	117
Restaurants	184
Catering contractors	69
Hotels, etc.	271
Cinemas, theatre, radio, etc.	106
Total	1,220
% of total employment	5.6

Sources: Table 1.2 Henley Centre for Forecasting (1985); Table 1.3 Corley (1982).

Plan of the Book

The rest of the book consists of a series of essays each of which, to a certain extent, stands alone, but also form a coherent whole. Chapter 2 reviews the history of ideas about the future of leisure, including utopian and other writings which foreshadow many of the current concerns about work and leisure. Chapter 3 is an appraisal of the idea of the post-industrial society and the place of leisure within it. Chapters 4 and 5 take as their starting point the proposition that we are entering a period of chronic work shortage and examine the proposals that have been put forward to deal with that problem. Chapter 4 deals with attitudes towards work – the question of whether the existence of a 'work ethic' is a hindrance to change and whether 'education for leisure' is a necessary or realistic proposition. Chapter 5 looks at the many ideas which have been put forward for sharing the available work more equitably to avoid high unemployment, and examines their implications for leisure. In Chapter 6, political attitudes and policies towards leisure are examined. Chapter 7 is concerned with the academic tradition of leisure forecasting and its development over the last two decades; it is therefore more technical than the other chapters. Chapter 8 considers the future of the commercial and public sector leisure providers. And finally Chapter 9 presents some concluding thoughts in the form of a set of propositions about leisure and the future.

2

Back to the Future: Philosophers, Visionaries and Utopians

Down the ages many thinkers and commentators on human affairs, from Aristotle to Asimov and from More to Marx, have expressed views on the place of leisure in the life of the individual and society and how this might change and develop in future. Most of these commentaries have been prescriptive in nature; they have been concerned with ideal societies – the way societies ought to be or might be at some time in the future.

The Classical View

For many centuries the classical Greek view of leisure as the ultimate purpose of life, as put forward for example by Aristotle, has been for most people a practical irrelevance. The Aristotelian view is exemplified by the following quotation:

> We choose war for the sake of peace, work for the sake of leisure, menial and useful acts for the sake of the noble ... For one must be able to work and fight, but even more to be at peace and lead a life of cultivated leisure, to do the necessary and useful things, but still more those of intrinsic worth.
>
> (Aristotle, 1962, p. 287)

Aristotle was talking about an ideal which was achievable only by a minority because of their wealth and the institution of slavery. Since the majority of people in the subsequent 2,500 years have had neither great wealth nor slaves the Aristotelian view of leisure has not been of any great relevance. But recent writers have suggested that, just possibly, in advanced industrial societies, technology may have brought wealth and slaves, in the form of machines, within reach of all, and opened up the prospect of 'Athens without the slaves'.

It should be noted that Aristotle's view of leisure is distinct from play, which is a necessary concomitant of work, as are rest, relaxation or *re*-creation. The question therefore arises as to how leisure should be spent:

> If not-working is preferable to, and is the end sought by, working, we must ask ourselves what are the proper activities of leisure. Obviously not play; for that would make play the object of living, our end in life, which is unthinkable. Play has its uses, but they belong rather to the sphere of work; for he who works hard needs rest and play is a way of resting, while work is inseparable from stress and strain. We must therefore for therapeutic reasons admit the necessity of games, while keeping them to their proper times and proper uses; taking exercise in this way is both a relaxation of the mind and, just because we enjoy it, a recreation. But the way of leisure that we are speaking of here is something positive, in itself a pleasant, happy existence which the life of work and business cannot be.
>
> (Aristotle, 1962, p. 302)

From this perspective therefore, coming home from work, switching on the television and drinking a can of beer is not leisure, it is resting. Even going on holiday may not be seen as leisure in this sense because it could be merely an extended form of resting – 'getting away from it all' or 'unwinding'. It is only when fully rested and recovered from the effects of work and faced with the question, 'What shall I do with my time?' that the individual can be said to face leisure. Quite clearly the word 'leisure' is not generally used in this precise sense. To avoid confusion it might be advisable to refer to the specific, Aristotlean, view of leisure as 'pure leisure'.

It could be argued that the average person never experiences pure leisure – most never have a long enough period away from work, paid or unpaid, to be really free of its influence. Even retired people may be so exhausted, mentally and physically, from forty years of work that they never fully recover before infirmity sets in. While the unemployed school-leaver or the long-term unemployed may have time and may be unaffected by work experience, they generally have low incomes and are faced with social and psychological problems which often make it impossible for them to convert their time into pure leisure, even if, technically it could be described as leisure. Women playing the traditional roles of child-rearer and housekeeper, as well as often engaging in paid work, are of course never free from work. For the future, therefore, a quite revolutionary change in the balance of work and leisure would be necessary for pure leisure in the Aristotlean sense to be widely experienced. Some commentators expect to see such revolutionary change by the end of the century.

A second aspect of the classical view of leisure is the question: what constitutes acceptable leisure activities in conditions of pure leisure? As, or if, society moves towards the society of pure leisure will people simply do more of what they do now, or is the current pattern of activity unduly influenced by the all-pervasive nature of the work experience? In the absence of work would people want to play more, would they want to relax as much or to be entertained? Aristotle had clear views on what ought to happen. During rest or play diversionary, relaxing activities were acceptable but when faced with pure leisure more consideration was required. Activities undertaken during pure leisure time should not themselves be materially necessary or useful – that would make them work-like. But they should give pleasure and fulfilment. In fact it was considered that only the enjoyment of music and contemplation were ultimately acceptable as pure leisure activities (De Grazia, 1962, p. 14). For the moment the precise activities favoured by Aristotle are less important than the fact that the choice of activity was considered important and that pure leisure activities were different from play activities. This is potentially relevant to the modern age; if we are to be faced with extended leisure time will we carry on doing more of the same, or will there – or should there – be a qualitative change? There may be a fair degree of consensus about the desirable outcome in broad terms, but problems and disagreement arise in considering the detail and the means of arriving at the outcome.

If it is held that leisure is freely chosen, can society, without interfering with that freedom, influence such choice so that people favour activities which are 'creative' and perhaps contribute to 'the improvement of society' rather than activities which are degrading to both the individual and to society? Such talk can quickly lead to paternalism and even totalitarianism. In fact governments – 'society' – have long been engaged in influencing such choices. Nearly all governments impose heavy taxes on gambling and alcoholic drink while at the same time subsidizing other activities such as the arts and sports. There is also much talk of 'education for leisure' to teach young people how to 'use their free time constructively'.

The classical view of leisure is therefore of interest because of the issues it raises in relation to the future possibilities for leisure in the late twentieth century. In discussing an ideal the ancient Greeks could have been discussing possibilities for our future. One modern Aristotelian is worth quoting at this stage because of the firmness of his views. The philosopher Mortimer Adler argues that the main purpose of life, towards which all should be striving, is to 'live a good life as a whole'. In discussing what constitutes 'a good life as a whole' he states:

> Only leisure activities – activities that are creative in the primary sense of being self-creative, not productive of other things – contribute, first of all, to the improvement of human society and the advancement of human culture . . . the activities of leisure make the greatest contribution to a good life as a whole.
>
> (Adler, 1970, p. 169)

Religion

Religion has, down the centuries, provided the parameters for leisure activity in the form of rituals, the sabbath, saints' days – holy or holidays – and religious festivals. Religion has been a means of absorbing leisure and directing it. Worship was seen as an acceptable way of using leisure – in fact often the *only* acceptable way. The idea that work and worship are virtuous and everything else is to be classed as idleness, and therefore sinful, is the basis of the 'Protestant work ethic' which is discussed more fully in Chapter 4.

Contemporary and traditional Christian attitudes towards leisure give rise to three issues relevant to our concerns here. The first is a positive approach to the subject as put forward by Pieper. He argues that leisure should lead almost inevitably towards worship as its finest expression.

> The soul of leisure, it can be said, lies in 'celebration' . . . But if celebration is the core of leisure, then leisure can be made possible and justifiable on the same basis as the celebration of a festival. That basis is divine worship.
>
> (Pieper, 1965, p. 59)

In an increasingly secular world the idea that divine worship should become the main focus of leisure activity seems hardly to be a likely possibility. But the increasing popularity of various Eastern religions in Western societies and of many all-embracing Christian sects, particularly in the United States, could be seen as a response, albeit probably not conscious, of some individuals to the question, 'What shall we do with our leisure time?'

A more negative perspective is presented by Ralph Glasser who argues that the disappearance of the historical regulatory role of religion could lead to severe problems in an age of leisure. He puts forward the proposition that individuals attempt in their lives to pursue some ideal identity or model which, in the past, was defined and projected by religion but which is currently being defined and projected by a basically amoral, commercial world. He states:

> The central question is a moral one, whether our society can muster the will to restore an authoritative consensus as to the model identity to follow, the aim of life in fact. Conventions about the model are ethical questions, how a person should feel, behave, respond to his neighbours and the environment; these conventions constitute the mortar holding the bricks of society together. The brick-work has not been attended to for a long time. To the extent that the mortar still holds it is a survival from the age of faith. We live on the ethical capital of the past. We face, therefore, not just the question of leisure, but whether humane society can survive.
> (Glasser, 1974)

In this perspective the absence of religion will leave a moral vacuum which will make it impossible for society to cope satisfactorily with the future growth of leisure. Of course it is possible to believe in the moral bankruptcy of the modern Western social and economic order without any reference to specifically religious beliefs, as contemporary Marxist commentators such as Gorz (1985) and Aronowitz (1973) show.

The third perspective to be considered here suggests that it is the continuing strength of the Protestant work ethic that is preventing modern Western societies from making the changes in attitudes which are necessary to cope with the changing relationship between work and leisure. Weber demonstrated the relationship between this religious philosophy and the development of industrial capitalism in the seventeenth and eighteenth centuries. 'Baptized in the bracing, if icy, waters of Calvinistic theology, the life of business, once regarded as perilous to the soul, acquires a new sanctity. Labour is not merely an economic means: it is a spiritual end' (Clemitson and Rodgers, 1981, p. 6). But the work ethic is no longer dependent on religion, it is believed to have become part of Western culture (although the equally strong 'work ethic' apparent in the East must presumably be called something other than 'Protestant'). There is however some debate as to whether the work ethic has ever been fully internalized by the working classes (Dubin, 1956; Goldthorpe et al., 1968). Contemporary commentators are arguing that the work ethic 'no longer fits the needs of the hour' (Clarke, 1982, p. 189), that it is necessary to 'escape from the shackles of the work ethic' (Clemitson and Rodgers, 1981, p. 174) and to 'renounce the false notions of the dignity of work, the necessity of work, self-fulfillment through work, and the right – and sometimes the duty – to work' (Hayter, 1978). These ideas are pursued more fully in Chapter 4.

Generally then, Western religion has not espoused leisure *per se*. Like governments, religions seek either to control leisure or to exploit it for their own purposes.

Utopia

The Idea of Utopia
Utopian thought is a rich source of ideas on how people might live and work and spend their leisure in some ideal future. Utopian writers have presented their readers with a wide range of possible, and impossible, futures for consideration.

> Utopias are about how people should live, about human nature, and the meaning and purpose of life. And thus they deal with perennial problems: happiness, good and evil, the state, religion, knowledge, work, sex, equality, liberty . . . [they] are concerned with three main relationships: firstly people's relationships with each other – democracy and marriage for example – secondly, people's relationships with nature; and thirdly, people's relationship with their work.
> (Tod and Wheeler, 1978, p.7)

The Garden of Eden is perhaps the original utopia. Although, by definition, it deals with our past, its idealism clearly points to a future paradise, characterized by innocence, plenty and certainly an absence of work. In folklore the 'Land of Cockayne' epitomizes the common people's fantasy that there exists, somewhere, a land of leisure and plenty. In their study, *Utopia*, Tod and Wheeler quote the folk ballad, 'Song of Cockayne':

> In Cockayne we drink and eat
> Freely without care and sweat
> The food is choice and clear the wine
> At fources and at supper time.
> I say again, and I dare swear
> No land is like it anywhere.
> Under heaven no land like this
> Of such joy and endless bliss.
> There is many a sweet sight,
> All is day, there is no night.
> There is no quarrelling, nor strife,
> There no death but endless life;
> There no lack of food or cloth,

> There no man or woman wroth . . .
> All is sporting, joy and glee,
> Lucky the man that there be.
>
> (Tod and Wheeler, 1978, p. 10)

De Grazia, one of the foremost American philosophers of leisure, in discussing the origins of leisure, refers to contemporary versions of the same notions, encapsulated in the song, 'The Big Rock Candy Mountain' (De Grazia, 1962, p. 363). These expressions of the common man's view of the ideal life from folklore, highlight the moral issues discussed earlier. Left to their own devices it would seem that 'ordinary people', presented with substantial leisure time and material prosperity, might not pursue the morally uplifting activities prescribed for them by their religious and secular leaders. If these songs are anything to go by they are more likely to spend their time in idleness and a variety of decidedly immoral activities. Thus it might be feared that the advent of a leisure society could herald not some idyllic state but the moral and physical decline of industrial civilization that would be reminiscent of the fall of the Roman Empire.

The word 'Utopia' derives from Sir Thomas More's book of the same name, written in 1516, in which he outlined in some detail an ideal society as he saw it. The book however conveys an ambivalence about leisure.

> The chief and almost the only business of the syphogrants (rulers) is to manage matters so that no one sits around in idleness, and to ensure that everyone works hard at his trade. But no one has to exhaust himself with endless toil from early morning to late at night, as if he were a beast of burden. Such wretchedness, really worse than slavery, is the common lot of workmen in all countries, except Utopia. Of the day's twenty-four hours, the Utopians devote only six to work. They work three hours before noon, when they go to dinner. After dinner they rest for a couple of hours, then they go to work for another three hours. Then they have supper, and at eight o'clock they go to bed and sleep eight hours. The other hours of the day, when they are not working, eating or sleeping, are left to each man's individual discretion, provided he does not waste them in roistering or sloth, but uses them busily in some occupation that pleases him.
>
> (Adams, 1975, p. 41)

These busy occupations included attending lectures, playing music, conversation and games 'not unlike our own chess'. But gambling is forbidden. As Adams points out, this timetable gives Utopians ten hours of leisure a day, but...

> More has done something to mitigate the dangers of leisure by allocating most of it to the early morning hours. If they go to bed at eight, as he says, and sleep eight hours, the Utopians will rise at four a.m. Work does not start till nine. There may be problems with this timetable but boredom is only one of them.
> (Adams, 1975, p. 41)

More indicated that Utopians needed to work only six hours a day because all members of the community were required to work – there was no idle class to support – and, in addition, a great deal of unnecessary work, such as the making of ostentatious clothing, would not need to be done. Indeed:

> the officials very often proclaim a shorter working day, since they never force their citizens to perform useless labour. The chief aim of their constitution and government is that, whenever public needs permit, all citizens shall be free, so far as possible, to withdraw their time and energy from service of the body, devote themselves to the freedom and culture of the mind. For that, they think, is the real happiness of life.
> (Adams, 1975, p. 44)

At the beginning of the seventeenth century Campanella wrote his *City of the Sun*, which described a Utopian society devoted to knowledge and science. Here also the hours of work were short.

> Since everyone in the city works, the working day is short, only four hours; and the rest of the time is spent in personal learning, debating, reading, storytelling, writing, walking and exercising of the mind and body. Again like Utopians, they have no dice or gambling, but they also forbid any game spent sitting down, including chess, and favour all energetic and sporting activities.
> (Tod and Wheeler, 1978, p. 43)

The Sports Council was obviously at work even in these far-off times!

In the early Utopian writings we therefore see the concern with the morality and suitability of leisure activities which we have already met in classical and religious contexts; but there is also something new: the idea that the working hours of the common people might be reduced. This is not based on fantasy but on logic: the idea that if all members of the community were required to work for their living and production for ostentatious life-styles were to be rendered unnecessary, then it would not be necessary for the many to work long hours in order to keep the few in idleness. This was almost the opposite of the classical outlook which took the labour of slaves for granted.

Utopian Planning

One tradition in Utopian thinking has been concerned with community planning and design. Some of these writings have found expression in real experiments in community design. The nineteenth century saw a plethora of such writings and indeed many experiments in new ways of living. Perhaps the most famous of these writers and experimenters was Robert Owen, a cotton manufacturer who established modern industrial communities in New Lanark in Scotland and New Harmony in Indiana, in which his socialist ideals were put into practice. In his *New View of Society* he indicated that leisure certainly had a place in his new scheme of things. 'Those then, who desire to give Mankind the character which it would be for the happiness of all that they possess, will not fail to make careful provision for their amusement and recreation' (Owen, 1972, p. 42).

Clearly Owen had not given any deep consideration to the question of the difference between 'leisure' and 'amusement and recreation'. Nevertheless there were moral overtones in the nature of the provision made for leisure in his model communities. His planned communities contained ample gardens and walks and 'rooms for innocent amusements and rational recreation'.

Some, however, envisaged communities in which attitudes towards work (and hence leisure) were transformed. In France, and later America, Charles Fourier promoted his vision of the ideal community known as 'Phalanx'. Among his principles was a system of free love and equality between the sexes and a novel approach to work and leisure.

> People were to work at a variety of jobs, and change jobs frequently, several times each day. Each person would do a minimum amount of work and receive a basic wage. Above that people's wages would be as varied as they wished to make them by the amount and kind of work they decided to do, though there should be no moral or social pressure exerted to make people work. By making work attractive Fourier hoped to liberate people from the work ethic as well as from the drudgery of work.
>
> (Tod and Wheeler, 1978, p. 91)

Modern notions of the 'social wage', which are discussed in Chapter 5, are a reflection of some of Fourier's ideas, as are the concerns of some that we should be looking at the humanization of the workplace rather than to leisure as a solution to the problems of modern society (Palm, 1977). The idea that people should not be confined to one type of work was also put forward as an ideal by Karl Marx.

William Morris was also of the view that salvation was to be found, not so much in leisure, but in changing work from mechanized drudgery to the means of producing beauty. In his book, *News from Nowhere*, which describes the experiences of someone transported to the twenty-first century, he describes a society in which work has become desirable rather than something to be avoided. As one of the characters in the book observes:

> There is a kind of fear growing up among us that we shall some day be short of work ... *all* work is now pleasurable; either because of the hope of gain in honour and wealth with which the work is done ... or else because it has grown into a pleasurable habit ... and lastly (and most of our work is of this kind) because there is conscious sensuous pleasure in the work itself.
>
> (Morris, 1973, p. 275)

Many of the Utopian community planners were concerned with the built environment as an expression of their philosophies of living. Ebenezer Howard, in *Garden Cities of Tomorrow* (1898), put forward ideas and plans for 'garden cities' as alternatives to mass city living. His ideas bore fruit in the form of Letchworth and Welwyn Garden City, both built in Hertfordshire in the early part of the century. Later the New Towns Act of 1946 and the ensuing programme of British new towns owed much to his thinking and that of the New Towns Movement that he founded. Leisure had a recognized place in Howard's dream:

> As it grows, the free gifts of nature – fresh air, sunlight, breathing room and playing room – shall be still retained in needed abundance, and by so employing the resources of modern science that Art may supplement Nature and life may become an abiding joy and delight.
>
> (Howard, 1898, p. 127)

Fifty years later, in introducing the New Towns Bill to the House of Commons, Mr Silkin, the Minister responsible, said:

> I want to see the new towns gay and bright, with plenty of theatres, concert halls and meeting places. I should like to see cricket and football played by the youth of the towns instead of being watched by them. I want to see them producing first class amateur teams and

> I should like to see golf courses made available for all ... The new towns should provide valuable experience in the best use of leisure, a commodity which is, and should become, more and more plentiful.
> (Veal, 1975, p. 2)

So a nineteenth-century idealist, Ebenezer Howard, provides a direct link between the earlier utopians and the modern concerns of planning for leisure in terms of facilities and opportunities, and Silkin provides a link to earlier writers with his moral concern for the appropriate use of leisure in an ideal society. Although many of the new towns which were built subsequently in Britain could be described as 'domestic' in style rather than 'futuristic', they can fairly be said to have fulfilled many of the hopes of their founders in relation to leisure. They indeed have generous amounts of open space and have been among the pioneers in the provision of indoor leisure facilities. But lack of some basic facilities in the early days contributed to dissatisfaction among some residents, particularly young people and housewives, which led to the coining of the term 'new-town blues', the virtual opposite of satisfying leisure (Veal, 1975).

The essence of the British Garden City was low density, organic development. This contrasts starkly with the approach of the 'modern movement' in architecture and planning, as exemplified by Le Corbusier and his 'La Ville Radieuse' proposals of the 1920s which concentrated people's homes and workplaces into enormous tower blocks. But the tower blocks were to be set in parkland.

> Since only 15 per cent of the ground is built over, there is plenty of space for garages, gardens, parks, nurseries, playing fields and swimming pools. Even the roofs of buildings are used for recreation, and the housing area as a whole is surrounded by a wide green belt, separating it from the factories, giving a city zoned into four main areas – housing, factories, culture and administration.
> (Tod and Wheeler, 1978, p. 40)

In the British experience, at least, the Corbusier dream in many cases turned into a nightmare, with mothers and young children isolated in tall tower blocks, and the spaces between them becoming windswept wildernesses rather than pleasant places of leisure. From the point of view of leisure, Gold suggests that Le Corbusier's grand designs were misconceived from the start (Gold, 1983). The Garden City concept of low-rise, neighbourhood-based development has therefore proved the more durable in Britain and, given the durability and the expense of replacing bricks and mortar, is likely to provide the physical context for life and leisure for many decades to come.

More recent architectural Utopians are Paul and Percival Goodman whose book, *Communitas*, published in 1947, presented three 'Community Paradigms'. The first, designed for 'efficient consumption', is not unlike 'La Ville Radieuse': surrounding a monolithic, highly concentrated city is a green belt described as a wild 'vacationland' where 'there is exchanged for the existence where everything is done for you, the existence where nothing is done for you'. But it also contains 'the imitation wildness of state parks and the bathos of adult camps'. And 'children are here conveniently disposed of in camps during the summer season'. But they also describe – or prescribe – a carnival for the city: 'when the boundaries are overridden between zone and zone, and the social order is loosed to the equalities and inequalities of nature' (Goodman and Goodman, 1947, p. 149).

This element in their ideal city is modelled on the Roman Saturnalia. Described as economically necessary to 'clear the shelves' for the new 'springtime fashions', the carnival sounds more like a necessary cathartic outburst from the population confined in the Goodmans' super-efficient city.

The Goodmans' second alternative involves the 'elimination of the differences between production and consumption'. Here the model is close to Owenite communities – small, organic communities producing goods primarily for their own consumption on a small scale – a theme taken up more recently by ecologists and others. The implications for leisure are not, however, fully spelt out in this scenario. In their third system, 'planned security with maximum regulation', the Goodmans put forward ideas which, while impractical, throw up issues which are relevant to current debates about work, leisure and the future. In many current views of the future which envisage a reduced role for work, the need for a subsistence allowance as of right, regardless of whether or not an individual works, is recognized; others see developments in areas referred to as the 'self-service economy' (Gershuny, 1977). In the Goodmans' scenario they suggest that a decent level of subsistence and the necessary goods to sustain that standard of living should be defined and that a part of the economy should be hived off and run as a state enterprise to produce that minimum set of goods and services. They estimate, ingeniously, that such a sub-economy would require about one-fifth of total available labour: people would be required to work for the subsistence economy for one year in five. For the rest of the time they could either be at leisure, while living at the basic subsistence level, or they could participate in the rest of the economy to a greater or lesser degree, according to their own preference. Such ideas are reminiscent of those of Fourier, outlined earlier.

Planning for Utopia has been brought up to date in Britain with a competition on designing 'Tomorrow's New Communities', sponsored by the Town and Country Planning Association (previously the Garden Cities Association), the *Guardian* newspaper and *Planning* newspaper. The results were exhibited at the Institute of Contemporary Arts in London in summer 1981 (ICA, 1981). The notable feature of many of the entries was the rejection of modern industrial technology and the embracing of alternative technology, energy conservation and self-sufficiency. While leisure facilities featured in most of the designs, these 'communities of the future' could by no stretch of the imagination be described as 'leisure societies'. If anything, the self-sufficiency, recycling and conservation of resources all seemed to promise a great deal of work for the citizens of the future. It seems that the labour-saving hard technology of the future is being embraced only by its creators and by some science-fiction writers – other modern Utopians are not interested.

From Sir Thomas More to the architecture students of the ICA exhibition has run a practical, community-based theme. But Utopia has also become an abstract, philosophical concept to which other writers have addressed themselves.

Utopian Philosophy
George Kateb (1973), in an essay entitled 'Utopia and the Good Life', considers how people should live their lives in the conditions of Utopia, conditions characterized by leisure and abundance. In a *laissez-faire* situation he considers the proposition that people would essentially spend their time in the pursuit of pleasure. But the problem is, *what* pleasures could be pursued which would give lasting satisfaction? Some activities which we consider to be pleasurable in our current, non-Utopian condition are, Kateb argues, only pleasurable because they are engaged in only infrequently and against a background of work or deprivation. Such activities are unlikely to provide the basis for continuing, Utopian, happiness. Their continuous pursuit would at best pall and at worst lead to physical and/or moral degeneracy. An obvious example of such an activity is eating and drinking engaged in as a leisure activity. While accepting that play, in its widest sense, would increase in importance in Utopia, Kateb nevertheless thinks that it would be insufficient to provide the whole focus for life:

> Can play, even in the most extended sense, be anything but one side of life, even a life of leisure and abundance? There is no doubt that beauty could become immeasurably more pervasive than it is now, that human feelings could be cultivated to the appreciation of beauty much more carefully than is common now, that a larger part of life could be given over to elaborate and hyper-civilised amusements

and involvements, that utopian citizens could be encouraged to develop all sorts of pleasurable but eccentric tastes and talents, that a life of continuous shifts in styles and fashions could be economically feasible, that life as a whole could be much more plastic than it is now: that is, the ability to switch roles frequently, to part easily with shreds of one's identity, to move around over the face of the earth, to play out one's fantasies, to 'experiment in living', could be enormously enhanced. Do these possibilities, however, add up to a *substantial* life? Or is it all frivolity? Surely a life of leisure and abundance can also be a life of seriousness?
(Kateb, 1973, p. 250)

He further rejects the view of the anthropologist Hannah Arendt, that political activity is the highest form of human activity since, he argues, when populations are counted in millions, only a few can be engaged as representatives in a representative democracy. He also rejects William Morris's view that we should be engaged in crafts. His conclusion is:

The good life is, to use the old solemn language, the contemplative life. To put it less solemnly, the good life is the life spent in the acquisition and use of learning, the self-delighting exercise of intellectual skills, the cultivation of responsiveness to the works of intellectual culture and perceptiveness to the beauty of works of art.
(Kateb, 1973, p. 255)

C. E. M. Joad, writing some years earlier, in 1935, came to the same conclusion. He envisaged a society in which material goods and services would be produced in four or five hours work a day. He first of all conjured up a future which he called depressing, despite its essential frivolity. In this future the English countryside was sold, 'complete with hedges', to 'American hostesses' on the look out for new stunts to amuse guests at smart dinner parties.

Pseudo-religions will spring up like mushrooms ... women will follow Great White Masters into the desert. Finally the sheer boredom of life made unendurable by wasted energies, servitude to pleasure and a craving for amusement which grows ever more difficult to satisfy, will lead to war, and men will be driven to kill one another in order to kill time.
(Joad, 1935, p. 70)

After due deliberation however, he comes to the conclusion that the life of contemplation is what abundant leisure *should* be used for if it is to avoid these excesses.

It is then, to a knowledge of the past in history or archaeology, to the understanding of the physical universe in science or of ourselves in psychology, to the alleviation of some social defect by the study of economics or sociology, to the solution of some problem in mathematics or philosophy, in short, to thinking, to reading, to writing and to creating, that our leisure, if it is to be a pleasure and not a burden, will in the future be devoted.

(Joad, 1935, p. 100)

But Kateb's and Joad's view and, as we saw earlier, Aristotle's, that play would ultimately be unacceptable, is not the conclusion of Bernard Suits, a Canadian philosopher, who puts forward an altogether less ponderous, but intricately elaborate, argument in his delightful book, *The Grasshopper: Games, Life and Utopia*. In his ultimate, highly theoretical, Utopia the need for 'any instrumental activity whatever' has been eliminated. Contemplation would not even have a place because:

just as we have supposed that they (the inhabitants of Utopia) have acquired all the economic goods they can use, we must assume that they have acquired all the knowledge there is. In Utopia, therefore, there are no scientists, philosophers or intellectual investigators.

(Suits, 1978, p. 170)

Even pursuit of the arts and sexual activity are dismissed, being products of the civilization of scarcity. All that is left is the playing of games:

In Utopia all instrumental activities have been eliminated. There is nothing to strive for precisely because everything has already been achieved. What we need, therefore, is some activity in which what is instrumental is inseparably combined with what is intrinsically valuable, and where the activity is not itself an instrument for some further end. Games meet this requirement perfectly. For in games we must have obstacles which we can strive to overcome *just so that* we can possess the activity as a whole, namely playing the game. Game playing makes it possible to retain enough effort in Utopia to make life worth living.

(Suits, 1978, p. 172)

Such an extreme scenario, developed for the purposes of philosophical argument, draws attention to an unmistakable trend in modern society. Sports superstars are undoubtedly the folk heroes of the day, despite the intrinsic futility of the actual activities they engage in. The

Olympic Games and World Cup soccer tournaments hold the world's attention through television. Fame and honours are heaped on those who climb mountains and circumnavigate the world single-handed in yachts. Essentially this is all the playing of games.

Alvin Toffler, in *Future Shock*, was however, impatient with the Utopias and Utopians who had gone before; he envisaged the study and design of Utopias as itself a significant activity in his own Utopian view of the future.

> Today we need powerful new utopian and anti-utopian concepts that look forward to super-industrialism, rather than backwards to simpler societies ... it may now be too difficult for any individual writer, no matter how gifted, to describe a convincingly complex future. We need, therefore a revolution in the production of utopias: collaborative utopianism. We need to construct 'utopia factories'.
> (Toffler, 1970, p. 421)

Utopians as Best Sellers
The nineteenth century and earlier Utopians were concerned with social reform. In the twentieth century a new form of Utopian (and sometimes 'dystopian') futurism has emerged in which the basis of the projected image of the future is technological change, its consequences and potential. H. G. Wells was the best-known forerunner of such futuristic thinking and a whole literary genre has developed in this area, namely science fiction. Wells provides a link between the reformist, ideal community writers of the nineteenth century and the later science-fiction writers who have combined idealism with fantasy and entertainment. In *A Modern Utopia*, published in 1905, he describes a Utopian London that might have been.

> Here will be one of the great meeting places of mankind. Here – I speak of Utopian London – will be the traditional centre of one of the great races of the commonality of the World State – and here will be its social and intellectual exchange. There will be a mighty University here, with thousands of professors and tens of thousands of advanced students, and here great journals of thought and speculation, mature and splendid books of philosophy and science, and a glorious fabric of literature will be woven and shaped, and with a teeming leisureliness, put forth. Here will be stupendous libraries and a mighty organisation of museums. About these centres will cluster a great swarm of people ... Then the arts will cluster around this city, as gold gathers about wisdom, and here Englishmen will weave into wonderful prose and beautiful rhythms and subtly

atmospheric forms, the intricate, austere and courageous imagination of our race.

(Wells, 1905, p. 243)

Clearly Wells subscribed to the 'contemplative' school of thought as regards desirable Utopian activity and, despite the chauvinistic overtones of his delivery, many of his ideas find reflection in contemporary commentaries. In much of his writing Wells was more concerned with work and the industrious application of science than with leisure. Indeed it is true to say that leisure has generally been a peripheral, incidental element of subsequent science-fiction writings. This does not make it any less interesting – in fact the unconscious attitudes towards leisure which are revealed have a certain significance *because* they have not been consciously and elaborately thought through.

In this futuristic, or other-worldly, literature the link with leisure is made in two ways; first, technology is seen to provide for new types of leisure activity or to speed up or extend present-day activities; and secondly the effects of technology are seen to reduce the amount of work necessary in society and therefore to increase the amount of leisure available to all or some members of society.

An example of the first type of phenomenon, in which technology directly affects leisure activities, is Douglas Adams's spoof, *The Restaurant at the End of the Universe* (1980), in which whole planets are taken over for rock concerts, playboys of the galaxy go 'flare-riding' into suns in specially built mini-spaceships, and the ultimate dining-out experience involves travelling forward in time to the restaurant from which the end of the universe can be watched as a sort of floor show, before returning to one's own time-period. Another, more serious, example is in Ray Bradbury's story, 'The Veldt' (1951), which centres around a child's playroom in a home of the future, in which any environment can be simulated, including the African veldt and its wildlife inhabitants which feature ominously in the story.

An example of the second type of scenario, in which technology affects the economic and social structure of society, is Kurt Vonnegut's *Player Piano* (1953), in which a small elite group of technicians and managers live in a compound, running the economy, and recruiting a few *hoi polloi* for certain residual menial tasks, but the masses live lives of apparent idleness, engaging in drinking and frequent carnivals, and posing a threat to the social order.

John Griffiths, analysing American, British and Soviet Utopian science-fiction writing, concludes: 'The worst feature of these utopias is the banality and astonishing bad taste of their leisure activities' (Griffiths, 1980, p. 101). In fact Griffiths suggests that leading science-fiction writers of the past decade have presented a profoundly depressing picture of the future of man. Science is no longer an agent of liberation and development, as earlier Utopian writers had seen it; it is a force which threatens to destroy man, morally if not physically.

> The Goths of science, the Visigoths of technology, and the Huns of bureaucracy have no human instincts to weaken. They are neutral and potentially more destructive, and more inspiring, than any barbarian. The trouble is that we seem to have given up all hope of taming them, even to have lost the will to try. The very intellectual elite which ought to lead the movement has surrendered. The monastic hideouts of human values are few and far between and are certainly not inviolable. We are entering another Dark Age and the prospects of a renaissant dawn are small. If the despairing SF writers of the West and the silent and conforming ones of the East are right in their image of what the future holds then there will be no tomorrow. Tomorrow has been cancelled.
> (Griffiths, 1980, p. 206)

This leads naturally and depressingly to the idea of 'dystopia' in which a horrific rather than desirable future state of affairs is presented. The most famous example is Orwell's *Nineteen Eighty-Four*, but this is such a desperate world that leisure barely gets a look in. Huxley's *Brave New World*, is however, a different matter. Here we are introduced to the children's game of 'Centrifugal Bubble-puppy', which is a complicated piece of apparatus which brings forth the following comment from an observer:

> Imagine the folly of allowing people to play elaborate games which do nothing whatever to increase consumption. It's madness. Nowadays the controllers won't approve of any new game unless it can be shown that it requires at least as much apparatus as the most complicated of existing games.
> (Huxley, 1932, p. 35)

Huxley's fertile imagination has no trouble in providing recreation in London's green belt of the future:

> They were flying over the six kilometre zone of parkland that separated Central London from its first ring of satellite suburbs. The green was maggoty with foreshortened life. Forests of Centrifugal Bubble-puppy towers gleamed between the trees. Near Shepherd's Bush two thousand Beta-Minus mixed doubles were playing Riemann-surface tennis. A double row of Escalator Fives Courts lined the main road from Notting Hill to Willesden. In the Ealing

stadium a Delta gymnastic display and community sing was in progress.

(Huxley, 1932, p. 58)

Westminster Abbey has become a cabaret venue featuring Calvin Stopes and his Sixteen Saxophonists and 'London's Finest Scent and Colour Organ: All the Latest Synthetic Music'. *Soma*, a hallucinogenic drug, appears throughout the book:

> Lenina felt herself entitled, after this day of queerness and horror, to a complete and absolute holiday. As soon as they got back to the rest-house, she swallowed six half-gramme tablets of *soma*, lay down on her bed, and within ten minutes had embarked for a lunar eternity. It would be eighteen hours at least before she would be back in time again.
>
> (p. 117)

We are also treated, in *Brave New World*, to a detailed description of a 'feely movie' with synchronized 'scent-organ'; children are encouraged to engage in 'erotic play' and people are conditioned to hate the country but to love country sports so that they maximize their consumption of transport and sports equipment. The standardized 'humans' in the book are however denied 'excessive' leisure – for their own happiness.

> Seven and a half hours of mild, unexhausting labour, and then the *soma* ration and games and unrestricted copulation and the feelies. What more can they ask for? True, they might ask for shorter hours. And of course we could give them shorter hours. Technically it would be perfectly simple to reduce all lower-caste working hours to three or four a day. But would they be any the happier for that? No they wouldn't. The experiment was tried more than a century and a half ago. The whole of Ireland was put onto the four-hour day. What was the result? Unrest and a large increase in the consumption of *soma*; that was all. Those three and a half hours of extra leisure were so far from being a source of happiness, that people felt constrained to take a holiday from them. The Inventions Office is stuffed with plans for labour-saving processes. Thousands of them. And why don't we put them into execution? for the sake of the labourers; it would be sheer cruelty to afflict them with excessive leisure.
>
> (p. 180)

So even in science fiction many of the issues which currently preoccupy society in thinking about the future are present. How many hours should people work and who should decide and on what criteria?

Who should work and who should not? What is the role of technology in changing the nature of leisure experience? Will people be able in practice to cope with extended leisure – or even permitted to try? It is, of course, the privilege of fiction writers not to have to consider either the probability or the desirability of the worlds they invent coming about.

Occasionally the more eminent science-fiction writers are asked to give a 'serious' view of the future. Thus Isaac Asimov, in 1976, wrote an essay entitled 'Future Fun', in which he made a fundamental point that despite technological change most leisure activity will continue in future much as it is at present, despite superficial modifications:

> Fun is where you find it and is always to be found in feasting and laughing and loving and roughhousing and gambling and hiking and noisemaking and yelling and moving chessmen and chasing rubber balls and sleeping in the sun and dancing and swimming and watching entertainers and risking one's neck for foolish reasons ...
> If we are to look into the future, then, and try to see what kind of recreation we are likely to have, let us agree to eliminate from consideration the kinds of recreation we already have. Much of this will continue unchanged and if some of it is to undergo modification, the alterations will not be essential. So television might go three-dimensional or movies might be piped directly into the home or a new dance may be invented – such things are trivial.
> (Asimov, 1976, p. 199)

He foresees developments of under-water living and concomitant under-water recreation, and speculates about recreation in moon settlements and earth satellites, the possibility of computer vs computer games becoming spectator sports and the use of hallucinogenic drugs.

We have examined the views and perspectives on Utopia as seen from religious, architectural, philosophical and science-fiction standpoints. Most of these remain in their historical or fictional milieux. They give us ideas and illustrate that the last quarter of the twentieth century is not the first time that the future of leisure has exercised people's minds. The factor which perhaps distinguishes the current age from previous ones is the overriding importance attached to economics. Some nineteenth-century and early-twentieth-century economists and commentators on economic affairs foresaw some of the issues facing advanced industrial economies today and provide us with a link between some of the historical perspectives described in this chapter and contemporary concerns.

Economic Futurists

Perhaps a link between some of the socialist Utopian thinkers of the nineteenth century and the economic realities of the twentieth century is the writing of Karl Marx. His view of the future, communist, society, though never very explicitly spelt out, was one in which all individuals would contribute freely to the community effort and in which the division between work and leisure would disappear because both would be engaged in freely and with pleasure (Rojek, 1984). Thus in *The German Ideology*, there is the famous passage:

> In the communist society, where nobody has one exclusive sphere of activity but each can become accomplished in any branch he wishes, society regulates the general production and thus makes it possible for me to do one thing today and another tomorrow, to hunt in the morning, fish in the afternoon, rear cattle in the evening, criticise after dinner, just as I have a mind, without ever becoming a hunter, fisherman, shepherd or critic.
> (Marx and Engels, 1846, p. 53)

In later writings Marx argues that the increasing productivity of labour offers increased freedom and leisure for workers. Indeed he equates increased leisure, or the freedom to take additional leisure, with national wealth and, in *Grundrisse*, quotes an anonymous earlier writer to the effect that 'there is ... no means of adding to *the wealth of a nation* but by adding to the facilities of living: so that wealth is liberty – liberty to seek recreation – liberty to enjoy life – liberty to improve the mind: it is disposable time and nothing more' (see Gorz, 1985, p. 59). The forces of capitalism will, however, want to maintain working hours to produce ever-increasing profits and capital accumulation. But he foresees a time when all energies will not need to be devoted to the production of material necessities.

> The actual wealth of society ... does not depend on the duration of surplus labour, but upon its productivity ... In fact, the realm of freedom actually begins only when labour which is determined by necessity and mundane considerations ceases; thus in the very nature of things it lies beyond the sphere of actual material production ... Beyond it begins that development of human energy which is an end in itself, the true realm of freedom, which, however can blossom forth only with this realm of necessity as its base. The shortening of the working day is its pre-requisite.
> (Marx, 1894, p. 820)

Thus Marx equates leisure with freedom. It is, however, notable that in his scenario, where the barrier between work and leisure has broken down, he does not include more mundane or unpleasant tasks in his list of activities. Would he sweep streets in the morning and mine coal in the afternoon without considering himself either roadsweeper or coalminer? Possibly he envisaged that these tasks would be performed by machine. Nevertheless, Marx's statements remain the first to draw attention to the possibilities which capitalism potentially offers for freedom and leisure.

John Maynard Keynes, writing much later, in 1931, in his essay 'Economic Possibilities for our Grandchildren', foresaw the reduction in working hours which technology could bring and the implications for leisure which this might have.

> It will be those people, who can keep alive, and cultivate into a fuller perfection, the art of life itself and do not sell themselves for the means of life, who will be able to enjoy the abundance when it comes ... those walk most truly in the paths of virtue and sane wisdom who take least thought for the morrow. We shall once more value ends above means and prefer the good to the useful. We shall honour those who can teach us how to pluck the hour and the day virtuously and well, the delightful people who are capable of taking direct enjoyment in things, the lilies of the field who toil not, neither do they spin.
>
> (Keynes, 1931, p. 331)

But he is not complacent about the possibility of achieving such an end.

> If the economic problem is solved mankind will be deprived of its traditional purpose. Will this be a benefit? If one believes at all in the real values of life the prospect at least opens up the possibility of benefit, yet I think with dread of the readjustments of the habits and instincts of the ordinary man, bred into him for countless generations, which he may be asked to discard within a few decades.... there is no country and no people, I think, who can look forward to the age of leisure and abundance without dread. For we have been trained too long to strive and not to enjoy. It is a fearful problem for the ordinary person, with no special talents, to occupy himself... To those who sweat for their daily bread leisure is a longed-for sweet – until they get it ... To judge from the behaviour and the achievements of the wealthy classes today in any quarter of the world, the outlook is very depressing! ... For they have most of them failed disastrously, so it seems to me – those who have an

independent income but no associations or duties or ties – to solve the problem which has been set to them.

(Keynes, 1931, p. 328)

Nevertheless he remains ultimately optimistic about the future of a society of abundance and of leisure.

> I feel sure that with a little more experience we shall use the new-found bounty of nature quite differently from the way in which the rich use it today, and will map out for ourselves a plan of life quite otherwise than theirs.
> (Keynes, 1931, p. 328)

A similar view was put forward by Bertrand Russell in *The Prospects of Industrialization*, written with Dora Russell and published in 1923, and in *In Praise of Idleness*, published in 1935. He contended that all material needs of society could be produced if everyone worked just four hours a day. But he argued that this was unlikely to happen because industrial society places means above ends.

> If every man and woman worked for four hours a day at necessary work, we could all have enough; ... it should be the remaining hours that would be regarded as important – hours which could be devoted to enjoyment of art or study, to affection and woodland and sunshine in green fields. The mechanistic Utopian is unable to value these things: he sees in his dreams a world where goods are produced more and more easily, and distributed with impartial justice to workers too tired and bored to know how to enjoy them. What men are to do with leisure he neither knows nor cares; presumably they are to sleep till the time for work comes round again ... Man's true life does not consist in the business of filling his belly and clothing his body, but in art and thought and love, in the creation and contemplation of beauty and in the scientific understanding of the world.
> (Russell and Russell, 1923, p. 50)

While the massive increases in productivity and prosperity envisaged by some of these commentators has materialized, the 'economic problem' remains the focus of society's political attention: the leisure society remains as part of some Utopian future.

Classical Greek philosophers, medieval and nineteenth-century Utopians, and twentieth-century economists, philosophers and science-fiction writers have all had something to say about the future potential for leisure. In the latter half of the twentieth century the study of the future has changed from being an occasional aside or diversionary essay for the observers of the day, to become almost a small industry in its own right. The 'futures industry', with its own journals, research institutes and self-made millionaires, is perhaps epitomized by the attention devoted to the concept of the post-industrial society, which is examined in the next chapter.

3

The Post-Industrial Society: An Appraisal

Introduction

The notion of a post-industrial society is a beguiling one: the idea that we, in the Western world, are about to move into a fundamentally different type of society, possibly in our own lifetime, is exciting to many: it opens up new possibilities and the prospect of throwing off some of the constraints of the old industrial society. It is generally propounded as a message of hope, even of revolution; it is the late-twentieth-century version of Utopia. There is a hint of the Old Testament prophet about some of the proponents of post-industrial and similar notions: the idea that only a few are blessed with the apocalyptic vision of what is to come; and it is only through the medium of their best-selling books that the rest of the world will come to know of it. Alvin Toffler conveys this most vividly:

> A new civilization is emerging in our lives, and blind men everywhere are trying to suppress it. This new civilization brings with it new family styles; changed ways of working, loving, and living; a new economy; new political conflicts; and beyond all this an altered consciousness as well. Pieces of this new civilization exist today. Millions are already attuning their lives to the rhythms of tomorrow. Others, terrified of the future, are engaged in a desperate, futile flight into the past and are trying to restore the dying world that gave them birth. The dawning of this new civilization is the single most explosive fact of our lifetimes ... We grope for words to describe the full power and reach of this extraordinary change. Some speak of a looming Space Age, Information Age, Electronic Era, or Global Village. Zbigniew Brzezinski has told us we face a 'technetronic age'. Sociologist Daniel Bell describes the coming of a 'post-industrial society'. Soviet futurists speak of the STR – the 'scientific–technological revolution'. I myself have written exten-

sively about the arrival of a 'super-industrial society' ... None of these terms even begins to convey the full force, scope, and dynamism of the changes rushing towards us or of the pressures and conflicts they trigger ... Humanity faces a quantum leap forward. It faces the deepest social upheaval and creative restructuring of all time. Without clearly recognizing it, we are engaged in building a remarkable new civilization from the ground up.

(Toffler, 1981, p. 23)

Toffler's most famous book, *Future Shock* (1970), alerted the Western world to the postwar pace of social change. Five hundred pages of breathless prose in the style exemplified above, packed with a mixture of insight, hyperbole and conceptual grape-shot, convinced hundreds of thousands of readers either that they had already arrived in the new super-industrial society or that they were careering, headlong and unstoppably towards it. *The Third Wave*, from which the above quotation is taken, was less original and made less impact, but the optimistic view of a super-industrial future remained. Our task here is to examine the concept of the post-industrial or super-industrial society or economy, to consider whether it has already arrived, is arriving or will arrive, and finally to consider the potential role of leisure in such a real or imagined society.

Origins and Definitions

Rostow's *The Stages of Economic Growth* (1960), was one of the first of the post-Second World War books to alert the world to the possibility of some sort of post-industrial transition. He divided economic history into five stages: traditional society; the preconditions for take-off; the take-off; the drive to maturity; and the age of mass-consumption. But he then raises the question of the stage beyond the age of mass-consumption and presents a range of possibilities:

> Will man fall into secular spiritual stagnation, finding no worthy outlet for the expression of his energies, talents, and instinct to reach for immortality? Will he follow the Americans and reimpose the strenuous life by raising the birth rate? Will the devil make work for idle hands? Will men learn to conduct wars with just enough violence to be good sport – and to accelerate capital depreciation – without blowing up the planet? Will the exploration of outer space offer an adequately interesting and expensive outlet for resources and ambitions? Or will man convert en masse into suburban versions of an eighteenth century gentleman, find in some mixture of the equivalent of hunting, shooting and fishing, the life of the mind

and spirit, and the minimum drama of carrying forward the human race, sufficient frontiers to keep for life its savour?

(Rostow, 1960, p. 91)

The term 'post-industrial society' is generally associated with Daniel Bell, but in his book, *The Coming of the Post-Industrial Society* (1974), he points out that although he was under the impression that he had coined the term in 1959, he subsequently found that others had used the term before him. David Riesman had used it in his 1958 essay 'Leisure and work in post-industrial society' (Riesman, 1958) and, much earlier, a book by Arthur J. Penty had been published in 1917 entitled *Old Worlds for New: A Study of the Post-Industrial Society* (see Bell, 1974, p. 37). Since there is no reference to Bell in Alaine Touraine's book *The Post-Industrial Society* (1974) it is possible that this was another independent coining of the word, albeit originally in French. Herman Kahn and his colleagues at the Hudson Institute can also be credited with the popularizing, if not the coining, of the term (Kahn and Weiner, 1967).

Riesman's essay does not explicitly define the post-industrial society. Ferkiss (1979), however, lists another ten papers in which the term is used in the title without being defined in the text, so this is by no means unusual. Kahn and his colleagues define post-industrial economies quite simply as those 'where the task of producing the necessities of life has become trivially easy because of technological advancement and economic development' (Kahn, Brown and Martel, 1977, p. 1), and a similar definition is advanced by Lasch (1972). All writers on the topic do not have exactly the same view of what constitutes the post-industrial society. Kahn's view seems to be more fundamental than Bell's, and Touraine's perspective is more political than that of either of the Americans. It is to Bell that we turn for the most detailed exposition of the subject. His most succinct definition is as follows:

> The concept of the post-industrial society is a large generalisation. Its meaning can be more easily understood if one specifies five dimensions, or components of the term:
>
> 1 Economic sector: the change from a goods-producing to a service economy;
> 2 Occupational distribution: the preeminence of the professional and technical class;
> 3 Axial principle: the centrality of theoretical knowledge as the source of innovation and policy formulation for society;
> 4 Future orientation: the control of technology and technological assessment;

5   Decision-making: the creation of a new 'intellectual technology'.
(Bell, 1974, p. 14)

At the time Bell was originally writing – in the late 1960s – only in the United States was a majority of the labour force involved in services rather than agricultural or manufacturing production. This is now true of Western economies generally, with the proportion in services rapidly moving towards two-thirds. But, as Gershuny (1977a) has pointed out, the growth of so-called service workers does not imply the growth of employment of people providing direct services for private consumers. In the market economies the opposite is tending to happen, with households providing their own servicing with the assistance of consumer durables, such as washing machines and private transport. The growth in 'service' employment over the last two decades has been partly in public services, particularly education, and partly in areas which serve the needs of industry, such as banking, computing, design, advertising and so on.

By the pre-eminence of the professional and technical class Bell appears to mean the tendency for such workers to increase in numbers, since presumably the professional and technical classes have always enjoyed pre-eminence in terms of salaries, conditions and, to some extent, power. However, he does not indicate how far he expects this process to go. Others have suggested that post-industrial societies will require only a small minority of professional and technical workers and that the vast majority of the people, far from finding themselves professionalized, would find themselves, as far as labour is concerned, economically redundant.

Bell sets great store by 'axial principles':

> In identifying a new and emerging social system, it is not only in the extrapolated social trends, such as the creation of a service economy or the expansion of the professional and technical class, that one seeks to understand fundamental change. Rather it is through some specifically defining characteristic of a social system, which becomes the axial principle, that one establishes a conceptual schema. Industrial society is the coordination of machines and men for the production of goods. Post-industrial society is organized around knowledge, for the purpose of social control and the directing of innovation and change; and this in turn gives rise to new social relationships and new structures which have to be managed politically.
> (Bell, 1974, p. 18)

Writing ten years later, and with very little apparent reference to Bell, Stonier's version of the new 'axial principle' is 'information' rather than knowledge; it appears to amount to much the same thing with perhaps computers doing more of it in Stonier's version than Bell's (Stonier, 1983). Stonier is at pains to point out that since the invention of the bow and arrow and the discovery of fire it has been knowledge, information and technology which has made all the difference between a successful community and an unsuccessful one, and it has been a key element, if not the key element, in economic change.

Bell's third, fourth and fifth components are closely linked and concern the importance, complexity and organization of knowledge, its gathering, its control, and its roles and uses in society. Stonier refers to the post-industrial *economy* rather than society: its defining characteristics being sevenfold:

(1) Primarily a service rather than manufacturing economy, with 'knowledge' industries predominating;
(2) The labour force is dominated by 'information operatives';
(3) The economy is credit-based rather than cash-based;
(4) The economy is trans-national rather than national;
(5) The economy is institutionalized rather than free market;
(6) Society is characterized by unprecedented affluence;
(7) Change takes place exponentially rather than linearly.

The first two characteristics reflect Bell's: the rest certainly typify the advanced capitalist stages of the late twentieth century but, as with the service/knowledge/information dimensions, the question is whether they are part of continuing trends in industrial economies or societies or whether they indicate some sort of fundamental change such that these societies can no longer be called 'industrial': Lasch's treatment of the topic (Lasch, 1972), for instance, merely seems to involve a drawing together of a number of trends in American society in the late 1960s and designating them 'post-industrial'. He draws attention to six characteristics of the post-industrial society:

(1) The Changing Character of Poverty – in post-industrial society poverty exists in 'pockets' and 'islands' and is not the general condition of the mass of the people.
(2) The Class Structure – in post-industrial society the industrial working class is no longer the largest class.
(3) The Decay of the City – this refers to the spread of car-based suburbs and the decentralization of cities.
(4) Superfluous Production – because productive power exceeds society's material needs, 'the continuing growth of the system now depends on the creation and satisfaction of false needs' and wasteful products.

(5) Neo-colonialism — suggests that the worldwide diplomatic and military role of the USA is brought about by the needs of the post-industrial economic system.
(6) The Central Importance of Education — this arises because of the need of post-industrial society for trained personnel but also because of its need for sophisticated consumers.

We return below to the question of whether post-industrial society is fundamentally different from industrial society or just a development of it. First we examine a rather different perspective on the post-industrial society, as put forward by Alain Touraine:

> A new type of society is being formed. These new societies can be labelled post-industrial to stress how different they are from the societies that preceded them ... They may also be called technocratic because of the power that dominates them. Or one can call them programmed societies to define them according to their production methods and economic organisation ... the most widespread characteristic of the programmed society is that economic decisions and struggles no longer possess either the autonomy or the central importance they had in an earlier society which was defined by the effort to accumulate and anticipate profits from directly productive work ... Nowadays it [economic growth] depends much more directly than ever before on knowledge, and hence on the capacity of society to call forth creativity. All the domains of social life — education, consumption, information, etc. — are being more and more integrated into what used to be called production factors.
> (Touraine, 1974, p. 3)

Whereas the other writers referred to are content merely to elaborate these tendencies in great depth and detail, and tend to see them as potentially beneficial, Touraine analyses them as the process by which the capitalist economic system, and those in control of it and benefiting from it, continue to maintain their control over society even when production of material necessities for survival is no longer the central problem. Thus the 'struggle' between the people and the ruling class is no longer about access to material goods and services, it is now much more directly about the culture and political power itself. For instance, how is it decided, and by whom, that more economic growth is required rather than, say, a more equal distribution of the current wealth? Writing in the aftermath of the events of May 1968 in France, Touraine devotes considerable attention to analysis of the role of the student movement in resisting the tendencies of the programmed society; he also argues that the traditional union/employer conflict in the class struggle is becoming less important and that the arena of contest for power lies increasingly outside employment, in areas such as consumption and leisure.

But is the post-industrial society to be welcomed? In his book Bell is neutral but excited about the changes he foresees, although in a later note he claims to be deeply pessimistic (see Stearns, 1975). Stonier, on the other hand, ends his book on a highly optimistic note. In terms reminiscent of those of Keynes and Russell in the 1920s and 1930s, he states:

> In late industrial society we stopped worrying about food. In late communicative societies we will stop worrying about all material resources. And just as the industrial economy eliminated slavery, famine and pestilence, so will the post-industrial economy eliminate authoritarianism, war and strife. For the first time in history, the rate at which we solve problems will exceed the rate at which they appear. This will leave us to get on with the real business of the next century. To take care of each other. To fathom what it means to be human. To explore intelligence. To move out into space...
> (Stonier, 1983, p. 214)

Touraine is, by contrast, pessimistic. His Marxist analysis portrays the prospect very much as one of struggle against the forces of control. Lasch is similarly pessimistic. He argues that behind the façade of success and stability the capitalist post-industrial society is inherently unstable and full of contradictions and tensions and 'may not even survive the twentieth century'. The question of timing is interesting because, whereas most writers on the subject see post-industrial society as a future or just emerging condition, Bell is of the opinion that it has already arrived in the advanced Western capitalist states.

Critics

The whole idea of a post-industrial society or economy is not without its critics. One of the most outspoken is Ferkiss, who asserts that: 'the term "post-industrial" as used by Bell and others who have adopted his usage has done more to obscure than to illuminate the phenomena of contemporary social life' (Ferkiss, 1979, p. 65). Bellini is critical of the bland approaches of writers such as Bell who do not see, or at least pay very little attention to, the problems of transition from industrial society to some sort of post-industrial Utopia.

> Millions of ordinary people across the industrial world have been the unsuspecting victims of a gigantic intellectual con trick. That

trick has been pulled by the economists and professors at a thousand universities and institutes who have painted pictures of Utopia and called them The Future. The child-like visions were coated in the sophisticated veneers of the academic style, which did nothing more than, to borrow a phrase of George Orwell, give an appearance of substance to pure wind. This Utopian dream goes by the name of the Post-Industrial Society. The many learned books and articles extolling its virtues and setting out its detail would fill a small library. But they are works of pure fiction.

(Bellini, 1981, p. 14)

Bellini argues that, while the post-industrial Utopia may materialize in some countries, in Britain, the passing of industrial society does not herald a new era of continued prosperity based on services and technology: it is more likely to signal economic decline and the re-establishment of feudal power relationships which, in his view, have never in fact been absent during the industrial period: the collapse of industry in Britain, and the growing crisis in the rest of the economy, will take the country back to its old habits of social organisation, based on the power of land and a traditional leisure class (Bellini, 1981, p. 19).

Others predict the emergence of a professional and technical elite in the labour force and imply that this elite will be in control – Bell's 'preeminence'. But Bellini sees it differently, the traditionally powerful class who owe their power to the ownership of property will continue to wield that power; they will control:

a small, closed world where knowledge is God and the altars are tended by a monastic order of information brokers. And there will be a vast backwater economy around it, where unemployment, menial work, crafts, moonlighting, barter and brigandry are the standard features of everyday life. For most people in Britain there will be no real life after industry. For them, post-industrial society will be a replay of the Hundred Years War. And they will find themselves on the losing side.

(Bellini, 1981, p. 21)

Other critics question whether Bell and company are describing something sufficiently different from industrial society to be called 'post-industrial' or whether what they are considering is the culmination, or simply another stage, in the process of industrialization itself. Stearns (1975) and Kumar (1978) argue that nearly all the features and trends identified by the post-industrialists can be traced back, often to the nineteenth century. Kumar points out, for instance, that the growth of service employment is a normal feature of industrialization at quite an early stage and that Britain is exceptional among industrial nations in ever having had a majority of its workforce engaged in manufacturing, and that it was only a bare majority for a short period. In most industrial economies the manufacturing labour force settles at around one-third; the tendency is for rapid reductions in the agricultural labour force and hence the 'norm' for industrial economies is for the largest group to be in services. Kumar is quite clear in his rejection of the post-industrial thesis:

> The post-industrial theory assumes that the structural features of the new society mark actual discontinuities with the patterns of the old industrial society: novel and to a large extent unexpected directions in the nature of economic activities, the quality of work, the shape of the occupational structure, the future of class conflict and so on. The theory postulates a 'system break' in the transition to post-industrialism. Such a break is largely illusory. What are projected as novel patterns of development turn out on examination to be massive *continuities* within the basic system of the developing industrial society. Essentially, and insofar as they are actually occurring, the trend singled out by the post-industrial theorists are extrapolations, intensifications, and clarifications of tendencies which were apparent from the very birth of industrialisation.
>
> (Kumar, 1978, p. 232)

The terminology itself tends to support Kumar's contention. As Ferkiss (1979, p. 71) puts it, 'Post-industrialism defines one alleged reality in terms of another chronologically preceding reality.' Before 'industrial economies' there were 'agrarian economies' – which may be described as 'pre-industrial', but their economic basis can clearly be identified as agriculture. In the industrial age the economic base is seen as manufacturing industry which derives its wealth from its ability to produce marketable manufactured goods in large quantities. But what is the economic basis of the 'post-industrial' economy? It cannot be 'post-manufacturing industry'. Kumar points out that the new age has been given a wide range of names, including 'post-modern', 'post-bourgeois', 'post-economic', 'post-scarcity' and 'post-civilized'. Rose (1985), though critical of the post-industrial idea, uses the term 'post-fabricative', Toffler (1970) uses the terms 'post-materialist' and 'post-service' and Gappert (1979) uses the term 'post-affluent'. All indicate what has gone before but not what is to come. They convey the writer's understanding of what characterises *current* society but not what is to characterize the new one – except that it follows after the current one. Some names have attempted to convey something about the basis of the new society, including such terms as the 'knowledge society', the 'personal-service society', the 'service-class society' and the 'technetronic era' (Kumar, 1978, p. 193). More recently Stonier (1983) has developed the notion of the 'information economy' and Gershuny (1977) has analysed the potential role of the 'self-service economy'.

What we are looking for is some indication of what a future society would be producing as its characteristic major product. Agrarian society is based on the production of food. Industrial society is based on the production of manufactured products and related services. What then is the characteristic product of the post-industrial society? One possibility explored by Bell is that such a society would be producing primarily *services*, while another possibility would appear to be the production of *information*.

Services seem to be promising as a basis for an economy, since the range of potential services which people might want seems limitless. But is this really radical enough to justify the term 'post-industrial'? Gershuny (1977, 1977a) demonstrates that the whole idea of the service economy is mistaken – or at least misunderstood. The myth of the service economy is based on the observation that an increasing proportion of the workforce comprises 'service' workers but the fact is that as many as half those 'service' workers are not engaged in producing services for final consumption, they are service workers working within or for manufacturing industry. Thus the growth of service workers reflects to a large extent the growth of 'white-collar' input into manufacturing industry. Computer programmers and management consultants are service workers but their function can be to produce programs or management advice for manufacturing industry. This of course conforms to personal experience – we know that over the postwar period services have become more expensive relative to manufactured products and that, far from increasing their consumption of services, people have reduced them – for example, substituting washing machines for the use of a laundry and television and videorecorders for visits to the cinema. There has, of course, been a large increase in public service workers which should not be ignored, and Gershuny's analysis does not preclude a shift into services in future, but it does show that we have not yet seen the shift to a service economy which some post-industrial theorists believe.

But what of the 'information economy'? Information or knowledge production and processing features prominently in Bell's definition of the post-industrial society. The idea is developed more fully by Tom Stonier in *The Wealth of Information* (1983). Stonier's title is of course a reference to Adam Smith's classic *The Wealth of Nations*, and the implication is that information is emerging as the main source of wealth in post-industrial society. Although knowledge has often been the major factor in transforming previous societies – for example, knowledge of fire, metal smelting, gunpowder manufacture, steam power, electricity generation, and so on – it is claimed that in post-industrial society the production of knowledge and the processing of information becomes the most important and pervasive activity in the economy. 'Information operatives' cover a wide range of occupations, including all managerial and clerical jobs, communications and media work and those concerned with research, marketing and education. Altogether these constitute half or more of the jobs in the advanced economies of the West. But as with services, it does not follow that because there has been a large increase in the number of workers engaged in handling information, individuals are increasing their consumption of information at the same rate. There is a limit to the amount of information the individual can use and absorb. The change in employment structures reflects the increased amount of research and information required to produce modern goods and services.

Thus the net effect of the increase in service and 'information' workers in the economy is still the production of, ultimately, food, manufactured products and consumer services. While there may be shifts from time to time in the balance of these outputs, there is little evidence to suggest a major shift in the near future. For example, while it might be expected that people will in future subscribe in increasing numbers to tele-text services such as Prestel and, through cable and satellite, gain access to a wider range of television channels, such services will not be a major expense for the average family – otherwise they would not become popular. They will not, therefore, represent a significant shift towards information or services consumption. In any case, at the same time one would expect, in a conventional economic-growth situation, to see a corresponding increase in the consumption of manufactured products, the increased penetration of the video-recorder, second television sets, second cars, more dishwashers and so on. The major area where a genuine shift of production and consumption might occur is education, by which Stonier sets great store. Education is labour intensive both in terms of the teachers and the taught. Thus, for example, another 100,000 teachers in further and higher education could occupy the time of maybe 1.5 million people as students. This would represent a significant increase in information processing and consumption. Because of the particular life-styles of students and of adults who have received higher education, such an increase in education would, as discussed in Chapter 5, have implications for leisure behaviour and leisure services. But what is not clear from Stonier's treatise is whether the massive increase in education which he calls for would come about naturally because the post-industrial economy would demand trained personnel, whether people would demand it for its own sake, or whether it would have to be artificially engendered by governments primarily motivated by a desire to take young people off the dole queues.

So while the production processes of advanced industrial economies involve more service and information workers and fewer and fewer direct production workers, it does not necessarily follow that relatively more services and information are being produced for final consumption. The transition from an agricultural to an industrial society actually saw a massive increase in the production of a particular type of output, namely manufactures, which transformed everyday life; there would appear to be no comparable change in the transition to post-industrial society.

If it is not distinguished by the nature of the product produced then perhaps the post-industrial society will be characterized by a different structure which will affect economic and social relations. Some believe that cheap and portable technology will make it possible for Schumacher's 'small is beautiful' philosophy to flourish. It is, however, difficult to see where the evidence for this lies. It is, more often than not, the large corporations which produce the cheap, portable, technological products. Industrial capitalist society is itself characterized as much by small businesses as large ones. The small software house begun in someone's spare bedroom is no different in essence from the millions of small businesses begun in millions of spare bedrooms since time immemorial. But the existence of small businesses does not mean that large corporations will not continue to dominate economic life, to which IBM and British Telecom stand witness. As Ferkiss states:

> What is crucial, of course, is not whether television, computers, and similar means of communication and control exist and are absorbing more and more of the material and personal resources of all societies, but, rather, what if anything this has to do with social structure and economic and political power. Does being an employee of IBM rather than US Steel make any difference in one's economic or political status *vis à vis* others?
>
> (Ferkiss, 1979, p. 72)

One view is that there *is* a fundamental difference between working for IBM and working for US Steel, a difference so significant that working in the new service-type occupations should not even be classified as work in the traditional sense. J. K. Galbraith, in *The Affluent Society*, said:

> The greatest prospect that we face – indeed what must now be counted one of the central goals of our society – is to eliminate toil as

a required economic institution. This is not a utopian vision. We are already well on the way. Only an extraordinarily elaborate exercise in social camouflage has kept us from seeing what is happening.
(Galbraith, 1958, p. 273)

He suggests that professional and quasi-professional 'workers', 'the advertising man, tycoon, poet, or professor', are a 'New Class', who are not engaged in work in the traditional sense of toil. They expect to work in pleasant surroundings and to be absorbed and stimulated by their work – just the sort of rewards one might expect from leisure activity. Therefore, Galbraith argues, one of the aims of society should be to expand the New Class as much as possible. One of the rewards of economic growth is to enable more and more people to join the New Class. Such a view links with that of Haworth (1984), who suggests that the solution to the growing shortage of work is to expand the professions and quasi-professions because such workers, as well as providing non-material services to the community, are self-motivated and themselves generate work and demand for their own services. This is of course almost the opposite of Illich's view that professionalization is an insidious process which has already gone too far (Illich et al., 1978).

The real break between industrial and post-industrial society would surely come if or when processes in the service sector as well as the manufacturing sector of the economy, became so automated that they too required, maybe as little as 10 or 15 per cent of the current labour force. Would something emerge to absorb the other three-quarters of the labour force? Two possibilities emerge as to how such a society would occupy itself and, therefore, what would characterize such a society. The first is that people would engage in work for themselves, producing what Gershuny has called the 'self-service' economy. Alternatively they would engage in leisure activities to produce a 'leisure society'.

The Self-Service Economy
The idea that there might be two economies at work, the formal economy in which people worked for money and an informal economy in which they worked freely for themselves or the community, was foreshadowed in the Goodmans' *Communitas* discussed in Chapter 2 and is also discussed by the British Ecology Party in their report *Working for a Future* (1981). Denis Pym (1980) suggests that the idea of a 'dual economy' should be encouraged. He argues that low productivity and underemployment are endemic in Britain and are symptoms of a 'retreat from employment'; this should be accepted rather than fought and people should be encouraged to leave the

formal labour force, so improving efficiency in the formal economy, and should be given a guaranteed income and allowed to 'do their own thing' in the domestic or informal economy. He implies that eventually the informal economy will become the dominant one and its 'central ethic' and 'dominant system' will be self-fulfilment and recreation, in contrast to the central ethic and dominant system of industrial society which are work and economics. Ivan Illich uses the term 'subsistence economy' to describe a society which has developed away from dependence on professional and industrial forces: 'Let us call modern subsistence the style of life that prevails in a post-industrial economy in which people have succeeded in reducing their market dependence' (Illich et al., 1978, p. 94).

The idea of the informal or self-service economy has been fully explored by Gershuny (Gershuny, 1977, 1979; Gershuny and Pahl, 1980), by Rose (1983) and by Robertson (1985), who has coined the term 'own work' to describe self-service activity. Because of technological change labour is expensive in the market place and, therefore, traditional direct services become increasingly expensive relative to goods. The manufacturing sector, however, increasingly provides us with the hardware to do things for ourselves – whether it be washing our own clothes, filling our own petrol tanks, or preserving our own food in domestic freezers. What is interesting here is the way these self-servicing activities, such as cooking, gardening, or handicrafts, *can* become leisure-like. As services they nevertheless have high economic value if measured by their labour input and their cost if bought on the open market. It is estimated that unpaid domestic work, if valued at an appropriate wage, would be worth some 35 to 50 per cent of GDP (Gershuny and Pahl, 1980; Rose, 1983). It is, however, not currently 'counted' as part of the formal economy. Gershuny suggests that:

> the complex of activities including recreation, education, housework and other production activities which might in the future be transferred to the informal sector, might become a viable alternative to employment in the formal sector.
>
> (Gershuny, 1978, p. 151)

Gershuny pursues his ideas further in developing the notion of the 'three economies': the formal, the household or self-service, and the 'black' or 'underground' (Gershuny, 1979; Gershuny and Pahl, 1980). Work moves between the sectors as circumstances dictate but the overall trend is away from the formal economy. Since the domestic economy is as large as 40 per cent of the formal economy and the 'black' economy is estimated by some to be as great as 10 per cent of

GDP, it can be seen that the 'non-formal' economy is indeed already highly significant.

It is possible to envisage a future scenario in which people's engagement in the formal economy is minimal – either people would work very few hours per week or per year, or for just a few years in their lives – but this minimal involvement would produce all of society's needs from the formal economy, including basic food-stuffs, mass-manufactured goods, and large-scale services; and it would generate the income for individual workers to pay for their share of this output. The bulk of people's time would be spent in self-service activities, or 'pro-suming' as Toffler calls it, and as such these would represent the major wealth of the community. Society would have come full circle: in subsistence agriculture there is little formal record of society's main source of wealth, its agricultural production, because for the most part it involves no cash transactions: it is for subsistence. So the major 'industry' and source of the society's wealth lies outside the 'formal economy'. A society in which 'the economy', producing the bulk of people's material needs and a large proportion of their services engaged only a minor part of people's attention would surely justify the term 'post-industrial'.

The question is whether the self-service activity would be primarily work-like or primarily leisure-like. To some extent this is a matter of definitions. Rose, in discussing the distribution of 'discretionary time,' groups 'unpaid housework and productive leisure' together, suggesting that such activities as cooking, do-it-yourself and gardening can be either leisure-like or work-like, depending on the circumstances. Stebbins (1982) coined the term 'serious leisure' for certain activities, like studying, which can be done in leisure time but with a serious purpose. The self-service economy therefore holds out the prospect of increased leisure, but the leisure will itself be of a 'self-service' nature.

A Post-Industrial Leisure Society?

But what of the more technologically orientated post-industrialists? What future do they see for leisure? Bell virtually ignores the leisure dimension and Stonier is not particularly forthcoming on the topic. Toffler is ecstatic about the possibility of 'experience industries' and an 'era of breathtaking fun specialism' – much of it based on sophisticated technology. It is appropriate to return at this point to Herman Kahn who divides industrial economies into the three conventional sectors: primary (agriculture and mining), secondary (manufacturing) and tertiary (services). But he adds the *quaternary* sector:

Eventually, in the 21st century, we should expect a transition to a different kind of service economy, to what we term a *quaternary*, or truly post-industrial economy. Here the primary, secondary and tertiary activities will constitute only a small part of human endeavours; more and more people will do things for their own sake, and even more than today ends will become more important than means.

(Kahn, Brown and Martel, 1977, p. 22)

The list of typical quaternary activities put forward by Kahn and his colleagues make interesting reading from the point of view of leisure:

(1) Ritualistic and aesthetic activities,
(2) The creation of taboos, totems, demanding religions, traditions and customs,
(3) Reading, writing, painting, acting, composing, musicianship, arts and crafts,
(4) Tourism, games, contests, rituals, exhibitions and performances,
(5) Gourmet cooking and eating,
(6) Hunting, fishing, hiking, camping, boating,
(7) Acquisition and exercise of nonvocational skills,
(8) Improving property – gardening, decorating,
(9) Conversation, discussion, debating and politicking,
(10) Other cultural and social activities,
(11) Most welfare and social security functions,
(12) Other 'recreations', including search for adventure, excitement, amusement,
(13) Many public works and projects.

(Kahn, Brown and Martel, 1977, p. 23)

Apart from items (11) and (13) (which one would have thought would have remained largely in the tertiary sector), this is entirely a list of leisure activities. So why not go the whole hog and call it the 'leisure society'?

Conclusion

There is then no consensus concerning the nature of, or the likelihood of, a post-industrial society. Daniel Bell believes that it has already arrived and is characterized by the service-orientated and increasingly knowledge-based economic activity we see emerging all around us. Others, such as Stonier, argue that this state is not yet here but is close at hand: the economy is not yet sufficiently service-based and knowledge-based to be termed post-industrial. Others argue that the changes defined by Bell as symptoms of a post-industrial society merely signal another stage in the development of the advanced industrial economy and do not constitute a fundamental change.

In these scenarios leisure is not generally seen as of fundamental importance. Increases in leisure time and activity would probably come about relatively slowly in line with economic growth as in the past. By and large people would continue to work: but their work would be in the 'knowledge' and 'information' industries. The second alternative, put forward by Gershuny, and to some extent Kahn, is that the post-industrial society will permit people to contract out of the formal economic system and engage in self-service or quaternary activities – in which leisure could feature prominently.

The discussion in this chapter has only considered *what* might happen in the future and has not considered the mechanisms of change. Many would argue that the trend in capitalist economies is always to maximize profits and for this it is necessary to expand production (and consumption) in the formal economy as much as possible. The growth of the informal economy would be counter to this trend and would therefore be resisted by those interests which stand to benefit from an expanded formal economy. Therefore attempts might be made to stimulate demand in the formal economy artificially, and leisure would be an obvious area to stimulate such demands. The role of the political process and the providers or producers of leisure goods and services is therefore of particular interest and is discussed in later chapters. But first we turn to questions of key attitudes in society which may affect change.

4

The Shortage of Work I: Changing Attitudes

Among the many commentators on the future of work and leisure over recent years there is a fair degree of consensus that there will in future be less work to be done in the advanced industrial economies. The question facing us, according to these many commentators, is what should be done about this 'shortage of work'? Solutions put forward seem to be of two basic types. The first involves changing the values of society – it suggests that a key factor in preventing societies from adapting to the changing economic and technological environment is ingrained attitudes. Two aspects of this question of attitudes are examined in this chapter: first, attitudes towards work and the 'work ethic' and secondly the role of education in instilling and sustaining attitudes. The second type of solution to the shortage of work is concerned with a variety of ways of sharing the work around so that everyone gets a share of the work available. These ideas are examined in Chapter 5.

The Work Ethic

The most frequent call for a change in attitudes concerns the so-called 'work ethic' sometimes referred to as the 'Protestant work ethic'. A number of writers have attacked the 'work ethic' in modern societies and have called for its replacement by some other sort of 'ethic'. Jenkins and Sherman, two British trade unionists who have written extensively on the future of work and leisure, espouse the idea of a 'usefulness ethic' to replace the work ethic:

> If it appears, as we suggest that it does, that society, both individually and collectively, would be happier, would be more harmonious and would have fewer problems if the work ethic were either destroyed or reconstructed, then why should it not be done?

> ... The need to be wanted is, we believe, the true human condition; the need for formal work is but a perversion of this, so that the concept of usefulness rather than work must be the future ethic.
>
> (Jenkins and Sherman, 1981, pp. 15, 185)

Clemitson and Rodgers, two Labour politicians, see the alternative as a 'life ethic':

> In short, we need to develop a 'life ethic' rather than a work ethic and the corresponding concept of 'full life' rather than 'full employment'. Such an ethic would be concerned with the full development of human beings and human potential ... a life ethic would cease to see a person's only and major contribution to society as being made through his or her employment.
>
> (Clemitson and Rodgers, 1981, p. 13)

Clarke, a worker–priest writing on the growing problems of unemployment in Britain, coins the term 'contribution ethic':

> Perhaps out of the ashes of the Work Ethic, which is seriously challenged by the loss of the ideal of Full Employment, there will emerge the concept of a Contribution Ethic – a belief that our humanity does find fulfilment in doing things for others. That God is glorified through our being of service to our fellows whether that be through employee/customer relationships in the paid economy or whether that service, that giving of ourselves, is manifested in some other way quite outwith the paid economy.
>
> (Clarke, 1982, p. 196)

Martin and Mason, two economic consultants working in the leisure field, want to see a 'leisure ethic':

> Now at the end of the twentieth century, a new set of values is needed, one which recognises both the changing role of work and unemployment in the Western World and the parallel changes that are taking place in the amount and nature of our leisure ... such a new ethic should be based on a view of leisure as a part of life that is of value in its own right.
>
> (Martin and Mason, 1984, p. 1)

Denis Pym, an economist, detects a 'retreat from employment' in Britain and the emergence of a 'dual economy' in which the most appropriate ethic will be a 'resourcefulness ethic' (Pym, 1980, p. 236). Lord Ritchie-Calder prescribes simply a 'non-work ethic':

> What we need is a non-work ethic. It is heretical but it is logical... I use the term 'non-work' deliberately. It comprises retirement, redundancy, unemployment, a shorter working week, a shorter working day, longer holidays, with pay. It is not slothfulness, that deadly sin in terms of the work ethic. It removes the stigma which has become attached to compulsory idleness – unemployment – giving the victim robbed of the use of his skills a demoralising sense of inadequacy. It is usually called 'leisure', doing what one wants to do, which might be personally productive like do-it-yourself, or creative, like inventing or painting, or writing, or music or physical recreation.
>
> (Ritchie-Calder, 1982, p. 16)

Andre Gorz, the French Marxist sociologist, does not give a name to his proposed new ethic but is quite clear about the need to abolish the work ethic:

> For 200 years or so societies have been dominated by the productivist ethic which has sanctified work as mortification and sacrifice, as a renunciation of life and pleasure, of the freedom to be oneself. It will certainly not be an easy matter to destroy it and replace it with an ethic which privileges the values of voluntary cooperation, self-determination, creativity and the quality of our relations with each other and with nature.
>
> (Gorz, 1985, p. 107)

What is the work ethic? How does it operate? Who subscribes to it? How powerful is it? The answers to these questions are far from straightforward. The work ethic, or the Protestant work ethic, or the Protestant ethic, is partly a historical phenomenon, partly a folk myth and partly a sociological concept.

The development of the Protestant work ethic was described by Max Weber in his book *The Protestant Ethic and the Spirit of Capitalism* (1930). While historically, labour had always been considered meritorious to the Christian, particularly to ascetics, the Puritans elevated all labour to the status of a 'calling'. As Weber puts it, the Puritan view was that:

> on earth man must, to be certain of his state of grace, 'do the works of him who sent him, as long as it is yet day'. Not leisure and enjoyment, but only activity serves to increase the glory of God... Waste of time is thus the first and in principle the deadliest of sins. Loss of time through sociability, idle talk, luxury, even more sleep

than is necessary for health ... is worthy of absolute moral condemnation.

(Weber, 1930, p. 157)

Thus Weber showed how the religious ethic which had taken hold in Northern Europe in the seventeenth and eighteenth centuries provided moral support for the rise of capitalism and many of its less desirable side effects, such as poverty and gross inequalities. Each individual's place in life was, according to the Puritan view, a calling ordained by God; wealth and success were signs of God's favour, and poverty a sign of failure in God's eyes. So well did the religious ethic and the 'spirit of capitalism' mesh together that the work ethic survived as an essential element of capitalism even though the religious basis faded:

The Puritan wanted to work in a calling: we are forced to do so. For when religious asceticism was carried out of monastic cells into everyday life, and began to dominate worldly morality, it did its part in building the tremendous cosmos of the modern economic order. This order is now bound to the technical and economic conditions of machine production which today determine the lives of all the individuals who are born into this mechanism ... with irresistible force.

(Weber, 1930, p. 181)

The Strength of the Work Ethic

Whether or not the work ethic was ever internalized as a value by working people is, however, a question for debate, and if it ever was internalized there is some doubt as to its continued strength as a moral force today. As Galbraith put it:

Over the span of man's history, although a phenomenal amount of education, persuasion, indoctrination, and incantation have been devoted to the effort, ordinary people have never been quite persuaded that toil is as agreeable as its alternatives.

(Galbraith, 1958, p. 269)

Even in its historical context the work ethic appears to have been resisted by the working classes. Historians writing on the subject of leisure repeatedly refer to the process of 'social control' – the process of the capitalist system seeking to ensure that there is a well-disciplined workforce available (Bailey, 1978; Walvin, 1978). In non-industrialized societies the rigours of absolute time-keeping are relatively unknown – the largely agricultural way of life follows the dictates of the weather and the seasons and the needs of plants and animals. The story of industrialization is, we are told, one of a constant struggle between the employing classes and the workers, with the former attempting to impose order and discipline and the latter attempting to maintain freedoms and to engage in activities, particularly leisure activities, which reduce their efficiency as workers and are inimical to the requirements of industry. Thus, during the nineteenth century in Britain, the number of public holidays was reduced substantially; many positive and negative measures were taken to discourage drunkenness among workers both at and away from the workplace and to encourage participation in more 'wholesome' leisure activities. So widespread was absenteeism on Mondays due to the 'excesses' of the weekend, that in some of the industrial parts of the country it became known as 'St Monday'. In the twentieth century licensing laws were introduced during the First World War in order to reduce workers' access to public houses and thereby increase war production. All this suggests that the sobriety, industry and discipline which are associated with the work ethic were far from universal among the working classes well into the twentieth century.

Work Centredness
The relative importance of work and leisure in people's lives has been the focus of extensive contemporary theoretical and empirical research by leisure sociologists (e.g. Smigel, 1963; S. Parker, 1971, 1983; Bacon, 1972; Clayre, 1974; Haworth and Smith, 1975) in fact it could be said that the work/leisure dichotomy has been almost an obsession with leisure sociologists.

Dubin (1956) coined the term 'Central Life Interest' in his work on the relative importance of work and presented evidence relating to American male industrial workers which suggested that work was not a central life interest. But in a follow-up study Orzack (1963) found that in the case of professional workers, in this instance nurses, most did see work as a central life interest. The opposite of viewing work as a central life interest is to view it as 'instrumental' – that is, seeing work primarily as a means of obtaining an income and having no value in itself. This view seemed to be held by the 'affluent workers' of the Luton car industry studied by Goldthorpe and his colleagues (1968). They suggested that the male car workers of the 1960s might not be typical of all workers at that time but might be an indicator of the future. They concluded that:

> The tendency will increase for industrial workers, particularly unskilled or semi-skilled men, to define their work in a largely

instrumental manner; that is, as essentially a means to ends which are extrinsic to their work situation ... And to the extent, then, that his out-of-work life becomes dominated by home and family concerns, the link between this and the worker's occupational life is likely to be narrowed down to one of a largely economic kind. In other words, a privatised social life and an instrumental orientation to work may in this way be seen as mutually supportive aspects of a particular life-style.

(Goldthorpe et al., 1968, p. 74)

Gorz suggests that this process has accelerated in the intervening years, with workers in many countries becoming increasingly alienated from their work:

Of all contemporary socio-cultural changes, this disaffection from work is the most significant. For example, in Sweden, according to polls the proportion of women and men for whom work is the most important part of their lives has fallen from 33 per cent in 1955 to 17 per cent in 1977. In West Germany, the proportion of people for whom free-time activity is more important than work rose from 36 per cent in 1962 to 56 per cent in 1976. An opinion poll in France in autumn 1981 put the following question to a sample of workers: 'If you had the choice, would you give up your job?' 61 per cent of those earning between 4,000–6,000F per month replied affirmatively, against 34.5 per cent of those earning more then 10,000F, the average being 44.9 per cent.

(Gorz, 1985, pp. 33–4)

In Holland a group of unemployed young people have formed the 'Dutch Association Against the Work Ethic' aimed at promoting the potential of life outside the formal paid-work context (De Vink, 1983).

Alternatives to Work and Leisure
Most sociological discussion on the relative importance and the meanings of work and leisure tends to be conducted in terms of precisely those two terms, as if they were direct corollaries. The remark of Goldthorpe and his colleagues draws attention to the fact that for the vast majority of people life is not divided into just two compartments, work and leisure: there is a large third component, namely, home and family. Technically it might be possible to classify many of the activities that take place in the context of home and family as either leisure or personal/domestic chores, but this would not be helpful if we are attempting to understand people's attitudes to different aspects of their lives. For while people may not see themselves as 'leisure orientated'

or as 'personal/domestic-chore orientated' many would certainly see themselves as 'home and family orientated'. In fact, if we are looking for a 'central life interest', then, for many, if it is not work then it is more likely to be home and family than leisure. Parker's review of central life interest research suggests that studies in Australia, France and Japan have confirmed this (S. Parker, 1983, p. 81). The work of the Rapoports (1975) also seemed to point in this direction when they posited the idea of three 'planes' of life – work, leisure and family – but they do not seem to have displaced the sociologists' central concern with the work/leisure dichotomy. The point is illustrated by a passage in Michael Rose's book, *Reworking the Work Ethic*:

> Leisure, it is said, whether enforced or chosen, must increase in the next half century, thus taking over the central cultural importance of work. This is fashionable nonsense. For the long foreseeable future, the greater part of the population will spend the greater part of their lives in paid employment, and nearly everybody will spend an additional period active in the *informal economy or performing domestic tasks*.
> (Rose, 1985, p. 39, emphasis added)

It is not necessary to assume that a decline in the relative importance of paid work will automatically lead to an increase in the relative importance of leisure: other forms of work and domestic activity and domestic concerns are also involved.

Some have argued that work is of paramount importance to people not just because of its economic and moral place in people's lives but because of its ability to provide structure and meaning to lives because of the discipline which it imposes and the social relations which it provides. As Kelvin puts it: 'Work provides structure because it specifies the time, place and nature, not only of what one does but with whom' (Kelvin, 1982, p. 21). But Kelvin falls into the trap of assuming that the only alternatives in life are work and leisure, since he goes on to argue that if work were to decline, leisure would be incapable of replacing the discipline and meaning lost. In the same conference volume however, Duffield puts the alternative:

> It is desirable to question whether it is only in the tight discipline of work that order and structure are to be found. There would appear to be other areas of our lives where a structural discipline is imposed, if not by economic transactions necessary for subsistence and survival, then by other no less pressing needs, the creation and sustenance of social, kinship and family relationships, the maintenance of home and community environment.
> (Duffield, 1982, p. 4)

International Perspectives

A more light-hearted, but nevertheless possibly profound, appraisal of Britain and the question of its work-centredness is contained in Bernard Nossiter's book *Britain: A Future that Works* (1978). While most observers see Britain's poor productivity and economic growth record as a sign of a British 'sickness', Nossiter, an American journalist, interprets it as indicating that the British are not locked into the work ethic:

> Britons, to the dismay of the textbook writers, appear to be *satisficing* rather than *optimizing*. Workers and managers do not seek the greatest possible income; they seek instead an adequate or satisfactory level of income. They prefer tea-breaks and long executive lunches, slower assembly lines and longer weekends to strenuous effort for higher incomes. This, to be sure, is a sweeping generalisation that obviously does not apply to all Britons ... The preference for leisure over goods applies chiefly to those toiling in the mines or on assembly lines, labouring at routine tasks in huge white-collar bureaucracies, public or private. Their work does not, cannot enlarge personality; quite the contrary. It diminishes it. They work because they must, to earn enough to support themselves and their families. It is these workers who have decided that there are limits to how long and hard they will labour for extra goods ... Britons, in short, appear to be the first citizens of the post-industrial age who are choosing leisure over goods on a large scale.
> (Nossiter, 1978, p. 88)

This conclusion is supported by the results of a survey conducted for the magazine *New Society* in 1977 in which over 1,000 adults were asked about their attitudes to work and the quality of life. When asked whether people should work as hard as possible to get as much money as possible or whether they should work only as hard as necessary to lead a pleasant life, 32 per cent favoured working as hard as possible while 59 per cent favoured working only as hard as necessary (Forester, 1977).

In the USA there has been concern in some quarters that the work ethic which 'made America strong', may be in decline, but at least one commentator (Berg, 1975) has expressed the view that the values of the work ethic are still widely held but are being undermined by the activities of corporations and managers, who no longer exemplify the idea of hard work and sober application bringing success. However, around 70 per cent of Americans in a wide range of surveys say that they would continue to work even if they could live comfortably without working, suggesting the continued strength of the work ethic in American society (Maccoby and Terzi, 1979, p. 33). A weakening of the work ethic has nevertheless been put forward as an explanation for the failure of the American economy to grow as fast as those of its competitors since the 1950s. Maccoby and Terzi see the traditional Protestant work ethic being replaced or added to by a number of different work-related 'ethics'. These included the 'Craft Ethic', which is less subservient to employers than the traditional Protestant ethic; the 'Entrepreneurial Ethic', which is that everyone can make their fortune through enterprise; and the 'Career Ethic', which commands great commitment to and involvement with work, but only as a means of 'getting on' and acquiring status in, usually large, organizations. They also suggest, along with Yankelovich (1979), that a 'Self-Development Ethic' is emerging in which people look for satisfaction and intrinsic rewards from their work and are dissatisfied, or move on, if this is not offered.

Both Britain and the US have suffered relative economic decline and, given the prevailing concern with economic growth, might understandably be concerned about the commitment to work, but this is surely not the case in the 'success' economies like Sweden and Germany? Apparently it is. Elizabeth Noelle-Neumann (1981) reports survey findings in Germany which indicate a definite decline in commitment to work values between 1960 and 1980 and concludes: 'We have the impression that people find it more difficult than ever before to be industrious . . . One might suspect that the Germans are in the middle of an all-out effort to change their national character'. As for Sweden, the picture is similar; commentators in the early 1980s, reporting the figures on declining work commitment already referred to in the quotation from Gorz above, confirm Yankelovich's American findings, that people are looking for more positive fulfilment from work, rather than simply money or status. They conclude:

> An increasing proportion of the population experience a conflict between their work, which does not particularly appeal to them, and their lifestyle outside of work, which really engrosses them. In this contest work often turns out to be the loser. The only ones not to experience this conflict are those who have work as a lifestyle.
> (Zetterburg and Frankel, 1981, p. 42)

In Chapter 7 the idea of using the 'comparative method' for leisure forecasting is discussed, in which possible futures are considered by means of studying other, more advanced societies. The idea that Britain is in fact the most advanced of the industrial nations, rather than one of the 'also rans', is an intriguing one. In a certain sense it cannot be denied; when Karl Marx laid out his theories on the workings of capitalism during the nineteenth century it was Britain that provided him with most of his data because Britain was the first and most advanced capitalist, industrial society. Britain has experienced industrialization for longer than any other nation: it is therefore in a very real sense 'the most advanced industrial society'. That does not make it the most wealthy or the most technologically advanced. But it may be that the social effects of industrialization are being seen in their most developed form in Britain. Is it possible that this advanced state involves a rejection of the values of work and the embracing of leisure?

Unemployment
It might be argued that the distress caused by unemployment is evidence of the existence of a work ethic. There is a great deal of evidence to show that people who are unemployed suffer both economically and psychologically from the loss of work and all that goes with it (Seabrook, 1982; Sinfield, 1981). Of course people who are unemployed suffer from feelings of inadequacy and rejection and, even in periods of high unemployment, may be viewed by those in work as 'work-shy' or 'scroungers' (Bacon, 1972). But there are other explanations which could be advanced for this, besides the idea of a deepseated 'work ethic'. First, it could be the very *dislike* of work which causes those in work to resent the position of those out of work, apparently living a life of enviable idleness, supported by the taxes of the employed. Second, lack of work is usually accompanied by lack of money, but even when it is not, there is still a feeling among some that they do not want to be recipients of 'charity' or 'something for nothing'. Again this does not necessarily imply a positive view of work but a feeling that 'dues should be paid'. Research suggests that many of the unemployed are bored and do not welcome the 'leisure time' which has been thrust upon them, and want to work if for no other reason than to occupy their time. Again, this may not necessarily indicate a desire to work so much as a desire to be occupied.

For those who have always worked, or who see most of their contemporaries working, or who have been brought up to expect to work, to suggest that they should somehow find the material and social resources to embrace a huge increase in anticipated leisure time seems very demanding. Leisure activity itself is often characterized in the minds of many people, certainly in traditional male roles, by its relationship to paid work: leisure is the reward for working. Therefore extended leisure in the absence of work is not something which most people would necessarily be equipped to cope with. This combination of attitudes could of course be interpreted as constituting a 'work ethic' but it would probably be more accurate to describe them as manifestations of a 'work-based culture'. The word 'ethic' implies deepseated, internally held values, whereas a culture describes the society we live in and the constraints it places on us as well as the values it entails.

Kelvin appears to be of a similar view, arguing on the basis of historical evidence, that the Protestant work ethic has never been adopted by British workers. He concludes that the existence of a widely held Protestant work ethic is a myth:

> The position is this: if indeed British society is moving into a time of much less demand for human labour, a time of widespread unemployment and, eventually perhaps, of leisure, it is not necessary to get rid of the Protestant Work Ethic. What has to be got rid of is the *notion* of the Protestant Work Ethic – a notion which, as an explanatory concept has the status of phlogiston; but which, by virtue of being invoked, has in relatively recent times, attained the potency of the myth; and has thus become, to some extent a self-fulfilling prophecy. The concept of the Protestant Work Ethic is a classic instance of the social construction of reality, which itself distorts reality, and is thus a barrier to the ability to grasp and cope with reality.
>
> (Kelvin, 1982, p. 16)

Education and the Work Ethic
Another area in which the work ethic is believed to be alive and well is in the education system. The idea of 'education for leisure' is discussed below but here the question of whether the existing education system attempts, successfully or unsuccessfully, to instil a work ethic among young people is considered. There does seem to be a paradox at the heart of the British, and indeed most Western education systems. On the one hand, it is averred that the education system is primarily concerned with work: its aim is to train people for work and to turn out young people, labelled and graded, for the job market. And yet even a brief examination of school curricula suggests that if training for work is the purpose of the system then it has a very curious way of going about it. No school leaver is particularly qualified to do any job on leaving school at 16, or even 18. Hardly any of the average school curriculum is vocationally orientated. The basis of the curriculum in British schools is the grammar school system of educating the 'gentleman'. A nineteenth-century 'gentleman' was not required to possess any vocational skills because he did not have to earn a living.

The education system is geared to educating the 'whole person', not developing particular vocational skills. It could be argued that the only *practically* useful skills learnt at school are English and mathematics – and a great deal of the latter is actually redundant; few school-leavers ever need to be able to solve simultaneous equations or make use of Pythagoras' theorem. The rest of the curriculum comprises such subjects as history, geography, English literature, science subjects, subjects which are obviously leisure oriented such as sport, music and the arts, and such subjects as religious knowledge and current affairs. For the relatively few who will go on to study these subjects in higher education they can be seen to have some relevance to work but, since even higher education is often viewed as general education and not vocational training, this is true for only very small numbers. The education system, in terms of curriculum content, can therefore hardly be seen as a vehicle for instilling the work ethic – it is concerned generally with the education of the 'whole person' and not with the provision of work-orientated skills.

Where the education system may be instilling work-ethic values is in its adherence to the examination and qualification system. Despite the fact that what is taught in schools is irrelevant to most employers, employers nevertheless look for evidence that young people have studied those subjects to a satisfactory level as an indicator of their ability and application. Despite its overt ideology that learning is for its own sake, the education system packages education so that it can be used as a passport to a job. A crisis develops when high youth unemployment devalues educational qualifications and breaks the implied contract between the education system and its clients.

Finally, it might be suggested that the very form of schooling, involving timetables and discipline, is a means of instilling some of the elements of the work ethic. To some extent this is plausible although the idea that children should be disciplined predates the industrial revolution and the rise of the Protestant work ethic. It is also perhaps worth noting that in the early years of schooling a relatively 'undisciplined' approach to learning, involving self-directed learning through play and exploration, is common, and similarly in higher education a less regimented approach is possible. In Britain, at least, it is mainly in the middle years, from 11 to 16 and then 18, that educational methods are traditional and often highly disciplined.

Overall, therefore, the role of education in instilling and maintaining the work ethic is at best ambivalent. Recent research by Roberts and his colleagues (1982) suggests that teenagers in Britain's inner city areas have, when work is available, a very casual attitude to work, involving dropping in and out of jobs as boredom or lack of money dictate: hardly the attitude of young people whom an education system has burdened with a powerful work ethic.

Considerable doubts, therefore, surround the whole notion of a work ethic and its influence on ordinary people. So it is perhaps surprising that so many commentators have attached so much importance to changing or removing it. The general argument appears to be: 'if people are to be content with less work then they must change their attitudes towards work'. But the evidence that people are gripped by a need to work excessively long hours is limited to say the least. Reductions in working hours have been sought, won and enjoyed by working people over the years. The fact that there is widespread overtime working, especially in Britain, and even moonlighting, is not conclusive evidence of the existence of a work ethic. Since overtime and moonlighting attract payment, very often at premium rates, their existence could equally well indicate the existence of a 'home and family ethic' as discussed above, or simply a materialist culture. The gradual reduction of working hours (and most reductions *are* gradual) does not seem to present a problem as far as people's values are concerned. Where values, and other issues, become a problem is when some people are thrown out of work altogether while others continue to work a forty-hour week. In other words the problem is not the total amount of work available and people's attitudes to it, rather the problem is one of the *distribution* of the work available, a question we return to in Chapter 5.

Changing Work Attitudes?
Before leaving the question of the work ethic we should consider the mechanisms by which attitudes might be changed, if indeed this were considered to be desirable. The advocates of change do not tell us how this change is to be brought about. It must be supposed that 'opinion formers', such as political leaders, the media and schools would adopt the idea, which would then lead to its acceptance by the population at large. The question of whether or not such a process could take place raises complex issues as to just how social attitudes are moulded and changed. One view is that it does not happen in this 'top down' manner, that political leaders and the media *follow* changes in attitudes rather than initiate and form them. Mainstream politicians in Britain have hardly been to the fore in discussing these issues, although some governments on the continent of Europe have been. But if, as some of the evidence discussed above suggests, the work ethic is not a widely held value among ordinary people, but is really only part of the rhetoric and ideology of the establishment, then it is only the establishment, the media and other 'opinion formers' who have to change, to move into line with the population at large.

A Marxist view of history would, however, see economic forces rather than ideas and attitudes as the driving force of change. This suggests that values will change in response to new economic circumstances. Thus it has been argued that the existence of material wealth in industrial societies has *necessitated* an increase in leisure time because otherwise the workers/consumers would have insufficient time to enjoy the fruits of their labours and would have no incentive to work and to buy (Galbraith, 1958). Reports from Japan (BBC TV, 21 Oct. 1984) suggest that this hitherto highly work-orientated society, in which the five-day working week is only now being introduced and in which workers commonly forgo their annual holiday entitlement, is becoming more leisure orientated as automation reduces the demand for labour and as the workers and their families require more leisure time to consume the fruits of prosperity.

One possibility for Britain and other countries experiencing high unemployment is that attitudes will be changed as the phenomenon of worklessness becomes more common and more familiar. If high unemployment persists it will, before long, be something which will have touched most of the population, either directly or indirectly through children, other relatives or friends. When it is realized that lack of work is not necessarily the fault of the unemployed, and that those in work are to some extent fortunate, then such resentment as exists towards the unemployed and some of the stigma of unemployment may abate.

While many academics and commentators of the left have been arguing for the disestablishment of the work ethic, others to the right of the political spectrum, including members of the British Conservative government, have been arguing for a need to return to 'Victorian values' of self-reliance and hard work. The belief here is not that people will need to work less in future but that they should work more and harder, and for less pay. Lord Young, the minister with special responsibility for job creation said in January 1985 that youth unemployment was caused 'not only by the state of the economy but also by the attitude of school-leavers'. Too often they were 'demotivated and lacked the personal qualities required' (Young, 1985). The belief is that the 1960s produced a decline in moral standards and even an 'anti-work' mentality which is buttressed by the welfare state. Michael Rose has examined this proposition in some detail and concludes, as we have done here, that there is some doubt as to whether the so-called 'Victorian values' were ever widely subscribed to by workers in general, but equally that the converse idea that a positively 'anti-work' mentality has become widespread since the 1960s is misguided.

So we have, on the one hand, pundits arguing that we are too committed to the work ethic and on the other politicians declaring that we have become work-shy. In truth it would appear that there is an enormous variety of attitudes towards work, depending on personality, domestic situation, work experience and the type of occupation an individual is in or aspires to. To pretend that there is one dominant 'work ethic' or 'anti-work ethic' is to misrepresent reality. It is equally misleading to imply that people are *either* work orientated *or* leisure orientated: there is another very important aspect of most people's lives to which they are likely to be primarily orientated, namely, their family. The relationship between work, family and home, and leisure cannot be neatly encapsulated in a single concept such as the 'work ethic'.

Education for Leisure

Some doubt has been raised as to whether modern education successfully instils the work ethic in the minds of young people. Another aspect of education is raised here, namely the proposal, which has often been put forward, that at least part of the solution to the perceived forthcoming shortage of work and surfeit of leisure is that there should be more education for leisure.

The 1963 Newsom Report on secondary education in England stated:

> In western industrialized countries, the hours which must necessarily be spent in earning a living are likely to be markedly reduced during the working lifetime of children now in school. The responsibility for ensuring that this new leisure is the source of enjoyment and benefit it ought to be, and not of demoralizing boredom, is not the schools' alone, but education can play a key part.
> (Newsom, 1963, p. 28)

The Chairmen's Policy Group report *Leisure Policy for the Future*, in a chapter entitled 'Education for Leisure', stated:

> When jobs for all could be expected, the education system could direct its efforts to fitting people to those jobs. Now that such certainties are gone, and people may spend more of their lives in leisure than in work, the education system faces a new task – to help the young towards a satisfactory life, and the adult in their adjustment to change.
> (Chairmen's Policy Group, 1982, p. 55)

In his critique of the concept of education for leisure, Basini (1975) quotes a typical self-interested academic assertion:

> History indicates that the downfall of great civilizations has been the result of a definite misuse of leisure time [therefore people] must be

educated to use leisure time wisely in addition to learning vocational and professional skills.

(Kinser, 1968, p. 57)

Denis Howell, the former Minister of Sport, has said:

> The education system is geared to education for examinations when its true purpose should be to educate people for life and its rich possibilities, and most of all, for showing young people how to use their leisure time.
>
> (Howell, 1972 – quoted in Basini, 1975, p. 113)

There is a burgeoning literature on the subject of education for leisure (Borrett, 1982). There is nevertheless a great deal of confusion and a number of contradictions surrounding the subject.

The Curriculum

We have already discussed what might be called the 'curriculum fallacy' – that is, the notion that the school curriculum is currently work orientated and should become more leisure orientated. We have noted that this is simply not so, that very little of the school curriculum is work orientated in the sense of being vocational or providing young people with skills usable in the work place. Indeed, the traditional liberal view of education as Entwistle (1970) has pointed out, is almost anti-work; he quotes MacIntyre, who epitomizes this view in arguing that the proper end of education is:

> to help young people discover activities whose ends are not outside themselves ... The critical ability which ought to be the fruit of education serves nothing directly except itself, no one except those who exercise it ... above all the task of education is to teach the value of activity for its own sake.
>
> (MacIntyre, 1964, p. 19)

We noted above that it was probably the form and organization of schooling which could be considered work-like rather than the curriculum content.

Free Choice

A second problem, or rather collection of problems, is what might be called the 'free choice conundrum'. Many believe that leisure is about free choice and that therefore 'education for leisure' must be concerned with educating young people to exercise such free choice. But is this not a contradiction in terms? In such a process of educating for free choice in leisure will teachers not inevitably be influencing their pupils' choice of activity and so negating the very essence of leisure? The problem is encapsulated in Kinser's statement about 'using leisure time wisely'. Who decides what is wise? The use of looser terminology, such as the Newsom Committee's helping young people to find 'enjoyment and benefit' rather than 'demoralizing boredom' or the Chairmen's Policy Group's 'satisfactory life', does not really avoid the problem. Such sentiments imply that in the absence of guidance young people's *totally* free choices of activity – or inactivity – would be judged unsatisfactory. If, for instance, a teacher is engaged with a group of pupils in discussing the process of 'choosing' music how will the teacher avoid directing the pupils in the direction of what the teacher considers to be 'good' rather than 'poor' music? Will not teachers extol the virtues of 'good' rather than 'trashy' television programmes? Will they not favour attending the theatre rather than going down to the pub and getting drunk?

This 'values problem' goes to the heart of educational philosophy in that education should presumably foster appreciation of the 'finer things of life', if they can be identified. But the things which some young people might consider to be the finer things of life might be considered by their teachers to be the baser things of life. In such cases 'education' and 'leisure' become uneasy bedfellows. Leigh (1971) and Peterson (1975) argue that teachers *should* commit themselves to value positions concerning what is and what is not excellence. Others duck this issue of values and speak of merely 'offering pupils or exposing pupils to a wider choice of activities', or of 'developing critical faculties' so that they are better equipped to make choices.

The belief in a wide choice as a positive value in itself is worthy of some consideration. It is enshrined in a great deal of thinking about modern leisure and is reflected in such things as leisure-orientated physical education and games periods in schools, with a wide range of options to choose from, and in the modern multi-purpose leisure centre offering twenty-five different sporting and recreational activities under one roof. The belief is that people are very different one from another and need to express those differences in a corresponding variety of activities. Such an idea seems so self-evident that it is rarely if ever challenged.

The idea could be challenged on the grounds that we have no evidence that people are always happier with a wide range of choice than with a limited choice. It is frequently noted that when young people are given a free choice as to how to dress they adopt a common uniform of training shoes and blue jeans: suggesting that they wish to conform rather than be individualists. There is again no evidence to show that when the only option in sport for young males was soccer in the winter and cricket in the summer, young males were less happy than they are now with twenty-five different sports to choose from at the local sports centre; or that drinkers were less happy with a choice of only mild or bitter in the local pub, than they are now with a dozen different brands of beer and lager to choose from.

Even if the individual is happier with a wider choice there is a potential loss in communal terms in fragmenting the community, or 'segmenting the market' as the marketing men would put it. Concern is often expressed about loss of community and alienation, but widening choice and segmenting the market ensures that those collective and communal activities – for instance getting twenty-two people together to play a game of football – lose out in favour of small-scale or individualistic activities – such as two people playing a game of squash. In addition, by spreading its efforts among a wide range of activities, an institution such as a school or a leisure centre could lose the collective experience which comes from the development of a local culture, a certain level of expertise, interest, support and social networks that can come from concentration on a narrower range of activities. The point can be illustrated by a situation where there is no choice but for everyone to join in the same activity: in a village everyone goes to the village fête because there is nothing else to do and 'community' is thereby fostered.

Breadth of choice has been equated with freedom of choice in leisure, which has been equated with freedom of choice generally, which in turn has been equated with freedom and then with happiness. Lest this argument be seen as some sort of totalitarian approach to leisure provision and education it should perhaps be stressed that it is not intended to denigrate the idea of choice totally but merely to suggest that there may be disadvantages in the pursuit of breadth of choice for its own sake.

There are other problems associated with widening choice as an aim of education for leisure. The first is that the range of activity offered in school may bear no relation to the range of choice available to the pupil outside of school; this might be called the 'facilities problem'. This has of course always been a problem for teachers, even with conventional activities such as playing football, since facilities are often more easily available to the school-pupil than to the school-leaver. This is one explanation for what was termed in Britain the 'Wolfenden Gap' – the fall-off in sports activity by young people immediately upon leaving school (Wolfenden, 1962). This problem is less apparent in the United States where so many young people continue in school into their late teens and community sport is focused on school and college facilities. In other areas of leisure lack of access is less of an excuse – for instance in Britain there is a widespread network of free public libraries so that no one need be short of a 'good read'. But while the school may have access to its own mountain outdoor pursuits centre or sailing centre at little or no cost to the pupil, or may be able to negotiate cheap matinees at the local repertory theatre, such opportunities are not so easily available outside of school.

A further problem with choice is the problem of 'dabbling'; the danger that children will flit from activity to activity and not achieve any competency in any one. Such an observation leads us back to the question of form as opposed to content. If leisure is seen by young people as effortless pleasurable activity then to force them to 'concentrate on something' may appear to be making the so-called 'leisure' work-like. If the choice is not available then pupils may be forced by circumstances to concentrate on one or two activities and become proficient in them. But if a wide range of choice is on offer then it might appear to be perverse to force them to concentrate. Again the values of education – which are concerned with 'learning something' and 'working at something' and acquiring skills – come into conflict with hedonistic, instant gratification ideals associated by many with leisure. A factor which can exacerbate the 'dabbling problem' is the limited range of skills of the average teacher ... who may not be *able* to take children beyond a basic, 'dabbling' level in more than a handful of activities.

This leads to a very practical problem with the 'wide-choice' approach to education for leisure, namely, resources. One solution to the limited skills of teachers is to employ more teachers with different specialisms or to send existing teachers on courses to widen their range of expertise. Both these options cost money. Further, the facilities and equipment required to give expression to the wide-choice philosophy also cost money, sometimes enormous sums of money. Such sums are rarely available, or, because they are often 'soft money' – for example, the weekly visit to the local swimming pool – are vulnerable to cuts in times of economic stringency.

Critical Faculties
The other declared aim of education for leisure, apart from simply exposing children to choice, is to develop critical faculties. This raises two issues, first, once again the 'values problem': the clash between establishment and educational values and those of popular or mass culture. Will practice at exercising critical judgement not inevitably be directed at showing that classical music is 'better' than pop music, that Shakespeare is 'better' than *Dallas*? Even if this is successful it may be seen by pupils as having nothing to do with leisure as they understand it. In fact the process could be counterproductive – that is simply *because* it is part of the school curriculum it will be seen as work-like and not leisure-like.

The second problem with the 'critical faculties' argument is that it throws the whole idea of education for leisure as a separate activity into doubt. The idea behind the development of critical faculties is that young people are going to be faced with increased leisure and a rapidly changing world without the certainties of past generations, and that in order to cope with this they will need all sorts of qualities and skills, including developed critical faculties and resourcefulness. But have we not heard this somewhere before? Are not these precisely the sorts of qualities which the whole of education is supposed to engender, to enable the child to cope with *life*? The development of these qualities is not a task peculiar to education for leisure, it is to do with the development of the individual as a whole. The idea that young people could emerge from the education system basically stupid but with all sorts of wonderful qualities enabling them to cope competently with an ever-changing world of leisure, but not much else, is far-fetched.

Education for Leisure for All?
The problems of education for leisure do not end here: it is caught up with one of the fundamental problems of education, namely, that while equality of opportunity is sought after, equality of outcome is not expected. In other words while all children may be offered the chances of an extended academic education with its prize of well-paid, highly skilled work, the prizes are not available for all. At an early stage in their academic career both pupils and teachers become aware of who is and who is not going to 'make it'. The question then arises as to whether the less intelligent or less academic child should have a different curriculum or simply a reduced menu from the academic curriculum. The danger is that 'education for leisure' will become an easy option for the academically less gifted child. The academically gifted do not have time for 'education for leisure' if they are to get their qualifications. But then irony is heaped on irony because if the academically less gifted children become the unskilled and unemployed and underemployed workers the evidence suggests that such groups are the very ones who reject, or cannot afford, the range of uplifting and personality developing activities for which education for leisure aims to educate them.

Continuity
A final problem with education for leisure might be termed the 'continuity problem'. One of the principles of education for leisure is more exposure of young people to a range of opportunity in the hope that something will 'turn them on' to a lifetime of interest, or at least that the memory and experience will lead to consideration of that activity in later life. Similarly leisure skills acquired in childhood will, it is

hoped, be useful in later life. Although it is popularly believed that once one has learnt to ride a bicycle the skill is never lost, it is not clear that this applies to other leisure skills. Thus it seems unlikely that the golf swing learnt at school will remain operational, if unexercised, until required in middle age. It is debatable whether efforts should be put into instilling a wide range of skills in young people while they are at school or whether such efforts would be better spent on making adult-education opportunities available as required. Bourdieu's (1980) concept of 'cultural capital' is a useful one: it is the set of values and skills passed on to children largely by their parents and is believed to affect children's life-chances in work and leisure. The laudable aim of education for leisure is to take on part of the burden of developing and passing on 'cultural capital'. This discussion has pointed out the difficulties in attempting to put this ideal into practice. It is intended to provide an antidote to some of the somewhat glib calls for 'education for leisure' as a solution to the problems of the 'leisure society'.

Alternative Views
Before leaving this discussion of education for leisure, it is perhaps advisable to express a note of caution lest it be thought that there is some sort of consensus about the need for 'education for leisure'. There are other views. In particular there is the view that the traditional approach to education, with its liberal perspective as exemplified by the quotation from MacIntyre above, is *too* leisurely and is devaluing work and failing to equip young people with the skills they require for work. In the speech in January 1985, referred to earlier, Lord Young said: 'We have to recognise that the preparation for work is a worthy, respectable, and above all essential objective in its own right' (Young, 1985).

The problem is that at the same time the minister decries specialization – 'our schools must on no account turn out specialists' – but wants flexible young people with general skills: precisely the output which the traditional, 'liberal' approach is aimed at. Harold Entwistle has consistently argued that the traditional liberal view of education is misguided and, far from being more leisure orientated, education should become more work and vocationally orientated:

> An education concerned with development of the whole man must bring him to the point where he is able to do a job of work with skill, intelligence, taste and a sense of responsibility . . . it has usually been argued that if most of our fellow men are to derive any satisfaction whatever from life, agreeable spare time recreations must be devised to compensate for soul-destroying work. However, the notion that worthwhile leisure activities can ever compensate for

degrading work is one of our less satisfactory myths. Similarly the assumption that under automation the problems of an abundance of leisure are all that need concern us is economically naive ...

On the contrary, he argues that an automated society will stress the importance:

not only of greatly expanded technical education, but also of moral, aesthetic and social education if our value systems and sociological competence are to be adequate to the challenge posed by radical technological innovation.

(Entwistle, 1970, p. 109)

At the centre of the debate about the future of work and leisure we therefore seem to have two very doubtful propositions. The first is that the work ethic is impeding change and should be replaced. But in fact it is not at all clear that the work ethic exists in any practical sense, and if it does, it is by no means clear how it would be replaced. The second is that young people should be educated for leisure rather than work. But we have seen that children are not generally educated for work at present and it is doubtful that education for leisure is a meaningful concept.

5

The Shortage of Work II: Sharing the Work Around

Many of the commentators on the future of work and leisure have suggested that if there is to be less work available in future then at least the work that is available should be shared out so that the average worker spends less time in work and has more leisure, and unemployment is minimized (Best, 1980; Jones, 1982; Handy, 1984; Townson, 1985). There are proposals to reduce the working day or week, the working year and the working life. Reducing the average working day or week involves reductions in the standard working week, reductions in the amount of overtime worked, and/or increasing the proportion of part-time workers, possibly as a result of job-sharing. Reducing the working year involves increasing annual holiday entitlements. Reducing the length of the working life involves raising the average age at which young people leave full-time education, increasing the availability of sabbaticals, and/or lowering the age of retirement.

Working Hours and the Working Lifetime

Before looking at these proposals individually it is perhaps worth looking at their relationship to each other in quantitative terms. If it is assumed for the present that, other things being equal, any reduction in hours worked by the existing workforce leads to an equivalent increase in jobs for the unemployed, then to absorb all of the unemployed in Britain in 1985 would require a reduction of some 15 per cent in the hours worked by the current workforce. This could be achieved in a number of ways. Let us assume that the average worker leaves full-time education at 17 years, works a forty-hour week, has four weeks holiday a year and retires at 62. A total working year would then consist of 1,920 hours work and a working life would be 86,400 hours. To absorb the 15 per cent unemployed these hours would need to be reduced to 1,630 and 73,440, respectively. Charles Handy, in his book *The Future of Work* (1984), refers to the current

'100,000 hour job' as being the norm, which would apply to males working in excess of forty hours a week from age 16 to 65, and suggests that this is 'crumbling down to 75,000 hours in many offices' and, in his view, needs to fall to 50,000 in future.

The reduction in hours from 86,400 to 73,440 could be achieved in a number of alternative ways:

(1) Reduction of weekly hours to thirty-four.
(2) Increase in annual holidays to eleven weeks.
(3) Lower the average retirement age (men and women) to 55.
(4) Raise the age of leaving full-time education to twenty-four years.
(5) Introduce seven years of sabbaticals for all workers.

A combination of these measures might be considered. One such combination which would achieve the desired results is:

(1) Reduction of weekly hours to thirty-eight.
(2) Increase in annual holidays to five weeks.
(3) Lower the retirement age of men to 60.
(4) Raise the age of leaving full-time education to eighteen.
(5) Introduce six months of sabbaticals for all.

Different people might prefer different options. For instance one hour off the working week gives forty-eight hours in a year which is equivalent to more than a week's holiday, and over a lifetime this would be the equivalent of more than a year's sabbatical. While sabbaticals have entered into some American union agreements they have only just crept into one or two white-collar union agreements in Britain outside the academic world. Over recent years the preferred option in Britain appears to have been an increase in holiday entitlement.

But such changes would not happen in a static situation. The whole point about technological change is that it increases the productivity of labour. Over the last three decades overall labour productivity has grown by some 2 per cent per annum. Microelectronics will, it is believed, accelerate this process. Suppose we take a ten-year view and anticipate that productivity will grow by 3 per cent per annum over the next decade. In the past there has been a tendency to take one-fifth of the increase in productivity in the form of reduced working hours and four-fifths in the form of increased incomes, that is, increased production. The increase in productivity over the decade, at a compound rate of 3 per cent per annum would amount to 34 per cent; some 27 per cent of this would therefore be taken in the form of increased incomes/production and 7 per cent in the form of reduced working hours. So total working hours would have to be reduced by 22 per cent to absorb the unemployed and take account of increases in productivity – so reducing the working lifetime to 67,400 hours. This would mean one or a combination of the following:

(1) Reduction of weekly hours to thirty-one.
(2) Increase in annual holidays to fifteen.
(3) Lower average retirement age to 52.
(4) Raise age of leaving full-time education to twenty-seven.
(5) Introduce ten years of sabbaticals for all.

These very simplistic calculations are presented to illustrate the scale of the changes that could be in prospect. The likelihood of their happening is another matter. From the leisure point of view the scale of change could be substantial, depending on the form in which the increased leisure time is taken and uses to which it is put.

Many, including the current governments of Britain and the United States and their main opposition parties, do not believe that the unemployment problem has to be solved by reducing working hours and sharing the work around. They believe that economic expansion will absorb the current levels of unemployment. And, of course, the creation of new jobs in the United States and Japan in 1983–84 suggests that they could be right – that current levels of unemployment are simply the by-product of economic recession combined with short- to medium-term structural problems, rather than symptoms of longer-term fundamental economic and social change. So while some governments, notably the French and the Belgian, will be taking measures to assist in the process of shortening working hours and sharing the work around, others will not: to do so would imply a loss of face since they are so firmly committed to economic expansion as the solution to all economic problems.

The second major problem in implementing any of the proposals to shorten working hours is the question of what it all costs and who is to pay. In the case of reductions in working hours resulting from increased productivity the question does not arise: the reduction in working hours and the increases in pay are paid for by the increase in productivity and are negotiated between employers and workers. But what of the reductions in working hours to absorb the unemployed? The way in which such measures could be financed varies according to the nature of the particular proposal and is taken up in the discussions below. These discussions deal first with reductions in the average working week/year, and second, the reduction of the length of the working life. In addition to the question of costings, the discussions also consider the practical feasibility of the proposals, the likely reactions of workers, employers and governments, and the possible implications for leisure.

Reducing the Working Week/Year

Here we discuss the possibilities of either reducing the length of the working week or increasing the length of holidays. Suppose this were to be attempted by legislation by means of a statutory holiday of eleven weeks for all without loss of pay. What would be the consequences? To maintain production employers would need to take on 15 per cent more workers, which would absorb the unemployed. But their wage bills would rise by 15 per cent and therefore prices would also rise, possibly by the full effect of the increase in wages, unless profits were squeezed. Demand for their products would therefore be expected to fall. But increased demand from the unemployed now with full wages in their pockets could offset some of this fall. Imported goods and prices in overseas markets would not however be subject to these price rises and so sales of British-made products could be decimated, depending on the amount of competition from foreign producers. A further effect is that there would be enormous savings to the exchequer which, if passed on in the form of tax cuts, could also offset some of the effects of increased prices and falling demand; alternatively it might reduce its borrowing in the money markets and so see a fall in interest rates, which would benefit industry and consumers. Overall, therefore, it is difficult to predict the precise net outcome.

Proposals leading to price rises as high as 15 per cent look unacceptable, but if they were phased in over a period of say five or six, or even ten, years, the impact might not be so severe. On the other hand, if the proposals were so phased in, they might get lost in the normal rounds of pay and hours negotiations and so would have very little net effect on jobs.

A further problem in attempting to create jobs by reducing working hours is that the reduced working hours may not in fact lead to a net increase in the equivalent number of jobs. The classic piece of evidence in this respect is the British experience of the three-day week during the miners' strike of 1973–4. In such conditions production should have fallen by 40 per cent but it rarely did; and in many reported cases there was no fall in output and even increases! In other words the amount of work people do is not entirely determined by the hours they work. The three-day week was, of course, a special case but there are likely to be many cases where this sort of phenomenon would occur and where employers would not increase their workforce by the full amount to compensate for the reduction in hours. There are certain types of job where extra jobs would be unlikely to be created because of their very nature – for example, top management, janitors and receptionists.

A further problem is that it is not in fact possible to separate changes in labour costs from the process of the introduction of labour-saving machinery. Any large increase in labour costs could have the effect of accelerating the rate of introduction of such equipment. Thus office managers, faced with a reduction of 15 per cent in their effective labour force, might suddenly introduce wordprocessors which, in the normal course of events, might have been introduced over a period of years. There would, therefore, be no net increase in jobs. In some cases the change in costs could tip the balance in favour of some sort of technology which would result in a net loss of jobs. Of course these sorts of scenarios would not take place everywhere, but where it did happen it would have reduced the effectiveness of the measure overall in creating jobs.

Worker Attitudes
In introducing such proposals, there is the question of how the workers themselves would react. In Britain, it is invariably argued, as we have already seen, that any reduction in the standard working week would be taken up in increased overtime working. Two points should be made in relation to this. First, if this is in fact the case, then it suggests that increases in holiday entitlements would be a more effective means of increasing jobs, since there is less evidence of workers doing overtime rather than taking their holiday entitlement. The second point is that increased overtime could be legally discouraged as is happening in France (Hantrais, 1984) and other European countries (Jenkins and Sherman, 1981, p. 28). But this would be difficult to enforce. There would certainly be exceptions to the rules, for instance, where a firm employs only one worker with certain vital skills, so there is bound to be 'leakage'. Besides, even if the basic proposal to legislate for reduced hours were acceptable to industry, it is unlikely that this more detailed level of 'interference' would be acceptable. In many cases the financial incentives for both employer and employee to break the rules would be so great that enforcement might be difficult.

But this all assumes that workers would attempt to maintain their normal hours of work with the same employer. In fact they might be tempted to 'moonlight'. For some the possibility of moonlighting might increase substantially, leading to a net increase in the number of hours worked. For example, workers who currently finish work at 5.00 pm may not be able to travel home and also work in a bar in the evening, starting at 5.30 pm. But if they finished work at 4.00 or 4.30 pm they might be able to undertake several evenings' work in a week. Again this sort of effect might be minimized if holiday entitlements were increased rather than weekly hours reduced. But even then longer holidays might enable full-time workers to take certain short-term seasonal jobs during their holidays, jobs which would otherwise have gone to the unemployed.

It should be emphasized that it is not being suggested that *all* workers, or even a majority, would want or have the opportunity to engage in moonlighting or increased overtime working. But, as discussed in Chapter 4 in relation to the work ethic, there are many who at particular times in their lives want to earn extra money and prefer this to increased leisure. The point is that this tendency would reduce the effectiveness of any policy to reduce working hours.

We should not ignore the role of employers in all this. A recent report by the British Trades Union Congress points out that firms who cut their labour during the depths of the recession in 1982 appear to have over-reacted, but instead of taking on additional workers in 1984 to make up any shortages, they have been offering increased overtime to existing workers. A news report points out:

> The increase in overtime is a blow to the TUC's attempts to encourage affiliated unions to negotiate agreements with companies which trade off reduced working hours for more jobs. Successive reports, notably by the Policy Studies Institute, indicate that shorter working hours have not led to an increase in employment. This is largely because companies increase productivity or overtime to deal with agreements introducing shorter basic working hours.
> (*Guardian*, 31 Dec. 1984, p. 3)

The TUC (1982) is committed, along with other European trade unions to the introduction of a thirty-five-hour week, and some success in moving towards this has been reported (*New Society*, 1980; Incomes Data Services, 1982).

All this suggests that there would be considerable difficulties in imposing measures to reduce working hours substantially, and there is considerable doubt as to the effectiveness of such measures in creating jobs if they were to be introduced.

Job-Sharing
A rather different way of sharing work by reducing average hours worked is the idea of job-sharing in which a full-time job is split into two part-time jobs (Olmsted, 1977; Billingsley, 1985). In this instance the individual worker is paid only half the full-time wage or salary so the cost of the measure falls on the worker. Minor extra costs do, however, fall on the employer because of the extra administrative costs

of employing two people instead of one. In fact there are a number of potential costs and benefits in the idea. It might be thought that, in certain jobs, there would be a loss of efficiency in having two people working at a job rather than one, and that there would be problems of continuity and communication. But presumably people involved in job-sharing learn to cope with these problems and educate the rest of the world to cope also. It can, however, be argued that there are potential gains to the employer – the employee who only has to work for twenty hours a week may bring more enthusiasm and concentrated work to the job and may be far more productive than full-time colleagues. The two people sharing the job may keep each other 'up to the mark' and the work may benefit from the attention of two brains rather than one. The employer and society as a whole may gain through not losing the skills and experience of a worker, where the alternative might be their temporary or permanent loss from the labour market. Equally of course all these positive things may not happen and personality clashes could lead to an unworkable or inefficient situation.

Job-sharing is likely to be an attractive proposition to people at particular stages in their lives, for instance, while they have pre-school children, or in the years prior to retirement. The idea is one which only the most enlightened employers are likely to introduce voluntarily, but since the cost to them is minimal, the introduction of the right to job-sharing for anyone who wants it, either through trade union agreement or through legislation, seems a not unreasonable proposition.

Part-time Working

Job-sharing is not the same as simply part-time working since it involves the splitting of a specific job. As such it is generally discussed in relation to professional jobs, but there is no reason why this should be so. Part-time work is already widespread, either because of the nature of the job, for example, office cleaning staff or the 'lollipop' wardens who see children across the road on their way to and from school, or because of the nature of the labour market, for instance, when women workers are required, or on many North American college campuses where large numbers of part-time jobs are available which students can conveniently take while also pursuing their studies. It is perhaps interesting to note that when they need labour of a certain type employers are prepared to adapt their recruitment policies accordingly. There is also usually an economic incentive: both women, despite equal pay legislation, and college students are attractive to employers because they generally command lower wages.

There is, however, one area where part-time work has not been widely adopted and where it might have considerable potential. While it is common for retired people to seek part-time work it seems less common for part-time work to be adopted in the years immediately prior to retirement. And yet the idea of 'easing' oneself into retirement via a spell in part-time work would seem to be a potentially attractive one. It would have all sorts of advantages: the older worker, say over 55, would benefit from reduced work pressures at a time when work may be becoming burdensome. Older workers taking part-time work would have time to accustom themselves to having extra time on their hands rather than this happening all at once. There is, of course, the question of money; at this stage in life many may be able to manage on less than a full salary when children are no longer dependent and mortgages may be paid off – and again there may be some value in being able to adjust slowly to a reduced income which will inevitably be experienced on retirement. It is possible, of course, that certain options could be exercised in relation to pensions so that part of a pension could be paid early to a part-time older worker.

Again the cost to employers of operating a part-time scheme for older workers would be minimal and therefore there seems no reason why such an option should not be legislated for as a right of all workers above a certain age. It could be argued that legislation is not necessary because if people want this they can seek out part-time work elsewhere. But it is well known that older workers have great difficulty in finding jobs in periods of high unemployment and many would not welcome the disruption of changing jobs at that time of life but might exercise the option if it were available in their current place of employment.

Part-time work has been promoted by a number of writers as a means of introducing flexibility and more satisfaction into people's lives. Goldring suggests that, depending on the time of life workers might hold one or two part-time jobs rather than one full-time one. In his book, *Multi-Purpose Man*, he states:

> The two-job man would probably try to take one job for the money and the other for its personal satisfaction. In doing so he would achieve many of the satisfactions associated with leisure while still gainfully employed.
>
> (Goldring, 1973, p. 103)

Andre Gorz, referring to French surveys in Aznar's study *Part-time for All* (1981), states:

> The situation where the man works full-time and the woman part-time is very far from being the most popular pattern among those

questioned. On the contrary, the most attractive situation is the household where both the man and the woman work part-time and share domestic responsibilities. And the 'ideal' is man and woman both working part-time and having another *shared* activity in their free time ... But at present the strong demand for reduced working hours, which would enable available work to be shared out among a greater number of workers, remains entirely unsatisfied.

(Gorz, 1985, p. 109)

Leisure Implications
What would the effect of these measures for reducing working time be on leisure, if they were to be introduced effectively? One way of exploring this issue is to ask people how they would spend additional leisure time if it were available. An early study by Faunce (1963) indicated that the most popular activities among industrial workers would be 'working around the house' (97 per cent of respondents) and 'spending time with the family' (77 per cent); only then did leisure emerge, with 54 per cent wanting to spend time travelling and 49 per cent wanting to attend sports matches. This supports the view expressed above, that home and family are potentially more important non-work activities than leisure. It is also likely that, depending on when the extra time became available, people would sleep more – as they do currently at weekends. The important point is that all reductions in work time would not automatically be translated into leisure time and leisure activity.

An important factor would be the timing and distribution of the newly available leisure. Maw (1974) has discussed the ways in which 'time blocks' affect people's ability to engage in leisure activities. If a worker arrives home from work at 6.00 pm, then has a meal, it may be 7.30 pm before he or she is ready to consider any sort of out-of-home leisure activity. If the local swimming pool closes at 8.00 pm that option is effectively excluded. In any case, at 7.30 pm, having been up since say 7.30 am, that worker may feel too tired to go for a swim. But if working hours are reduced so that there is time before the evening meal for a swim, or the evening meal can be brought forward, then the worker can take a swim. Thus in some situations, even an extra half an hour of free time in the day could make it possible to engage in some sort of leisure activity which itself might take an hour or more. Equally the extra half hour might enable some people to work in the garden or take their child for a walk, resulting in less time spent watching television. Thus 'home and family' activities might be substituted for an, admittedly passive, leisure activity. Finally, as discussed above, some might be enabled to take on additional part-time paid work or moonlighting.

Generally speaking, larger 'blocks' of time would be expected to give rise to more additional specific leisure activity. For instance, an extra day off per fortnight might be planned for and might involve specific activities, whereas the equivalent time of three-quarters of an hour a day spread over two weeks would hardly be noticed. If the time became available in the form of increased holidays (more than four weeks a year) then this is likely to be even more the case in that trips away from home are more likely to be planned. An overall increase in leisure demand is to be expected which would be felt by providers of facilities in both the private and public sectors. But in addition to an overall increase in demand the result might be a reduction in peak demand, since people would have more choice as to when they engaged in leisure activities. So that, for example, a family wanting to go to the seaside is more or less constrained to go on Sunday at present; with more days off, on a weekly or annual basis, they could go on other days of the week.

Finally, we should refer to the question of fatigue, which was briefly referred to above. In Chapter 2 the Aristotlean concept of what was called 'pure leisure' was discussed, in which the choice of leisure activity is completely unconstrained by the effects of work. It was suggested that the modern worker rarely if ever experiences this condition: work is always there in the background, being recovered from, unwound from, or prepared for. As workers gain more and more time off, so they move nearer the Aristotlean ideal, when leisure activities are engaged in for their own sake rather than as recuperation from work or resting in preparation for work. Time is a necessary resource for this to happen. Domestic work and child-care activity will of course always be there for the mass of the people. But if paid working hours are reduced then the likelihood of domestic work being shared, rather than being a constant burden for one member of the household, increases.

Reducing the Working Life-time

The working life-time can be reduced in three different ways: by lowering the retirement age, by raising the age at which young people enter the labour market, or by introducing some sort of sabbatical or retraining system so that people leave the labour markets for periods during their working lives. Each of these possibilities is discussed in turn below.

Retirement
The *de facto* average retirement age is falling because of voluntary early retirement schemes and the fact that redundant older workers have

only a poor chance of regaining employment in a period of high general unemployment. While the retirement age is a matter of negotiation in some industries, such as mining, for most the question is determined by the state through the availability of state retirement pensions and increasingly through the minimum rules imposed by occupational pension schemes.

Compulsory and voluntary early retirement schemes have become increasingly familiar features of the manpower planning policies of both individual employers and the state (Dept of Employment, 1978; McGoldrick, 1982). In Britain the state Job Release Scheme enables older workers to retire early and draw their pensions provided that their job is refilled. Early retirement schemes are becoming increasingly popular in the United States (McGoldrick and Cooper, 1978) and are being encouraged by the European Commission (Commission of the European Communities, 1980). Early retirement is considered here in three ways. What is its (potential) effect on the level of unemployment? What is the likelihood of its being widely introduced? And what would be the effects on leisure?

Other things being equal, every person retiring from a job creates a vacancy which could be filled by a younger, unemployed person. In reality other things are not equal. If employers are generally looking for ways of reducing their labour forces then, in the absence of any restrictive conditions, such as those which exist with the Job Release Scheme, additional jobs will not necessarily be created. There is then the question of what the retired workers themselves might do. If they obtain part-time or even full-time jobs the benefit from their retirement is partly or entirely lost. In fact the chances of older workers obtaining full-time jobs might be expected to be low, and there may be pension-related restrictions on their ability to earn money after retirement, but part-time work is more of a possibility. Some retired workers might become self-employed and set up businesses, which could result in jobs being created. Overall, therefore, the effects of reductions in the retirement age are uncertain and would depend on the circumstances in which the reductions were achieved.

We have already noted that earlier retirement is beginning to happen on a voluntary basis, and very occasionally compulsorily, but this is generally on a firm by firm or single industry basis or is very much up to the individual; it therefore affects only a minority. What is the likelihood of a permanent, compulsory reduction in the retirement age? In the United States the opposite has happened: organized groups of the elderly (such as the 'Grey Panthers') have obtained rulings to prevent compulsory retirement on the basis of age alone. The European Court of Human Rights has recently ruled that women in Britain may not be compulsorily retired at the age of 60 but have the right, if they wish, to work until the age of 65, the same as men. Generally it might be expected that people would welcome earlier retirement rather than resist it, provided that pension rights were not affected. One move which would be likely in the UK, especially in the light of contemporary views on sexual equality, would be to reduce the retirement age for men to 60 to bring it in line with the traditional retirement age of women.

The major problem is one of cost, or, more accurately, of financing. Pensions are funded by contributions from workers and employers (sometimes from employers alone) during their working lives. In the case of occupational pension schemes the system works on strict insurance principles with the pension being paid from the fund created by the contributions – although in periods of high inflation certain employers may 'top up' the fund. In the case of the state pension in Britain the connection between contributions and payments is more tenuous. In theory they are linked on the insurance principle but in practice current pensions are paid from current contributions and taxes, rather than from an accumulated fund. In one sense it ought to be possible to do two things: either draw a reduced pension over an extended period of retirement or increase contributions so that the 'fund' is large enough to fund the pension over the extended retirement period, or a combination of the two. The first option is not realistic for the basic state pension since it is generally considered to be at or even below the subsistence level, and any reduction in pensions would frequently have to be made up in supplementary welfare payments; it could, however, be a possibility for income related occupational pension schemes. The second option, of increased contributions, is a possibility, but it would take time for the fund to build up if the strict insurance principle were to be followed.

As far as state pensions are concerned, reducing the retirement age should be attractive to government in a period of high unemployment because the effect would be simply to replace one group dependent on the state (the unemployed) by another group (the retired), but with the added advantage that the politically sensitive unemployment figures would be reduced. Financially it would mean that instead of paying taxes to finance unemployment benefits workers and employers would be paying a similar amount but in the form of increased contributions to the pension fund. Since the sums paid to pensioners and to the unemployed are similar, the net additional costs should be negligible. In fact, if the unemployed taken off the register are people with families there would be a net saving since they would have been receiving higher benefits than older people with no dependent children.

Research indicates that one of the major problems facing both the retired and the unemployed is loss of income (Long and Wimbush, 1981; Parker, 1982). For those dependent upon the state pension, therefore, the prospect of earlier retirement may not be viewed very favourably.

What are the implications for leisure of earlier retirement? In so far as the retired would be replacing a similar number of the unemployed as members of the 'leisure class' and would have similarly low levels of income, any effects would result from the differences in age of the two groups and to some extent differences in family or household structure. But neither the unemployed nor the retired are particularly active in out-of-home leisure activities, if for no other reason than lack of money. Change would arise from the increased expenditure of the young people given jobs. Overall an increase in participation in more active forms of leisure would be expected as the younger age group found themselves with more money in their pockets.

Extending Full-time Education
The second way in which the working lifetime can be reduced is to extend the time that young people spend in full-time education. Extension of adult education in its various forms is also a possibility and that is discussed below in relation to sabbaticals. In the United States 80 per cent of young people receive full-time education until the age of 18, and some 50 per cent receive at least some higher education beyond 18. The provision of that scale of education would have a dramatic effect on Britain's youth unemployment figures.

In practice in Britain education is being extended, or rather *training* is being extended through the programmes of the Manpower Services Commission (MSC). This quango, which provides a number of job creation and youth training programmes, has been one of the fastest growing institutions of the 1980s. The MSC claims to be able to provide one or two years training or 'work experience' for every school-leaver without a job. The reluctance of many school-leavers to take up these opportunities, because of low remuneration and because they believe that the prospects of getting a job subsequently are low, has led the government to introduce measures which will prevent school-leavers from claiming unemployment or social security benefit if they refuse to accept a place on an MSC scheme. In effect, therefore, the government has raised the school-leaving age to 17 or 18 but has, in the last two years, replaced school with MSC training and work-experience programmes. This results in a once and for all reduction of some 2 per cent in the size of the formal market labour force.

Whereas in the 1960s youth emerged as the new affluent group – a new 'market' – the raising of the school-leaving age from 15 to 16 and now the exclusion of the majority from the formal labour market until they are 17 or 18 is having the effect of prolonging a relatively unprosperous adolescence. As Simon Frith puts it:

> the direct consequence of wide-scale youth unemployment is to give school leavers a new institutional position, as cheap, dependent labour, clearly demarcated from both adult workers and their peers in further and higher education. This seems a very different position from that occupied by 1950s and 1960s working class teenagers, who had money in their pockets, jobs to choose from, were irresponsible and cocky as they set the leisure pace for everyone else.
> (Frith, 1984, p. 62)

This solution to unemployment, of taking young people off the labour market, is being adopted by government partly because it is a minimum-cost measure and partly because young people are the easiest group in society to 'order around', having no organization or power base from which to resist. But other motives on the part of society may be at work. We have already referred to the process of 'social control' in relation to the era of industrialization. Part of that process is the learning of work discipline. The unemployed teenager is not learning useful skills and is not getting used to the discipline of the workplace for when he or she may be required. Indeed the purposelessness of unemployment could be making some of today's youth permanently unemployable. Again to quote Frith: 'if school leavers can no longer acquire work discipline simply by getting a job, then state agencies have to step in to provide it – hence the development of the Youth Training Schemes' (Frith, 1984, p. 61).

But there are potentially even more serious consequences of youth unemployment which society fears, and that is social unrest. The government White Paper, *Sport and Recreation* (Dept of the Environment, 1975), referred to the problems of young people experiencing 'urban frustration' which could lead to anti-social behaviour. The Scarman report on the disorders in London, Liverpool and the West Midlands in 1981 stated:

> Without close parental support, with no job to go to and few recreational facilities available, the young black person makes his life on the streets and in the seedy commercially run clubs of Brixton. There he meets criminals who appear to have no difficulty in obtaining the benefits of a materialist society.
> (Scarman, 1982, p. 29)

A leading politician has gone so far as to say: 'It does not seem particularly fanciful to discern, in high rates of long-term unemployment among the young, the seeds of a threat to our democratic system' (Owen, 1984, p. 97). With such dire possibilities in mind, therefore, even 'monetarist' governments readily find the money at least to attempt to combat youth unemployment.

The work-experience and training opportunities are however short term: while they may cater for the 16 year olds, when they reach 17 many will return to the dole queues. Other countries, notably the United States, have a less elitist attitude to higher education than Britain. While opening up the formal education process to more young people would be a means of absorbing the unemployed, and presumably would be beneficial to the economy in the form of an increased pool of trained labour, it is an expensive option, especially in Britain where traditionally government has provided student grants for living as well as the education service itself. At the time of writing, however, the future of student grants is under review. Professor Tom Stonier suggests a massive increase in the education system, both as a means of absorbing labour, in the form of both the teachers and the taught, and to provide the necessary highly trained labour force for the future 'information' economy:

> The best strategy to effect a smooth transition from an industrial to an information economy is by means of a massive expansion of both education and research and development ... The expansion of ... education is required to upgrade the human capital to make the workforce economically more productive ... to create an informed citizenry capable of manoeuvring effectively in an information economy; and to keep everyone from going neurotic in a rapidly changing information environment.
>
> (Stonier, 1983, p. 13)

As far as leisure is concerned, widespread youth unemployment and the exclusion of young people from the labour market by various means is highly significant in terms of consumption of and participation in 'youth culture'. The provision of government training schemes is likely to have little impact on the leisure behaviour of the young unemployed. The training schemes are poorly remunerated and so are unlikely to generate a buoyant 'youth market'. They are also very often effectively part-time in nature so they do not necessarily have a significant effect on the leisure time available to young people. It might be thought that the young unemployed are some form of new 'sub-leisure class' but research shows that lack of financial resources and other factors make them a relatively inactive group as far as formal leisure activities are concerned (Hendry et al., 1984). As for those on Youth Training Schemes, Bob Hollands has recently revealed how limited their leisure opportunities are, mainly again because of their financial circumstances (Hollands, 1985).

If higher education were opened up on any significant scale, however, some notable changes might be expected. Students are among the most active groups in society in sport and cultural activities and their particular situation often generates an intense social life. Some of this may be partly because of the current correlation between class background and access to higher education, but since social-class status can also be affected by the educational process there is some reason to believe that the education experience itself may give rise to the higher rates of activity. A further factor is the influence of the educational institution which usually makes provision for cultural and sporting activity on a collective and/or subsidized basis. The leading role played by college sports in the sporting life of the United States is an indication of the potential impact which an expanded higher-education sector could have on at least one aspect of leisure.

A traditional measure which has the effect of taking substantial numbers of young people out of the labour market for a period is conscription to the armed forces. This remains in force in certain countries such as Switzerland and Sweden, but has largely disappeared from Western societies. While those who experienced 'National Service' in Britain often refer to its beneficial effects in terms of 'making a man' of them, and the desirability of reintroducing this experience to 'make men' of today's youth is often proposed in bar-side conversations, it is not a serious possibility in peace-time in Britain. Variations on the theme, such as conscription to some sort of social-service task force, are however occasionally mooted – President Kennedy's 'Peace Corps' being one such variation.

Overall it would seem that the trend towards keeping young people out of the labour market for longer and longer periods is inexorable. Young people will simply not be required in the labour force until at least their later teens. When labour forces are being squeezed certain groups will suffer first: young people have even less power than the older people at the other end of the age range who have votes, experience, skills and trade unions on their side. Thus young people are currently making the greatest contribution to 'sharing the work around', but because of expediency rather than any conscious planning.

Sabbaticals
Sabbaticals – the taking of extended leave from a job – have traditionally been available in certain occupations, notably in higher education. Academics are granted sabbaticals to pursue research. Research has always been seen as an important part of an academic's work and in

order to make progress it is often necessary to have a continuous period to concentrate on research, uninterrupted by teaching or administrative duties. In addition, it is often considered necessary to travel, either to work with a particular research team or simply to get away from the distractions of the regular workplace. For many academics such sabbaticals are formal or informal rights of the job, for instance, for one term of sabbatical leave in three years or one year in seven. The origin of the term sabbatical is a Biblical reference to the Mosaic Law that land should lie fallow one year in every seven (Goyder, 1977). The practice is built into the academic system with teachers expecting to 'cover' for colleagues while they are away, on the understanding that they will in turn cover for them, timetables are shuffled to facilitate the absence, or precious funds are used to buy in temporary lecturers to cover the absentee's work.

While the academic sabbatical is definitely 'work' or 'training' and not 'leisure', it is nevertheless viewed as a 'perk' of the job and has many of the characteristics and functions of an extended vacation, such as getting away from it all, relief from pressure, and recharging batteries. One ironical term for the sabbatical is 'the leisure of the theory class'! Many academics on sabbatical no doubt work very hard on a tight research schedule, but equally some are in effect coasting for a term or two and do the minimum of writing for appearances' sake. To the employer, the university or college, much of the value of the sabbatical must be seen in the same light as any other perk, rather than as something with an immediate payoff. Returning academics are somewhat beholden to the institution and their colleagues: 'they have only just had their sabbatical' so they will be expected to more than pull their weight and in some way show their gratitude. Equally, academics expecting to take a sabbatical in the near future need to pull their weight in the department or their request may be turned down. The sabbatical system is therefore a complicated one with a number of subtle payoffs for employer and employee.

Sabbaticals can then have two functions from the employer's point of view: a direct one concerned with education, training or some sort of project useful to the employer, or an indirect one where it is seen more as an extended holiday or 'perk', which is intended to reward loyalty and hard work and to boost staff morale and productivity. In the former case the extension of sabbaticals is a matter for employers' training policies: if they feel that employees need extended periods of training they should be prepared to facilitate and pay for it. There is, however, in Britain, a curious trend for employers to expect more and more of the costs of training to be borne by the state, as witness the collapse of the apprenticeship system and the levy-based Industrial Training Boards. If the state were to take a role, therefore, it would be possible to envisage a system in which every worker would be entitled to a certain amount of state-financed post-school education which could be taken at any time in their working life. The basis of this exists at present, in that anyone who gains a place on an undergraduate course in Britain is entitled to a (means-tested) grant to cover fees and living expenses at a 'student' level. Extending the system would involve widening the range of courses for which such 'mandatory' grants were available and making more generous arrangements than exist at present for mature students with family and other financial commitments. The popularity of the Open University in Britain suggests that there is considerable demand for education among older people, but three years full-time commitment is rarely a realistic possibility. This sort of proposal links to the earlier discussion about extending post-school education. There is a case for considering the extension of educational entitlement generally rather than just in the immediate post-school period.

If sabbaticals are viewed, and administered, as perks in the form of extended vacations then they are no longer in the sphere of educational or training policy but enter the realm of collective bargaining about holidays or pension entitlements. Agreements might be struck to entitle all or some employees to take sabbaticals, or possibly for employees who wish to do so to 'save up' some of their holiday entitlement from one year to another and to take it in a larger block as a sabbatical. Employers might wish to offer extended leave as a reward for long service. Best (1980, p. 170) reports a number of such agreements in the United States, including one involving steel-workers dating from 1967. One firm in California gives a year's paid leave to all employees with six years' continuous service. Alternatively, a sabbatical might be seen as taking a portion of one's retirement early. It would be financed out of the pension fund and would therefore be negotiated as part of pension rights: more sabbaticals would result in a lower pension on retirement, or would require larger pension contributions.

A sabbatical system could of course be imposed by legislation, in which case it would be seen as a cost of labour rather like employers' pension contributions or holiday pay. Melching and Broberg (1974), in calling for a national sabbatical system for the United States, suggest that a system involving a year's sabbatical every seven years, financed from taxation, would cost $32 billion or 3.5 per cent of the country's personal income.

It is likely that the main leisure implications of sabbaticals would lie in the area of tourism since leisure-orientated sabbaticals, and to a lesser extent educational ones, would be likely to be used for travel. If the average British worker has four weeks holiday a year, or 1,800 weeks in a working lifetime, a six months sabbatical would add less than 2 per cent to this total, which is an indicator of the comparatively low cost of a sabbatical system, but also an indication of the marginal impact it would have on the tourism or leisure industries. As with several of the changes we have discussed, the extra demand for leisure would be likely to a large extent to be off-peak or off-season, which would be welcomed by most leisure and tourism enterprises.

Extended education, periods of part-time working, flexible pension plans and sabbaticals are all ways of achieving what Fred Best calls 'Flexible Life Scheduling'. In his book with this title he calls for all these measures and others to be introduced to break the 'education–work–retirement lockstep' (Best, 1980).

Time Management

The problem with many of the proposals designed to reduce working time in order to share the available work more equally is that they cost money. If working hours are reduced in some way by, say, 10 per cent and wages stay the same, then clearly the employer is, other things being equal, getting 10 per cent less work done for the same money, or is having to employ 10 per cent more workers and increase the wage bill by 10 per cent in order to get the same amount of work done. It has been argued that if the employer involved is the state then the net cost is less, and may in fact be zero, because the extra staff employed come off the dole queue and so do not claim social security benefits and, in addition, they return part of their income in direct and indirect taxation. But private sector employers would also be involved in most of these proposals and, unless the government devised some complex system of transfer payments, these employers would bear the whole cost of the proposals with no offsetting cash savings.

A suggestion has emerged from Belgium which could make savings to offset the increased labour costs of the reduction in working hours. It is referred to as 'time management'. Professor Fache (1983) of the University of Ghent reports that the Belgian government has set aside a substantial sum of money and temporarily suspended certain employment regulations in certain areas to facilitate experiments in changed patterns of working. One such experiment would involve the introduction of shift working for all. This could entail, for example, two six-hour shifts a day for five days a week, resulting in a thirty-hour working week for the individual worker. But, since there would be two shifts, offices, shops and factories would be utilized for sixty hours a week. This would result in a 25 per cent reduction in working hours for the individual but an increase of 50 per cent in the utilization of plant. The cost savings to employers would therefore arise through working their plant more intensively. Other cost savings would accrue to the community through reduced peak-time demand on transport facilities and possibly on other utilities such as electricity.

Clearly there is a number of imponderables in such an idea, hence the Belgian proposal to experiment in order to explore the advantages and disadvantages. In industries which already operate shift systems there would be no gains and if they were forced to offer a thirty-hour week then their costs would rise. Even for other employers it is not exactly clear how the balance of costs and savings would turn out. It is possible that labour productivity per hour would rise as it did in Britain during the three-day week in 1974. But this could be a short-lived phenomenon. For the scheme to work financially the saving in plant operating costs would need to be at least equal to the increase in labour costs which would be of the order of one-third. This might be the case in capital intensive industries, but these are likely to be the very ones already operating a shift system. Since the government would be one of the main beneficiaries of the scheme, in that there would be a reduction in the dole queues and corresponding welfare payments, there could be some transfer from government to employers participating in the scheme.

Time management is not only a macro, social-planning concept, it also applies to individuals and families. How, for instance, would members of families co-ordinate themselves so that they were all working the same shifts at school, office or factory? And what would be the effects on patterns of friendship and leisure activity? We have evidence to show that current shiftworkers resent the abnormality of their hours of work and leisure which prevent them from enjoying the depth and continuity of social relationships which conventional hours permit, even when, as is normally the case, the *amount* of leisure time available is no different from that of the person working conventional hours (Chambers and Roberts, 1985). Perceived problems are exacerbated by the rotating shift system where the pattern of work and leisure time varies from week to week. But if shiftworking were the norm and people could opt for a more or less permanent (early or late) shift, which fitted in with family and friends, then these problems might not arise.

There would also be implications for leisure providers. Opening hours of places of entertainment and broadcasting would all have to adapt to the idea of two or more groups of people with different time patterns. Again one of the difficulties experienced by current shiftworkers, as reported by Chambers and Roberts (1985), is that opening hours of such places as pubs, are not suited to their needs. This would have to change if the whole of the population was 'on shifts'. Examples of this sort of response to work patterns already in operation are the traditional concessions to pubs in market areas such as Billingsgate in

London where, because the local workforce works unconventional hours, the pubs also have unconventional opening hours.

A variation on the five six-hour shift pattern would be three ten-hour days a week, enabling workplaces to operate two three-day weeks. This has its antecedents in the United States four day forty-hour week movement, which has been extensively researched, notably by Riva Poor (1972). A number of firms adopted this system in the USA in the 1960s, giving their workers, in effect, a three-day weekend. A paper in Poor's book also reports on eight British cases of four-day forty-hour weeks and nine in Australia (Richmond, 1972, 1972a). Research was done on the leisure impact of the system; showing that all leisure activities tended to increase under the four-day arrangement. While simply resting and relaxing showed the biggest absolute increase in levels of participation, operators of public swimming pools would be interested to note that the largest percentage increase in participants was in swimming and boating. A fascinating film by Granada Television, from the late 1960s, studied the effect of a four-day week on workers in a Lancashire factory. Some were so busy gardening, working on caravans and similar pursuits that there were not enough hours in the day, while others were totally bemused by the prospect of a whole extra day a week to fill (Granada, 1968).

A Social Wage

The idea of a universal 'social wage' has frequently been put forward as at least part of the solution to the problem of work scarcity. The idea of the social wage is that everyone should receive a basic income from the state regardless of their circumstances and whether they have a job or not; they could then choose whether or not to add to this basic income by taking a paid job. One of the earliest proponents of the idea was Major C. H. Douglas who, in the 1920s and 1930s, propounded a 'Social Credit' system to solve the economic and social problems which an increasingly automated economy would throw up. 'Douglas had a vision of an automated society in which all individuals could enjoy freedom and leisure, but he insisted that this could never be achieved unless his new way of distributing incomes to consumers was adopted' (Jordan and Drakeford, 1980, p. 167). Modern versions of the idea have a variety of names, including: a National Dividend (Roberts, 1982), a Social Dividend (H. Parker, 1983), a National Income/Tax Credit Scheme (Ecology Party, 1981, p. 30), a National Income Scheme (Handy, 1984, p. 106), a 'Social Income' (Gorz, 1985, p. 44), simply a 'guaranteed income for all' (Samuelson, 1973; Clemitson and Rodgers, 1981, p. 93; Jones, 1982, p. 243) or a 'basic income payment' (Ball, 1984).

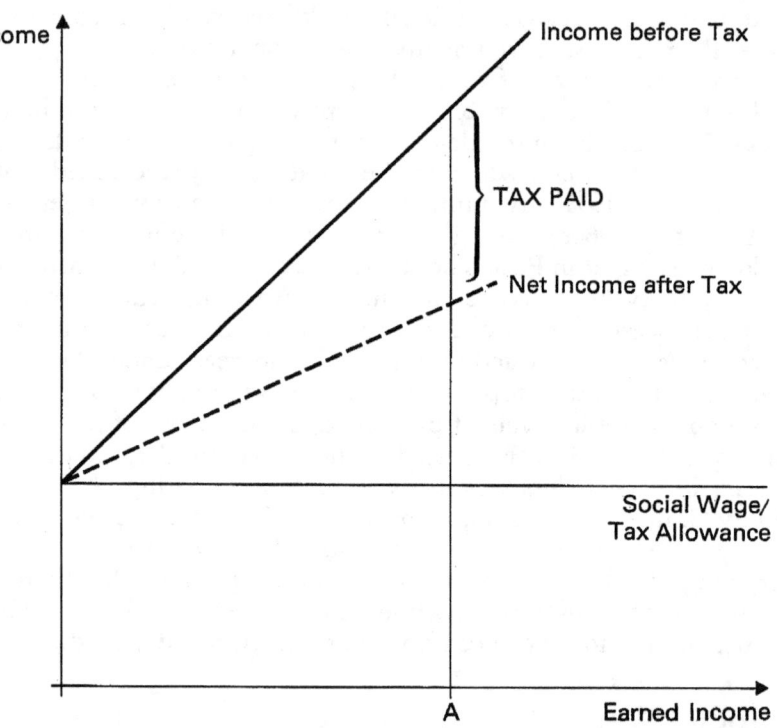

A: Point at which tax paid = social wage.

Figure 5.1 Negative income tax/social wage system.
Source: After Roberts (1983).

It might be argued that some sort of social wage system already exists in the form of the social security system, but there are two vital differences between this and the social wage. First, the social wage would generally be pitched at a higher level than typical social security payments. Secondly, the social wage would be payable to all as of right and would not depend on the individual's work contribution or social or economic circumstances. This would reflect a fundamentally changed attitude in society towards the relationship between work and income. Work would be seen as an option rather than a necessity. Similarly a life of leisure would be chosen rather than thrust on people in the form of unemployment.

Social wage systems generally need to be considered along with the taxation system in order to see how the resultant distribution of income would work out in practice. When combined with the question of taxation it is difficult to see how they differ from the more longstanding notion of 'negative income tax'. In recent years this has been associated with Milton Friedman (Friedman and Friedman, 1979, p. 149) but has also been proposed by, among others Alvin Toffler (1984, p. 58), Tom Stonier (1983, p. 213), David Owen (1984, p. 110) and in a discussion paper by the Conservative government in 1972 (Great Britain, 1972).

The negative income tax involves giving every individual or family a basic income tax allowance which would be set at the level of subsistence and would replace all existing welfare payments. A person or family would receive this allowance in cash. People with earnings would lose say one pound of allowance for every two pounds earned. At this rate of deduction the tax paid would be exactly balanced by the allowance received when earnings were double the allowance. Beyond this 'break even' point income tax would be paid in the normal way. This is illustrated in Figure 5.1. Milton Friedman sees this as a system not only to rationalize the current complex social security system but also to maintain an incentive to work even among the poorest. It is seen as a means of abolishing the 'poverty trap' by which the poor, especially with large families, can be better off out of work than in work. Clearly the difference between this system and the social wage system lies mainly in its motivation with the negative income tax proponents concerned to encourage people to work and the social wage proponents wanting to make it possible not to work. In practice, the effects of the systems are similar once income tax is taken into account since income tax is paid on all earned income in both schemes. Any differences would arise in the differences in the levels at which the social wage or the basic income tax allowance might be set.

One curiosity, pointed out by Roberts (1983, p. 64), is that despite the popularity of Milton Friedman's monetarist ideas with governments on both sides of the Atlantic, his negative income tax proposals have been virtually ignored. And yet they are very much part of Friedman's package of measures which are designed to solve unemployment and defeat inflation; at the same time, their claimed qualities include rationalization of the welfare system and an increase in work incentives for the lower paid – both issues about which Mrs Thatcher's government expresses concern. The previous Conservative government even went so far as to publish a discussion paper on the subject using the term 'Tax Credit', but this has never been followed up.

Should a social wage system be implemented the implications for leisure could be far reaching, depending on the level at which the social wage was set and the numbers of people who opted not to work at all or to reduce paid work substantially. There are clearly two fundamental questions: first, what would it cost – and therefore what is the likelihood of its being implemented? Secondly, if such a scheme were to be implemented would it work as its proponents suggest?

At least two of the organizations supporting the social wage idea have costed it. The Ecology Party estimated that the net annual cost of implementing their National Income/Tax Credit Scheme in Britain, at 1980–1 prices, would be £20 billion. This would finance certain housing benefits plus payments of £7 per week for every child under 5, £10 for children aged 5 to 18, £20 for those up to the age of 60 and £28 for those aged over 60. These figures, including the overall cost, would be some 40 per cent higher at 1985 prices. The £20 billion would be financed by increasing income tax to 40 pence in the pound, raising VAT on luxury items and 'redirecting government expenditure', particularly away from armaments.

The European Centre for Work and Society (Roberts, 1983) have costed a scheme for a National Dividend for the UK which, at 1979 prices, would cost a net £11 billion (a figure which would increase by 50 per cent to reflect 1985 prices). The scheme would be financed mainly through increased VAT payments which, in the context of a radically changed taxation and government finance system, could be set at a rate of 100 per cent!

The prospect that governments of the main political parties would implement such a scheme in current circumstances seems remote. But Tom Stonier argues that such a scheme is not only desirable but is inevitable. He sees oil-producing states leading the way and cites the case of Alaska where oil revenues became so large by 1980 that, in addition to abolishing state income tax, the authorities disbursed $1,000 to each Alaskan resident. He sees other industries becoming, through the application of technology, equally capital-intensive and revenue-yielding and makes a direct connection between this sort of development and the future of leisure.

> At the moment this Alaskan situation is regarded as a freak occurrence. It is not; it will happen more and more often as technology converts more and more non-resources into revenue-yielding resources. Sometime in the first quarter of the next century technological progress will have been enough to make worries about money less and less relevant. As more people come to perceive this altered state of affairs, they will generate political pressures to modify the current economic institutions ... Early in the next century, as we gain the experience of successfully tapping new sources of energy, material and food – as we discover how to automate virtually all materials-producing systems – we will learn to live off the backs of the robots as the ancient rulers lived off the backs of their slaves. Everyone an aristocrat. That is the shape of the future as far as material satisfaction is concerned.
>
> As our material resource base becomes sufficiently large to assure

everyone a guaranteed annual income, our social and economic preoccupations will shift to fulfilling human psychological needs. What does it mean to be human? Assuming that we do not live by bread alone, just what does it take to make us happy?

(Stonier, 1983, p. 212)

In such a scenario of abundant material wealth it can be imagined, if the scenario as a whole can be imagined, that a social wage system of some sort would work. Until such a time, however, strong doubts need to be expressed about the idea. In its negative income tax form, designed to 'tidy up' the welfare and tax allowance system, the proposals might well be viable, although one suspects that critics from the left would see a right-wing introduced system as being designed to save money at the expense of the poor. The social wage system, however, assumes that there is a level of income which society, even a society of the future, could afford to pay, which would be sufficiently high as to attract a significant proportion of the population out of the labour market altogether. The problem is that unless and until we reach a position of general material satiety, as Stonier implies, poverty will always be seen as a relative thing and those on the 'social wage' alone would always be seen as the poor.

Clive Jenkins and Barrie Sherman illustrate the problem when they say that 'An income of at least national average earnings should be available to all' (Jenkins and Sherman, 1981, p. 82). This means that anyone on less than average earnings should have their income raised to the average, so average *earnings* become the minimum *income*. So people living on the social wage alone would, by definition, be the poorest people in the country. We already see with current welfare systems that there are few people prepared to opt for this situation voluntarily. It might be argued that this is because current welfare payments are too low in absolute terms – but if we take standards of living in many Third World countries, or in Europe say fifty or seventy-five years ago, as some sort of measure of absolute poverty, we see that poverty in most advanced industrial nations is a *relative* rather than an absolute concept, but no more acceptable because of that. Recipients of the 'social wage', like current recipients of social security payments, would be seen as poor because they would be the least well-off members of the community. For this reason, unless there was a substantial movement against the material values of society, the social wage system would not be acceptable and would not work in the way its proponents hope.

In this chapter we have reviewed a variety of methods which have been proposed for sharing work more equitably in order to relieve unemployment. They all have implications of some sort for leisure. In every case there are financial and practical implications for government, employers and workers. On balance it would seem that it is these potential costs and practical problems, together with fear of the unknown, which are preventing implementation of such proposals, rather than the sorts of attitudinal issues discussed in Chapter 4. One of the difficulties in discussing these matters is the apocalyptic tone used by some commentators on the problems. Often it seems that drastic measures must be taken *tomorrow afternoon* to solve problems which will arise *tomorrow morning*. As Levitan and Belous put it over a decade ago:

> One major problem blocking serious consideration of changes in worktime has been the general tendency to praise or damn such approaches excessively. Advocates have often unrealistically sung reduced worktime's praises and ignored real problems, and critics have often failed to find any redeeming features in such policies. Reduced worktime by itself is no long-run solution to unemployment. However, it could be an effective tool if combined with traditional stimulus and counter-cyclical job creation measures.
> (Levitan and Belous, 1977, p. viii)

The measures discussed in this chapter are not short-term, 'at a stroke' policies which will cure all the ills of Western capitalism. They are more suited to phased introduction over a five-, ten- or even twenty-year period. In that context, and in the context of co-operation between government, trade unions and employers, the costs would be minimal and the result would be a more humane society. The disturbing feature of the situation is the apparent failure of mainstream parties and governments in Britain to give serious attention to these issues. The political dimension is discussed in Chapter 6.

6

Political Dimensions

Leisure has become a political issue. Until recently only certain aspects of leisure, such as sport or the arts or children's play, have exercised politicians' minds, and leisure as a whole has not been seen as a topic for serious consideration by serious people. As Bramham and Henry (1985) demonstrate, in the UK at least, leisure has not traditionally been a significant part of any political manifesto. This has begun to change. Such a change is obviously important for the future of leisure since politics is all about the future. Political philosophies are expressions of how groups of people would like to see, and intend or hope to shape, the future. So what sort of future do the politicians hold out for leisure?

Perhaps the politician who has put leisure most firmly on the political map is President Mitterrand of France who, on coming to office in 1981, created a Minister for Free Time, who immediately set about introducing measures to reduce the working week to thirty-nine hours, with plans to reduce it to thirty-five hours by 1985. Other policies included extension of holiday entitlements, encouragement of participation in voluntary activities and the fostering of 'creative' use of leisure time (Henry, 1982; Hantrais, 1984). The ministry was, however, shortlived and was later subsumed under the Ministry of Youth, Sport and Free Time.

The Right

The views of the political centre and left are discussed in more detail later in the chapter but first we consider the views of the political right. In Britain, the Prime Minister, Mrs Thatcher, struck a significant note in 1983 when, in an interview in *The Director*, she declared:

> There is much industry to be had from people's pleasures. We must expect that a lot more of our jobs will come from the service industries – from the MacDonalds and Wimpys, which employ a lot of

people and from the kind of Disneyland they are starting in Corby. Leisure is a big industry.

(Thatcher, 1983, p. 22)

This led to front-page headlines in the national press such as 'Maggie's Mickey Mouse Jobs Plan: Thatcher Backs a Leisure Boom to Cut Dole Queues' (*Daily Mirror*, 26 Aug. 1983).

This theme has been further developed by the Thatcher Administration and its supporters. A report from a committee chaired by a Conservative Member of Parliament, Robert Banks, echoes Mrs Thatcher's terminology in its title: *New Jobs from Pleasure* (Banks, 1985). It focuses primarily on tourism and quotes a British Tourist Authority report (Morrel, 1982) which stated that tourism would create another 250,000 jobs in Britain by the end of the decade. The Banks report seeks to persuade the government to reduce restrictions on the tourism industry, such as licensing laws, in the belief that this booming element of a generally flagging economy should at least not be hindered by government regulations. But the political bias in favour of private rather than public enterprise is very clear:

> Tourism is Britain's biggest growth industry. According to the English Tourist Board it employs about 1,300,000 people, has a turnover of £10,000 million and generated £4,150 million in foreign exchange earnings last year. It is creating more new jobs than any other industry – about 50,000 a year. Tourism is an unsung hero of the British economy ... the focus of this report is best summed up by saying that new jobs can be created by the commercial provision of pleasure and recreation to foreign tourists and Britons in their leisure time. The key is to understand the need for commercial provision. Too often, people expect their leisure to be subsidised. There are no jobs to be had there – only higher taxes. When people pay for their own pleasure they create a job for someone else.
>
> (Banks, 1985, p. 1)

Only months after the publication of the Banks report an official government report was produced from the Cabinet Office Enterprise Unit with much the same message. Lord Young, previously Director of the Manpower Services Commission, had been elevated to the peerage and given a job in the Cabinet with specific responsibilities for job creation. It is significant for the subject of this book that one of his first reports and sets of proposals for action should be entitled *Pleasure, Leisure and Jobs: The Business of Tourism* (Young, 1985a). The report is glowing about the prospects for the leisure and tourism industries:

Tourism and leisure are one of the UK's success stories – but one which is still not fully recognised. If it were, there would certainly have been a rash of articles seeking to analyse the economic secret and apply it to other sectors, especially those which, unlike tourism, are facing declining world market shares and a reducing employment base ... For the future signs are bright. On the international front, when only 7 per cent of US citizens yet have passports, when new prosperity in the Middle East and Far East brings millions more people into the market for international tourism, when liberalisation of air travel is on the increase, there is clearly much to play for ... although many people in the UK will continue to take holidays abroad, the scope at the same time for growth in holidays, weekends and day visits in this country offers good (and increasingly discriminating) business to the UK industry ... it is hardly surprising therefore, that the British Tourist Authority has foreseen the continuing growth of UK employment in tourism at the rate of some 50,000 jobs a year. The Government's concern is to make that growth of jobs easier to achieve.

(Young, 1985a, p. 2)

Again the political belief in the private enterprise system comes through, with such statements as: 'Private enterprise is the backbone of the industry and it has never looked to Government for handouts', and, 'The success story of tourism and leisure is essentially a flowering of private enterprise'. So leisure to the British Conservative Party, as expressed by its government and supporters, is a source of jobs – work – and also a rare symbol of a still flourishing private enterprise system.

At the local level, however, a different picture seems to be emerging: part of the government's 'privatization' programme involves requiring local authorities to contract out many of their services to private sector operators. One of the ways in which private operators can reduce costs below local authority levels, and thus win the contracts, is by reducing staffing levels, thus making leisure services a source of unemployment rather than expanding job opportunities. This, is, however, a complicated issue which is discussed more fully in Chapter 8 on the future of leisure providers.

But this is not the only view emanating from the Conservative Party: the struggle between the 'wets' (the old-style, middle-of-the-road Tories) and the 'dries' (the right-wing, monetarist supporters of Mrs Thatcher) is reflected in conflicting views on the future of leisure. Peter Walker, though retaining a job in the government, is considered to be a 'wet'. Perhaps the fact that he manages to retain his position is reflected in the way in a newspaper article in 1983 he avoided discussing difficult political matters directly and was more concerned with the general challenge of the 'information society'. 'Britain', he declared, 'stands on the brink of a social revolution as big as the switch from an agricultural to an industrial society 200 years ago'. Nevertheless he did provide some lively copy on a political theme, which smacks more of Liberalism than Toryism:

> The information revolution will speed up the process of liberation for people, including liberation from big government, big business and big unions... The information society spells the end of capitalism as we know it, and it will make old fashioned state socialism impossible. It will be a liberating force for those in the lowest, most mundane jobs. That is why the Tories should rejoice at the prospect. This new freedom for all is why socialism is about to become an endangered species. In the information age people will not want to be bossed about by big government or dragooned into joining big unions.
>
> (Walker, 1983)

He therefore harnesses 'Stonierism' to the Tory bandwagon, expounding the advantages for jobs and industry which the information revolution will bring. He rounded off his piece with a vision of leisure which these changes will bring.

> With care and thought we can now have a better lifestyle, with possibilities of education being a continuous process throughout our life. And possibilities for time for far more pleasure, for travel, for reading and for those activities that bring genuine happiness and enjoyment to the individual. It is a whole new concept of life that the information society is going to provide. We have the unique opportunity of creating Athens without the slaves, where the slaves will be the computer and the micro-chip and the human race can obtain a new sense of enjoyment, leisure and fulfilment.
>
> (Walker, 1983)

Francis Pym's views are sufficiently 'wet' for him to have left his job as Foreign Secretary in Mrs Thatcher's government and to lead a vaguely oppositional ginger group within the Conservative Party, attempting to change its policies. This difference is reflected in his views on leisure which provide a challenge for the parties of both left and right. In a speech to the Oxford University Conservative Association in 1983, entitled 'The Revolution *Laissez-faire* and Socialism Cannot Handle', he expressed the view that economic growth under current circumstances will not produce sufficient jobs to cure the problem of unemployment: 'A fully automated factory is what it says:

fully automated'. He speculated that in fifteen years' time we might only need half the working hours required now and that this should be achieved by reducing working hours in a variety of ways. He then discussed the potential social implications:

> The reduction of the working life would be a great benefit to us all, but it will only be so if we find satisfying things to do with the increased leisure time. In a way, the most frightening freedom of all is the freedom to choose what we do with our time because it forces us to fall back on our own inner resources, to use our time creatively, and not to succumb to a life of boredom and inertia.
> (Pym, 1983)

In his book, *The Politics of Consent*, Pym concludes that neither the economic policies of the left nor of the orthodox right are adequate to deal with the coming changes, and argues that a 'middle way' is needed, one which rejects 'the traditional notions of employment', and seeks instead to examine how to distribute 'the total number of working hours needed to produce what we can sell'. He adds:

> It depends entirely on how we approach it. If we think of it as 'unemployment in manufacturing industry is doubled', it is a *problem* of huge proportions. If we think of it as 'the working week is halved', it is an *opportunity* of huge proportions.
> (Pym, 1984, p. 177)

Thus the Conservative views of leisure appear to range from a purely utilitarian conception of leisure as a creator of jobs, via an optimistic, technological, information-age scenario with a leisure fringe, to a 'shortage of work'/'sharing work' scenario as put forward by Pym. Needless to say it is the hardnosed, utilitarian views which currently hold sway with the government.

The Centre

In the middle of the political spectrum in Britain is the newly formed Social Democratic Party. In his book, *A Future that Will Work*, the leader, David Owen, devotes several pages to discussion of the future of work and its leisure implications. He expresses views similar to those of Pym, that conventional economic measures will not be able to solve the problem of unemployment and that work will need to be shared by reducing working hours. He discusses the various ways in which working hours might be reduced but notes that this would only be possible in the context of rising productivity, so that unit production costs do not rise. Apart from tax and social security changes to make part-time working and early retirement more attractive, he sees very little role for government in bringing about change; the process is largely one for agreement between workers and employers. As with his Tory counterparts he is able to conjure up, with suitable rhetorical flourishes, an inspiring vision of a future leisure society.

> If the scourge of unemployment is to be removed from Britain we shall need not only faster economic growth and more active labour-market policies, but also new thinking about the relationship between work and leisure. People must be encouraged and helped to stay longer in full-time education and training; to retire earlier; to welcome the opportunity to work fewer hours per week or take longer annual holidays; or to take sabbaticals in the course of their working lives in order to retrain for new careers or simply to engage in private pursuits. We need to look afresh at the role of the volunteer and the voluntary movement. In every case, the aim must be to help people see the changing work patterns and greater leisure made possible by the advent of the microelectronic era as a gateway to the achievement of fuller and more satisfying lives.
> (Owen, 1984, p. 103)

Also somewhere in the middle-left of the political spectrum is the Ecology Party, which recently changed its name to the Green Party, but is not nearly as popular electorally as its counterparts in other European countries. In their report *Working for a Future* (Ecology Party, 1981), the party demonstrates perhaps the most radical thinking of all the political groupings about the relationship between work, leisure and society. We noted elsewhere their advocacy and costing of a National Income/Tax Credit Scheme which would provide a basic income for all regardless of their economic role. The basic platform of the party is, of course, the fostering of an economy which does not exploit the environment and does not pursue growth and technology for its own sake regardless of the consequences. They nevertheless see technology reducing labour requirements and opening up possibilities for reduced working hours, and possibly reduced incomes, in the formal market economy. But they see the slack being taken up not in leisure but in work in the 'informal economy' – a concept which we discussed in more detail in Chapter 3. In fact they are dismissive of what they call the 'Chimera of the Leisure Society' and the 'megafantasy of the "leisure society"' (Porritt, 1984, p. 68).

We need therefore to be suspicious of those who push the 'self-evident merits' of a self-sustaining post-industrial 'Leisure Society'.

Leisure in itself does not create wealth, neither real wealth, nor the phoney substitutes that people use to measure wealth today. The notion that technological advances will provide an opportunity to increase the amount of leisure time, without a relative loss of conventionally assessed income, is sadly mistaken.

(Ecology Party, 1981, p. 18)

The Ecology Party is, of course, setting up a number of 'Aunt Sallies' here. It is curious that they should share a widespread misconception that a service such as leisure has nothing to do with a society's wealth. The term 'wealth-producing industries' has entered the language, generally referring to manufacturing industry and implying that other industries are not 'wealth producing'. Clearly the ability of a society to produce leisure services — whether they be television programmes, swimming pools or greyhound races — is as much an indicator of its wealth as its ability to produce ships, motor cars or food, or education or medical services. If a society was unable to produce adequate output of these more 'serious' products and only produced leisure services then it would be in trouble. But a society which could only produce 'basics' and was unable to produce leisure services or enable its citizens to have time to enjoy leisure would be poverty stricken indeed. They further exaggerate in suggesting that proponents of a 'leisure society' believe that increased leisure can be obtained without a 'relative loss of conventionally assessed income'. As was argued in Chapter 1, there is always a trade-off between work time and leisure time: no one could seriously take issue with the Ecology Party on this.

They argue directly against the sort of view put forward above by Peter Walker:

Work (we are told) is nothing but drudgery, and its constant replacement by machines signifies progress of such magnitude that we will eventually be relieved of the 'necessity' to work. Thus the displacement of labour is presented to us as evidence 'that mankind is solving its economic problem' (Keynes). One may wonder why such nonsense has become so influential.

(Ecology Party, 1981, p. 19)

Rather than leisure being promoted as an escape from unpleasant labour they believe that technology should be used to improve working conditions, reduce rather than increase alienation, and make room for people to engage in satisfying work for themselves. As with William Morris in the nineteenth century, therefore, they envisage work not being abolished but being humanized and, in appropriate small-scale and creative forms, celebrated.

The Left

The left of the political spectrum presents a very mixed picture. We have already noted President Mitterrand's initiatives in France but such a concern for leisure time is exceptional among left-wing governments or major parties. Governments and parties of the left have generally been more concerned with substantive leisure issues than their centre or right-wing contemporaries partly because of their more interventionist stance overall. Leisure, or aspects of it, could be co-opted as a social service, or as a vehicle for the exercise of more democracy or more economic or physical planning, all of which are of generally greater overt concern to the left. Thus in the 1970s the British Labour government stated in a White Paper that recreation was now 'part of the general fabric of the social services' (Dept of the Environment, 1975). The Labour Party has had plans to democratize the Arts Council and, in response to the recreational pressures on the countryside, established first of all a National Parks Commission in 1947, and then a Countryside Commission in 1968. Finally Tourist Boards were created in the early 1970s in recognition of the economic importance of tourism. This sort of pattern of response is typical of Western left-of-centre governments, but it does not amount to a policy for leisure as a whole. At the time of writing the British Labour Party has established a committee on leisure under the chairmanship of the leader, Neil Kinnock – so it is possible that the situation is about to change.

A number of commentators from the middle and far left have, over the years, attempted to persuade their comrades in the labour movement to recognize the importance of leisure for the future. During the 1960s Antony Crosland was a leading strategic thinker of the Labour Party and in his book *The Future of Socialism* he wrote:

> We realize that we must guard against romantic or Utopian notions: that hard work and research are virtues: that we must do nothing foolish or impulsive: and that Fabian pamphlets must be studied. We know these things too well ... Now the time has come for a reaction: for a greater emphasis on private life, on freedom and dissent, on Culture, beauty, leisure, and even frivolity.
> (Crosland, 1964, p. 357)

In 1978 Dianne Hayter, the General Secretary of the Fabian Society noted that the Labour Party, then in power, was hardly looking beyond the next few months or years, let alone considering the 'ideals and causes it will champion in the eighties and nineties'. Leisure was one of the key issues to which she believed that socialists should be addressing themselves.

The challenge which has to be taken up is to reject the current glorification of work and to grasp the possibility of using the benefits of technological and economic progress to renounce the false notions of the dignity of work, the necessity of work, self-fulfilment through work and the right – and sometimes the duty – to work. Thus the priority should be to break out of . . . that inherited tradition whereby a man works 48 hours a week for 48 weeks in each year for 48 years of his life . . . Progress and Socialism should not be measured solely in terms of material rewards – take-home pay or even the social wage – but in terms of life chances, enjoyment, leisure, work variety, friendships, pleasures, appreciation of the arts, contentment, and all the ingredients of a happy life, be these some land to garden or the opportunity to participate in sport, to travel, or to widen one's experiences. The choice is whether we take the American path to ever more gadgets and superfluous consumer durables or whether we use the increased wealth for more time, more recreation, more fun.

(Hayter, 1978)

The following year the leading trade unionists Clive Jenkins and Barrie Sherman published their book, *The Collapse of Work*, with its detailed analysis of the change in the demand for labour in the British economy and its ringing call for the labour movement to develop leisure policies. In 1981 Clemitson and Rodgers, both ex Labour Members of Parliament produced their book, *A Life to Live*, in which they advocated a 'life ethic' to replace the work ethic, as discussed earlier in Chapter 4. The book has a foreword by Neil Kinnock, written before he became leader of the party, in which he is moved to assert: 'The simple alternative between employment and unemployment must be transcended by policies which are designed to provide creative and positive non-work alternatives to both employment and unemployment'. The lack of any apparent follow-up to this sort of sentiment in terms of Labour Party policies is foreseen by Clemitson and Rodgers themselves when they say:

To have to rethink such long-cherished concepts as full employment and, at a deeper level, to replace socialism based upon a work ethic with one which is not, will be seen by some as striking at the very heart of institutions whose very names and functions have been so closely related to work, and to those who perform it. The Labour Movement, after all, claims to be the political and industrial representative of that section of society known as the 'working class', and there will, no doubt, be those who will regard what we have said as a betrayal of it.

(Clemitson and Rodgers, 1981, p. 137)

The picture of changing awareness and attitudes in the British labour movement is completed by the remarks, already noted in Chapter 4, of Denis Howell, the previous Labour Minister for Sport and Recreation, concerning the importance of education for leisure, and the views of Len Murray, the former leader of the Trades Union Congress, who declared in 1983:

> I don't think full employment is necessary or desirable. I don't see why we should accept full employment axiomatically. A 48 to 50 hour week was seen as the goal when Lord Beveridge prepared his report (1944). But things have changed and we should not assume that our working patterns today should be the pattern of the future. We have been raising the school leaving age and lowering the age of retirement. It's a good thing that people should have more time to engage in creative unemployment. Inevitably we are moving into a situation where leisure is forming an important part of our everyday life. So the issue is that in order to preserve living standards there will have to be an agreement about who gets what and how work is divided. We must try to get a proper distribution of work and that can only be done by tackling the question of leisure as well.
> (Murray, 1983)

Such sentiments are then firmly entrenched in certain parts of the labour movement, and they have been given a fair airing in recent years, but they have yet to emerge in the form of policies.

The left is however blessed, or possibly blighted, by a greater outpouring of academic and quasi-academic literature on the subject than the right. The current period, when governments of the right, particularly in Britain and the USA, appear to look to academic gurus, such as Milton Friedman, for guidance and philosophy, is unusual – on the left such a phenomenon is more common. The greatest guru is of course Karl Marx and we have already referred, in Chapter 2, to his vision of the leisured communist society. But Marx's views on leisure were not very fully developed (Rojek, 1984) – his main message was concerned with how the world of *work* should be organized and his followers have mostly concentrated on work to the exclusion of leisure. But there are exceptions.

The French sociologist Andre Gorz is a Marxist in his outlook but believes that the left is mistaken in continuing to ignore the importance of leisure. He outlines his views in two books published in English, *Farewell to the Working Class: An Essay on Post-Industrial Socialism* (1980) and *Paths to Paradise: On Liberation from Work* (1985). His argument is that modern technology could facilitate the abolition of work, or at least the tyranny of work over people's lives but that the workers themselves and the organizations which claim to represent them are slow to realize this. He stresses the aspect of Marxist philosophy which emphasizes freedom and the right of individuals and communities to control their own lives – a right which is continually denied by the forces of capitalism which wish to keep people enslaved, both to work and to consume the products which the system needs to produce and sell and profit from. Gorz suggests that workers and the labour and socialist movements have become so obsessed with paid work and the struggle between worker and employer that they have failed to realize that the productive power of the advanced industrial economies means that workers need no longer be enslaved by the system. They could if they wished create space and opportunity to 'do their own thing' – that is, to achieve a measure of freedom. In other words, in practical terms, if the worker in the modern economy wishes to work only part-time, say half-time only, he or she would not starve. In fact they would be as well-off materially as the full-time worker of the 1950s. Similarly if American or German or Swedish workers reduced their working hours, and their incomes, by a third or a half they would still be as well off as the full-time British worker. This is potentially a source of freedom. People could, as the economy developed, opt increasingly to contract out of the capitalist system, to make do with less material wealth and have more time to themselves – more freedom.

The problem is that people are caught up in the struggle between worker and employer and on the treadmill of expectations of ever-increasing material prosperity. Gorz argues that the essence of the traditional struggle between workers and capitalist employers was the struggle for freedom – freedom from the tyranny of wage labour. But workers and workers' movements have become obsessed with the struggle and have lost sight of its ultimate purpose. He contrasts paid work with 'self-determined' or 'autonomous' activity. As we have argued in Chapter 4, the corollary of paid work is not necessarily leisure alone, it may include work for oneself or the community or general social/family interaction. It is potentially a realm of freedom, of 'self-determined activity'. Gorz' central theme is that this area of freedom should be expanded, and he adopts the slogan of the 'abolition of work':

> The demand to 'work less' does not mean or imply the right to 'rest more', but the right to 'live more' . . . The outlines of a society based on the free use of time are only beginning to appear in the interstices of, and in opposition to, the present social order. Its watchword may be defined as: let us work less so that we may all work and do more things by ourselves in our free time. Socially useful labour, distributed over all those willing and able to work, will thus cease to

> be anyone's exclusive or leading activity. Instead people's major occupation may be one or a number of self-defined activities, carried out not for money but for the interest, pleasure or benefit involved. The manner in which the abolition of work is to be managed and socially implemented constitutes the central political issue of the coming decades.
>
> (Gorz, 1982, pp. 2–4)

He suggests that the aspirations of working people, or the 'post-industrial proletariat', have become controlled and determined by the capitalist system so that the potential of automation to relieve people from work is not perceived.

> There is a rapid decline in the amount of labour-time necessary to reproduce not *this* society and its mechanisms of domination and command, but a viable society endowed with everything useful and necessary to life. The requirement would be a mere two hours a day, or ten hours a week, or fifteen weeks a year, or ten years in a lifetime.
>
> (Gorz, 1982, p. 72)

People do want freedom, but the freedom they manage to obtain is based on privatized consumption which reinforces the system which is denying them, or from which they are not demanding, genuine freedom.

> Essentially, the 'freedom' which the majority of the population of the overdeveloped nations seeks to protect from 'collectivism' and the 'totalitarian' threat, is the freedom to create a private niche protecting one's personal life against all pressures and external obligations. This niche may be represented by family life, a home of one's own, a back garden, a do-it-yourself workshop, a boat, a country cottage, a collection of antiques, music, gastronomy, sport, love, etc. . . . It represents a sphere of sovereignty wrested (or to be wrested) from a world governed by the principles of productivity, aggression, competition, hierarchical discipline, etc.
>
> (Gorz, 1982, p. 80)

Such a view is also shared by another Marxist observer, Stanley Aronowitz, who observes 'the gradual disappearance of daily social life beyond the workplace in American society', and the tendency of the family or innovative institutions such as communes, to become 'a protection against the tyranny and the terror of the everyday world' (Aronowitz, 1973, p. 412).

Despite the assertions of many commentators that leisure is one of the most important issues to face society in the coming decades, it can hardly be shown to be a central issue in live politics. To some extent the main political parties are caught in a cleft stick. In a period of recession and high unemployment it is impossible for either the party in power or those in opposition to conclude that the problem of high unemployment is insoluble through conventional economic growth. To do so would be to admit that their policies, of either a free enterprise or socialist nature, will not work. And the criterion on which the success of policies is largely based is their ability to produce economic growth of a traditional kind. If Western economies were to return to the high growth, low unemployment pattern of the 1960s then probably all talk of the leisure society and of the urgent need to share work would disappear. So it appears to be politically impossible for the major parties to reorientate their policies, either in a period of stagnation or in a period of growth. It might be argued that as unemployment mounts then parties, governments and electorate *must* change, but in the UK this was being said when unemployment was less than 2 million and it is now over 3 million, so no one can be sure how high unemployment would have to rise in order to trigger such a change. If the major political parties were to change it is possible that it might come about as a result of the threat from the electoral success of smaller parties. In other countries of Europe, notably Germany, the Greens are making a considerable impact on politics but this is not happening in the UK to anything like the same extent. At the present time the only example of the government of a major country adopting a more leisure-orientated stance is the French, but the economic troubles of Mitterrand's France have not inspired others to follow suit. Meanwhile the comparative success of Reagan's work-orientated America in creating jobs and growth in the old style has caused politicians elsewhere to be cautious about predicting the imminent demise of the work society and the emergence of a leisure society.

It is possible, then, to distinguish a number of different perspectives in the politics of leisure and the future. First, there is the view of the current British government which might be termed the 'leisure as enterprise' perspective, which sees leisure as an industry with exceptional growth prospects and which demonstrates the continued vigour of the private enterprise system. Secondly, there is the 'Athens without the slaves' perspective of Peter Walker, in which a small-scale free enterprise system allied with technology and the information society will offer material prosperity and leisure to all. In the middle of the political perspective, including the 'centre ground' of the main parties in Britain, there exists the view that there will continue to be a shortage of work even if growth returns and that the available work should be shared. The by-product of this 'work-sharing perspective' is increased leisure, but also there is the beginning of a view that voluntary work will become more important and should be encouraged. As befits 'middle of the road' politics such a view is not very overtly political in a traditional sense; it is motivated primarily by a concern to solve the problem of unemployment. The 'Green perspective' agrees with the foregoing analysis, that technology means the end of full employment in the formal economy as we have known it, but sees this as an opportunity to opt out of the growth economy and turn to a more environmentally acceptable self-service economy with increased leisure hardly featuring at all. Finally, the 'liberation from work perspective' of Gorz sees technology as the means by which the workers can finally free themselves from dependency on wage labour and capitalism; the by-product is more 'self-determined activity' which would include leisure as an expression of newfound freedom.

7
The Leisure Forecasting Tradition

Since the 1960s there has been a burgeoning literature on leisure forecasting. Forecasting is different from the theoretical discussion and speculation considered in previous chapters. The main difference is that it tends to be quantitative: it aims to produce precise predictions of how many people will be engaging in what activities at some point in the future. In the 1960s, when researchers, planners and policymakers involved with leisure began to turn their attention to questions of forecasting, the environment in which they were working was entirely different from the situation in the 1980s. In the 1960s the full effects of postwar economic growth and increased prosperity were being felt. Real incomes were rising rapidly, even in Britain and the USA, which experienced lower growth rates than other economically advanced and advancing nations. In particular two important changes were taking place which, it was realized, would affect leisure. These two changes were the growth in population and the growth in car-ownership.

In 1965 the projected population of the UK predicted for the end of the century was some 77 million – a projected increase of 23 million. The population was therefore set to rise by 2 million every 3 years. In absolute terms this represented an enormous task for the planners: the equivalent of two cities the size of Birmingham would have to be built every 3 years. Similarly in the USA the population was expected to *double* by the end of the century (ORRRC, 1962). While the main concerns of governments and planners in this situation were housing, industry, transport, shopping and educational needs, at least some attention was given to the recreational implications of this growth – hence the spate of national and regional surveys of recreational participation mounted during the 1960s, and the establishment of such organizations as the Countryside Commission, the Sports Council and the Tourist Boards in Britain and, in the USA, the Outdoor Recreation Resources Review Commission, followed by the Bureau of

Outdoor Recreation and later the Heritage, Conservation and Recreation Service.

Clearly these national organizations and regional and local government were faced with an enormous task. If, for example, only 10 per cent of the additional population wanted to take part in sport in the UK then another 2 million sports players would have to be catered for by the end of the century simply because of the effects of population increase, in addition to any increase in participation which might arise through increasing prosperity or increasing leisure time. Even more dramatic would be the effect on the countryside. As many as 50 per cent of the population would want to use the countryside for formal and informal recreation — another 10 million people pouring into the National Parks and other rural areas.

But the increase in population was only half the story. One of the key findings of the early leisure surveys was that owners of private cars were more than twice as likely to take recreational trips to the countryside and coast as those without access to cars. And even participation in sport was higher among car-owners. The number of cars in England and Wales in 1966 was 9 million and one forecast was that it would rise to 26 million by 1980 (Lacey, 1966). This factor alone, without any population increase at all, would have rapidly increased the demand for recreation. Add the two factors of population growth and growth in car-ownership together and a potentially explosive situation was in prospect.

The ORRRC estimated that the doubling of America's population would be accompanied by a threefold increase in demand for outdoor recreation. No quantified forecasts were available in Britain at the time, but the urgency of the situation was conveyed by Michael Dower's famous 1965 term, the 'Fourth Wave':

> Three great waves have broken across the face of Britain since 1800. First, the sudden growth of dark industrial towns. Second, the thrusting movement along far-flung railways. Third, the sprawl of car-based suburbs. Now we see, under the guise of a modest word, the surge of a fourth wave which could be more powerful than all the others. The modest word is *leisure*.
>
> (Dower, 1965, p. 1)

But now, in the mid-1980s, the projected rate of growth of population has plummeted. A population of no more than 57 million is expected in the UK by the end of the century, an increase of less than 2 million over the current level, or under 100,000 a year. Because of the fall in the birth rate, the relentless pressure of increasing population is no longer an urgent problem. Similarly, growing car-ownership is no longer the explosive phenomenon which it once was. The level of car-ownership has indeed grown substantially over the last twenty years as predicted, although it has slowed with the economic recession of the 1980s. But having reached almost 70 per cent of families, the level is reaching its peak and the *proportionate* rate of increase is therefore falling. The birth rate could, of course, rise again, and any resurgence of economic growth rates could result in car-ownership resuming its rapid upward growth as two-car households became more common. But the short term with which planners and providers are largely preoccupied, presents a comparatively static picture.

A third factor which was often seen as important in the 1960s was the changing age structure of the population. As the population grew, so the relative size of the younger age groups grew. Being more active in many areas of leisure than older people, this growth in the importance of the younger generation intimated even greater increases in the demand for recreation facilities, especially of a more active kind. As the various 'baby bulges' have aged, this is again no longer as important a phenomenon, indeed it is more likely that an overall aging of the population will take place. The leisure demands of older people do, however, now receive greater attention, so this itself could become a source of growth.

Thus leisure forecasting of two decades ago was concerned not so much with changing tastes and trends in leisure activity, although that did feature, but with the long-term effects on participation of underlying demographic and socioeconomic changes. Because these factors, traditionally associated with quantitative forecasting, are no longer changing so rapidly and because other concerns, such as unemployment and the future of work, have emerged, this type of forecasting seems to have fallen out of favour.

There are, however, additional reasons for quantitative forecasting falling out of favour. One was that the methods available were simply not capable of producing accurate results. This was found particularly in the United States, as discussed below. But even if the forecasts had been reliable, it became clear that the decision-making model implicit in the forecasting-based approach to planning was, if not invalid, then at least inoperable. The model was of the form: first predict demand, then planning will be undertaken and resources allocated to provide the facilities and services to meet that demand. This is the sort of planning model utilized in other areas of public policy such as education and housing. The problem is that the demand for leisure is a much more slippery concept than the demand for such services as education or housing. For example, for a given child-population the demand for school places is known and the consequences of not providing that number of places would be all too apparent. In the case of leisure the situation is different. Demand cannot be so precisely determined – the numbers of people who want to play sport, visit the countryside, or take part in arts activities is not known. The consequence of not providing facilities for these activities is that people do something else with their leisure time, such as watching more television. There are no statistics on the 'sports centre-less' or the 'arts centre-less' equivalent to the statistics on the homeless. In general, planning and policy-making for leisure has been more pragmatic and opportunistic than the forecasting model assumes. Certainly at local level in the UK it is hard to find a single example of a public body which has based its provision on quantified forecasts of demand.

Is forecasting dead? This would certainly be an exaggeration. Some commercial agencies continue to provide quantitative forecasts of leisure expenditure and participation and these find a ready market. There is continued interest, at national and local level, in the results of forecasting exercises, at least as a background to the planning and policy-making process.

In this chapter we review the variety of techniques available for forecasting, both quantitative and qualitative. This provides a framework for a review of some of the examples of leisure forecasts which have been produced in the last twenty-five years.

Measuring Leisure

A key aspect of any forecasting exercise is the decision about how the phenomenon under consideration is to be measured. Some five different measures of the scale of the leisure phenomenon can be identified, as set out below:

(1) *The Participation Rate* – the proportion or percentage of the population which engages in specified leisure activities, for example: '6 per cent of the adult population swim at least once a week'.
(2) *Number of Participants* – the number of people from a given community or geographical area who engage in specified leisure activities, for example: '20,000 *people* in Blankshire swim at least once a week'.
(3) *The Volume of Activity* – the number of visits made or games played in particular activities in a particular area over a given time period, for example: 'There are 1.2 million *visits* to swimming pools in Blankshire in a year'.
(4) *Time* – the amount of leisure time available to the individual or collection of individuals, in a specified time period, for example: 'The average working male has three hours leisure time per day'.
(5) *Expenditure* – the amount spent in pounds or dollars on leisure by

individuals, families or communities in a given time period, for example: 'Consumer expenditure on leisure in Britain in 1983 was almost £50 billion.'

(Veal, 1980a, p. 3)

There are certain relationships between a number of these measures, particularly the first three. The Number of Participants is equal to the Participation Rate multiplied by the population of the area under study. The Volume of Activity is equal to the Number of Participants multiplied by the frequency of participation. Expenditure on a particular leisure activity is equal to the Volume of Activity multiplied by the expenditure per visit.

Of particular importance to all these measures is the *time period* to which they relate. This is obvious in the case of the last three measures which relate to volumes of activity, time, or money which must be related to a time period to make any sense. But it is also true of the first two which relate to levels of participation. Information on levels of participation in leisure is largely obtained from social surveys. Many of the early leisure social surveys asked people what leisure activities they had participated in over the previous *year*. This had the advantage of covering all seasons, which is particularly important for many outdoor leisure activities, but had the disadvantage of straining respondents' memories about events up to a year ago and thereby possibly introducing errors into the results. Generally the trend in surveys has been to reduce the period of recall in the interests of accuracy. In Britain, for instance, the General Household Survey asks respondents what activities they have done in the *four weeks* prior to interview. This has the effect of excluding many, although not all, of the less frequent participants, so producing apparently lower levels of participation than surveys based on a one-year period. The level of participation recorded is therefore dependent on the period of time referred to and is dependent on people's own accuracy of recall.

All the measures outlined above have their uses and users. The commercial sector is more interested in the volume of activity and expenditure, whereas the public sector provider is very often more interested in increasing the participation rate and the number of participants. Broadcasting organizations are particularly interested in the time measure of leisure activity. All these measures are used in forecasting.

Forecasting Techniques

The range of forecasting techniques available to the social scientist has been much discussed (Bell, 1964; Encel *et al.*, 1975) and most have been utilized in some form by leisure forecasters (Burton and Veal,

1971). Here we review techniques under nine main headings: speculation, trend extrapolation, respondent assessment, the Delphi technique, scenario writing, the comparative method, spatial models, cross-sectional analysis and composite methods.

Speculation
The term speculation is used here to cover all those predictions which appear to be based on writers' own experience, knowledge, thoughts and informal observations rather than on some explicit, formal technique. Such speculation can be a source of ideas both for policy-making and research. Much of the work of the 'visionaries and philosophers' discussed in Chapter 2 would come under this heading. Contemporary examples include Burton's essay 'The Shape of Things to Come' (1970), Bailey's *Futuresport* (1982), Jennings's (1979) paper 'Future Fun' and Asimov's (1976) paper of the same name. Some of the speculation in such papers is based on observation of current trends – such as Burton's prediction that team sports would decline in popularity relative to individual sports or Jennings's prediction of the growth of non-competitive games. Others rely on some creative thinking about the possible implications of science, technology and space exploration for leisure.

Trend Extrapolation
Trend extrapolation or 'time series analysis' simply involves examination of the pattern of increase or decrease in a particular phenomenon in the recent past and extending, or 'extrapolating' this into the future to obtain a forecast. Examples are given in Figure 7.1 relating to visits to US National Parks and attendances at cinemas in Britain.

In its simplest form this is clearly a very unsophisticated approach. It is based on little more than a hunch that what has gone on in the past will continue to go on in the future. It can produce some unlikely results if not used with care. For instance a straight line extrapolation in Figure 7.1(B) would suggest that cinema attendances in 1990 would fall to zero, whereas in practice they are more likely to 'bottom out' before then, even if at a very low level. At the other extreme there are times when certain activities experience booms in participation – for instance, squash in Britain in the 1970s – when, if current trends were continued far enough into the future, the whole population would be doing little else! In common with most others, this technique is not able to predict sudden changes in trends: for example, at the time of writing, British cinema attendances have recovered from their long-term decline, at least for one year, and have shown a 35 per cent increase over 1984. The technique, in its simplest form, is therefore only suitable for short- to medium-term forecasting – say, over a

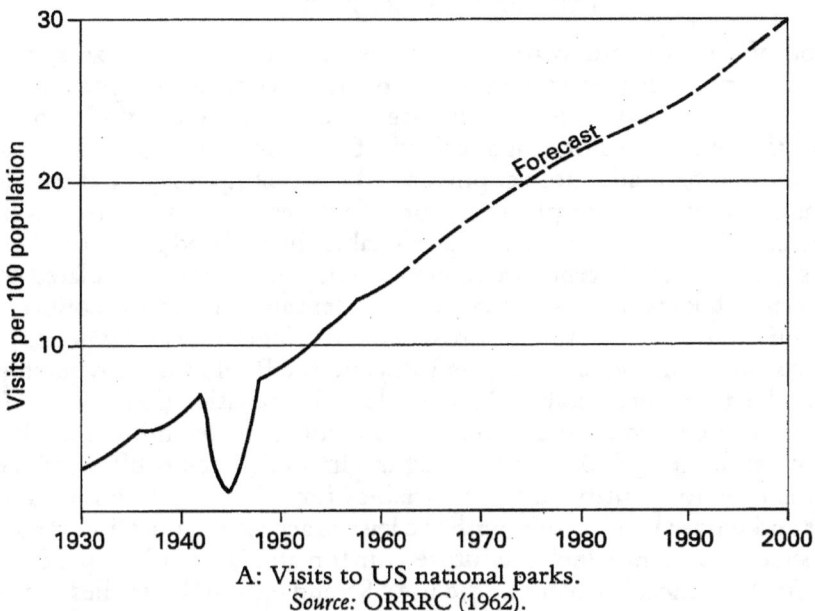

A: Visits to US national parks.
Source: ORRRC (1962).

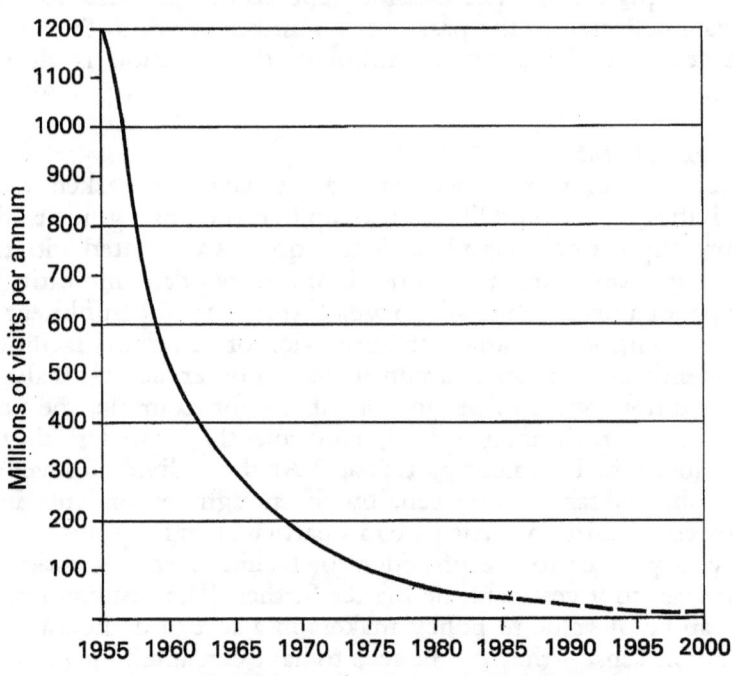

B: Visits to the cinema in Britain.
Source: Central Statistical Office, *Annual Abstract of Statistics* (London: HMSO).

Figure 7.1 Trend extrapolation.

period of three or four years in most leisure forecasting exercises, and even then must be treated with caution and be constantly updated.

An unsophisticated technique needs to be handled with some sophistication if it is not to make fools of the forecasters. Trend extrapolation can be made more sophisticated by looking not just at trends in the activity or other phenomenon of interest but also at trends in some additional, more basic, or predictable, but related series of data. Thus, for example, trends in cinema attendances might be related to the sales of television sets and video-recorders and trips to the countryside might be related to the growth in the level of car-ownership. Television set and video-recorder sales and the level of car-ownership might be more predictable than the leisure activities themselves. If more than one underlying variable is included, the techniques evolve into what Stynes (1983) calls a 'structural model'. The problem for the forecaster is to identify suitable variables for which reliable forecasts exist and whose relationship with the leisure activity in question can be expected to continue into the future (Burton and Veal, 1971, p. 88).

A final practical problem in the use of trend extrapolation lies in the absence of adequate data. The method depends on the existence of a series of data collected in the past over a number of years. Such data series are few and far between, although the situation is slowly improving.

Respondent Assessment
In a number of leisure surveys respondents have been asked what leisure activities they would like to take up in future, as a guide to the likely future popularity of activities. The problems associated with the use of such questions are numerous. Is the respondent indicating a wistful hope, or a firm intention? To what extent does the fulfilment of the wish or intention depend on the provision of additional facilities, the respondent's own personal circumstances or other factors? If all the external conditions were to become suitable – for example, the provision of a new, reasonably priced, conveniently located facility – would the individual actually participate? At the individual level all sorts of problems can be foreseen, but if enough respondents in a survey express a desire to participate in a particular activity this would give a strong pointer to the providers of facilities, commodities or services at least to investigate the matter further. The results of such exercises can be of value to policy-makers in a sort of democratic or public relations sense – they can be seen to have consulted the public – but in practice they would need to be treated with extreme caution.

Examples of the use of the approach in Britain were the *Pilot National Recreation Survey* (BTA/Keele, 1967) and the *Leisure in the North West* survey (North West Sports Council, 1972), both early examples of leisure surveys in Britain. More recently the approach seems to have fallen out of favour in national surveys, but is used at local level to guide local authorities in their decision-making.

Another approach of this general type is to ask people about their past patterns of leisure activity. What activities have they dropped and why? What activities have they taken up and why? Some of the answers would be related to changing personal circumstances and the life-cycle but it might be possible to detect changes and trends in tastes as well (Hedges, 1983).

The *Pilot National Recreation Survey* (PNRS) included this type of 'life history' question and the results were analysed in terms of changing relative popularity of different activities. It was concluded that the sporting activities with the greatest relative growth potential were winter sports, archery, motor rallying and racing, sea sailing, golf and riding (the study was largely confined to sport and outdoor recreation). Many of these activities have indeed grown relatively fast over the succeeding twenty years, but some of those activities expected to show a slow rate of growth or a decline – team games, cycling and athletics – have also shown growth.

The Tourism and Recreation Research Unit at Edinburgh University devised a number of 'indices of growth potential' based on past and current participation and future intentions of Scottish people. The results are summarised in Table 7.1 for the seven overall most popular activities. On the basis of this analysis they identify nature studies, swimming, sailing, golf and sea-fishing as activities with the most growth potential, and cycling and youth hostelling as declining activities – showing some agreement with the PNRS results. As with PNRS, the Scottish surveys were largely concerned with sport and outdoor recreation. But as Coppock and Duffield themselves point out, 'interesting and informative as such subjective measures may be, they cannot stand alone'. They look to more 'objective' techniques to 'add statistical and quantitative support to such subjective indices'. In particular they favour the cross-sectional and spatial techniques discussed later in this chapter.

A further variation on this theme is to ask people how they would spend additional time if their working hours were to be reduced. An early study carried out by Faunce with American car-workers found that the most popular use of such time would be not leisure but work around the house (97 per cent) and the second most popular was not a specific leisure activity but 'spending more time with the family' (77 per cent). Travel (54 per cent), watching sports (49 per cent) and fishing and hunting (42 per cent) were the next most popular activities among this all-male sample (Faunce, 1963, p. 92).

As with so many of the forecasting exercises reported on here, the

Table 7.1 *Recreational Activities in Scotland: Indices of Growth Potential*

Activity	Index A %	Rank	Index B %	Rank	Index C %	Rank	Index D %	Rank	Index E Total Score	Rank
Swimming	45	1	60	3	27	9	14	9	22	5
Golf	43	2	70	1	37	6	12	8	17	3
Angling	39	3	60	5	33	7	14	10	25	7
Sea-fishing	37	4	56	7	39	5	7	3	19	4
Nature studies	37	5	69	2	45	2	8	4	13	1
Field sports	34	6	64	4	21	13	6	1	24	6
Sailing	29	7	58	6	54	1	7	2	16	2

Index A: Number of people participating within last year divided by the number of those who have ever participated, multiplied by 100.

Index B: Number of people participating within last year divided by the number of people participating within the last five years, multiplied by 100.

Index C: Percentage of recent participants who claimed that their interest had increased in the twelve months prior to interview.

Index D: Percentage of recent participants who claimed that their interest had decreased over the twelve months prior to interview.

Index E: Summation of rank scores for indices A, B, C, D.

Source: Coppock and Duffield (1975, p. 84).

practicalities of actually testing the validity of these methods mean that very few have ever been evaluated. It would be necessary to repeat the surveys of the 1960s using the same wording for this sort of test to be done. The declining interest of funding agencies in forecasting means that the substantial funds necessary to carry out such repeat surveys are rarely available.

The Delphi Technique
The Delphi technique can be used for both quantitative and qualitative forecasting but is particularly suited to the latter. It was developed in the early 1960s for the RAND Corporation of America, and is a means of producing a consensus of expert opinion about future events.

The technique involves three or more stages. First, a panel of experts in the particular field of interest is each presented with a series of questions concerning the likelihood of a range of events happening in a given time period, or alternatively they are themselves asked to suggest developments which they see taking place in the field of interest over the given time period. In the second stage the answers from the experts are collated; average probabilities are assigned to each of the developments, based on the experts' answers, or a list of possible developments and their possible timings, as put forward by the panel, is drawn up. Members of the panel are then sent this collated list and asked to revise their own opinions, if they wish, in the light of the information presented on their colleagues' views. These replies are then collated and the process repeated until a stable situation is reached. The technique is therefore a process of distillation of expert views on the future. Of course its success depends to a large extent on the choice of a suitable panel of experts.

Shafer and his colleagues (1975) conducted a Delphi exercise on the future of leisure in the United States using a panel of 400 professionals and academics who were mainly expert in the area of natural resource aspects of recreation management. The exercise involved four 'rounds' of questioning. Panel members were asked to indicate the most significant events, in their own areas of expertise, which they thought had at least a 50–50 chance of happening by the year 2000, assuming a stable political situation and sustained economic growth. These events were grouped into five areas: natural resources management, wildland recreation management, environmental pollution, population-workforce-leisure, and urban environment. Within the wildland recreation management and population-workforce-leisure sections, the following are some of the events predicted:

By 1980: Computers used to advise recreationists where to go for recreation.
By 1985: Maximum noise levels enforced in recreation areas.
Most people work a four-day, thirty-two hour week.
By 1990: Year-round skiing on artificial surfaces.
US Census of population includes questions on recreation activities and needs.
Most homes have video-tape systems.
By 2000: Waste-disposing bacteria incorporated into recreation equipment.
Small recreational submarines common.
Average retirement age is 50 years.
'Weekends' distributed throughout the week.
After 2050: Self-contained under-water resorts.
First park established on moon.
Average worker has three month annual vacation.
Twenty per cent of the available workforce used to produce goods and services for the entire population.

Already many of these predictions have been proved premature or unduly cautious. The purpose of the exercise was, however, not to produce hard and fast predictions but to 'stimulate the thinking of the decision-makers ... and provide direction for formulating policies to deal with future environmental problems'.

A similar exercise was carried out in the USA by Chai (1977) using a panel of only thirty-six people and was also concerned with changes likely to take place by the year 2000. In Britain the 'Matrix' management consultancy firm conducted a Delphi-style exercise on leisure futures for a consortium of commercial companies considering investment options for the future. Their TAROT (Trend Analysis by Relative Opinion Testing) method is a modified, less formal form of the Delphi method. Their panel of experts was first of all interviewed individually in a semi-structured way. The results of the interviews formed the basis of an initial report which was sent to the experts who were then interviewed again and a final report prepared. There was also an element of 'scenario writing' in their approach in that leisure trends were examined in the context of possible shifts in such factors as political power, oil prices and unemployment levels. The panel of experts included investment advisers, journalists and marketing and advertising consultants as well as those involved academically and professionally with leisure. It is not possible to quote the results of this research because of its commercial nature, but the project does demonstrate that the Delphi technique, or something very close to it, is sufficiently well thought of for hard-nosed businessmen to use it to guide them in investment decisions.

Other examples of the use of the Delphi technique in the leisure area are Kaynak and Macaulay's (1984) study of tourism potential in Nova Scotia, and Ng, Brown and Knott's (1983) work on manpower needs of the leisure industry in Canada.

The technique appears simple but can be very time consuming to set up and administer (Moeller and Shafer, 1983). While it has the advantage of throwing up possibilities which other methods could not, it is still ultimately dependent on the quality of the experts chosen; the experts may or may not be gifted with 'Delphic' vision.

Scenario Writing
Discussion of the Delphi technique and its derivatives leads naturally to a consideration of 'scenario writing' as a means of looking at potential futures. Scenario writing involves the drawing up of alternative hypothetical futures as characterized by key variables and the relationships between them. For example, one scenario might involve a future of high economic growth and low unemployment and all that flows from that, while a second, alternative scenario would involve low economic growth and high unemployment. The implications for leisure would then be explored within these 'scenarios'. The aim is not

FORECASTING

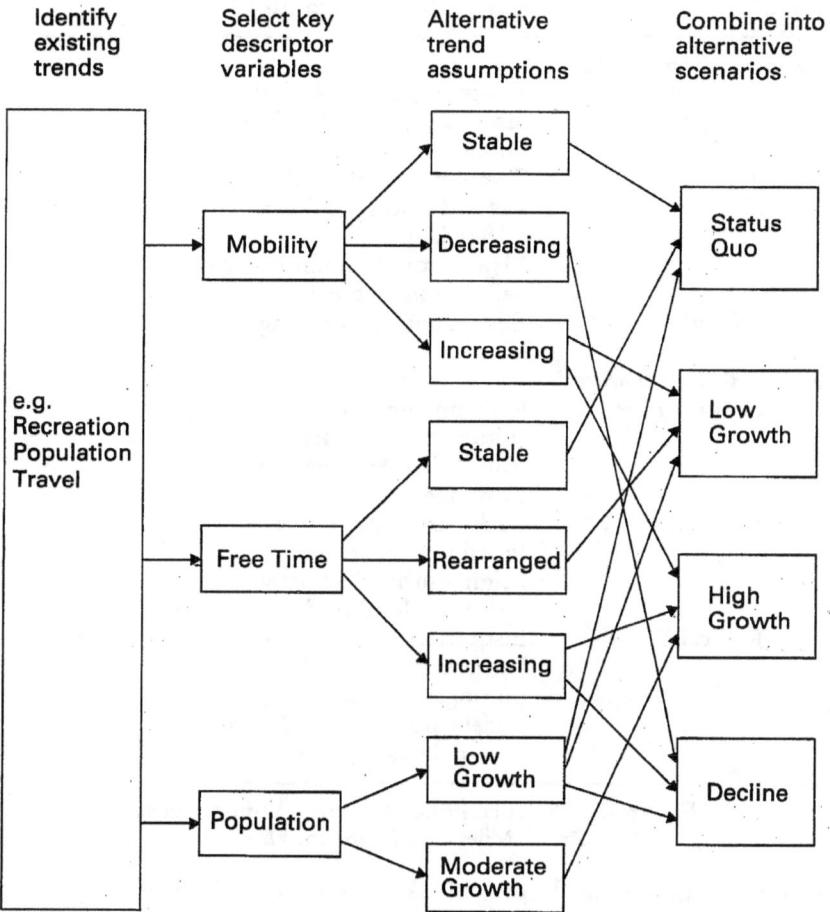

Figure 7.2 McCalla's future scenarios for Ontario.
Source: McCalla (1976).

to produce hard predictions but to present policy-makers with alternatives so that they are prepared for all conceivable eventualities.

An example of the use of the method in recreation forecasting was developed in Ontario, Canada in the mid-1970s as part of a project to aid in transport planning (McCalla, 1981). Three 'key descriptor variables' were selected as being likely, from past experience, to determine the level of recreational travel: mobility, free time and population level. Mobility and the ratio of incomes to travel costs were assigned three alternative trend assumptions: stable, decreasing or increasing. Free time was also assigned three alternative trend assumptions: stable, increasing and 'rearranged', the latter meaning that free time might

Scenario	Leisure Activities Expected
High growth/more equal	
Conservative	'Cultural delicatessen' of pre-packaged leisure. Tourism important.
Reformist	Re-animation of traditional arts and culture, cultural eclecticism. Major growth of innovative/personal mass media.
Radical	Educational/'improving' leisure.
Low growth/inegalitarian	
Conservative	High unemployment and cultural poverty. Rise of stimulus-seeking leisure, e.g. gambling.
Reformist	Backward-looking mass media. Possibly some rise of neighbourhood sports as search for local pride.
Radical	Institutionalized passive barbarism, violence and pornography. Sporting and social clubs associated with para-political groups.

Figure 7.3 Science Policy Research Unit scenarios.
Source: Miles *et al.* (1978, pp. 302–3).

become available in larger blocks such as sabbaticals and longer weekends. Finally, population level was given two alternatives: low growth and moderate growth. Figure 7.2 illustrates the approach. All possible combinations of these trend assumptions would give a total of eighteen possible scenarios. But it was not considered necessary to examine all of these in order to obtain some idea of the range of possible futures. In the Ontario exercise four of the scenarios were explored in detail, referred to as status quo, low growth, high growth and decline.

The Science Policy Research Unit of Sussex University also used a scenario approach in their book *World Futures: The Great Debate* (Miles *et al.*, 1978). They explore a twelvefold set of scenarios developed along two main dimensions. The first dimension is concerned with economic growth and equality. Four possibilities are put forward: high growth/more equal, high growth/inegalitarian, low growth/inegalitarian and low growth/more equal. The second dimension is a political one with three possibilities: conservative, reformist or radical. In addition, they consider the possibilities not only for advanced economies of East and West, but also the Third World. Leisure is one of seventeen topics explored using this framework. Some idea of the scenarios for leisure can be seen from the high growth/more equal and low growth/inegalitarian alternatives reproduced in Figure 7.3.

A further example was developed by Martin and Mason (1981, 1982), two consultants working in England, who present a fourfold set of scenarios for the future, based on the two dimensions of 'economic growth' and 'social attitudes'. Economic growth can range from high to low and social attitudes can range from 'conventional' to 'transformed'. Conventional attitudes conform to the assumed current consensus which places importance on increasing incomes and material wealth; transformed social values involve rejection of materialism and the embracing of more ecologically aware attitudes – a 'Green' approach. Thus the four scenarios are designated Conventional success (high economic growth/conventional values), Transformed growth (high economic growth/transformed values), Frustration (low economic growth/conventional values) and Self-restraint (low economic growth/transformed values), as illustrated in Figure 7.4. Some of the implications which Martin and Mason see in these scenarios for leisure are as follows:

Conventional success	Work hard, play hard. Leisure as rest and entertainment.
Frustration	More leisure at work. Leisure as an escape.
Transformed growth	Deliberate choice of extra free time. Leisure as personal and social development.
Self-restraint	Leisure used partly for productive purposes. Blurring of distinction between work and leisure.

In their more detailed work on leisure expenditures these alternative scenarios are explored in depth to show the implications for consumer expenditure on leisure goods and services.

Scenario writing can be seen as complementary to other, more quantified forecasting. In the past some forecasters have simply assumed that the political, social and economic environment would not change radically over the forecasting period and that such

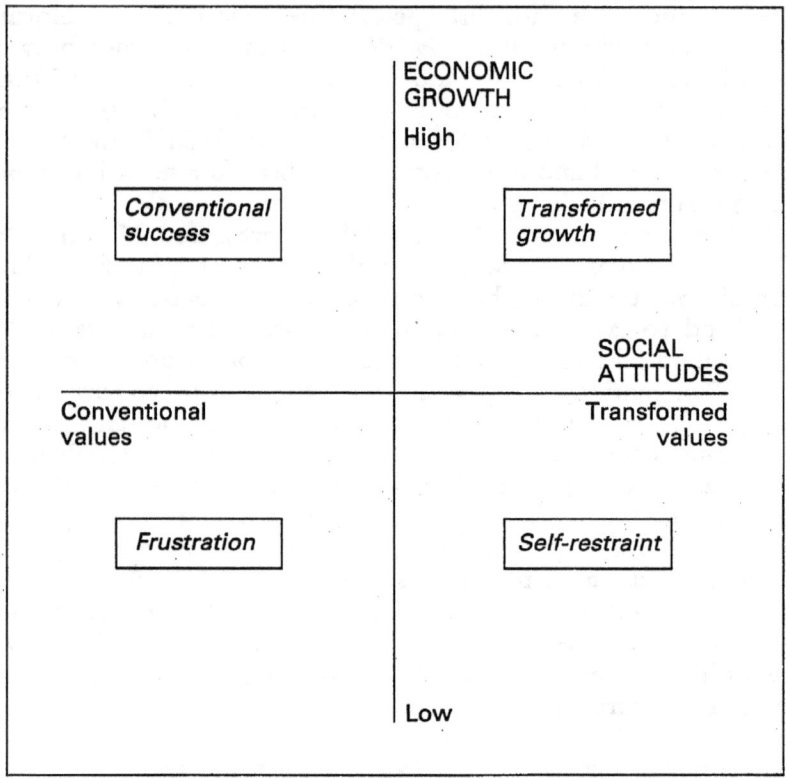

Figure 7.4 Martin and Mason: Four possible futures.
Source: Martin and Mason (1981).

phenomena as economic growth would continue. In the 1980s such assumptions have become less tenable. Economic growth seems less assured and political values have become polarized in the West. Forecasting must, therefore, of necessity, involve alternative scenarios.

The Comparative Method
Joffre Dumazedier, in his book *The Sociology of Leisure* (1974) put forward a threefold classification of sociological forecasting methods:

(1) temporal elasticity – which is essentially trend extrapolation;
(2) social elasticity – which is in effect the cross-sectional method outlined below;
(3) comparative spatial elasticity – comparison of other, more-advanced societies with the society under observation.

It is the third of these which is highlighted here. Dumazedier suggests that society A can consider its future by reference to society B, a more advanced society. Thus he suggests that Western societies in general should look particularly to the United States as a means of studying their own futures. He refers to America as the first society to pass into a post-industrial state.

Dumazedier recognizes that differences in cultural, political, historical and environmental contexts will make comparison difficult. He attempts to outline a method by which the essence of leisure and the causal relationships between leisure and other aspects of life can be isolated. Unfortunately these ideas are outlined only briefly in the closing pages of the book and are not tested empirically. In fact the culmination of his thought appears to be a call for a general monitoring of international statistical trends in leisure and related phenomena rather than proposals for a specific project.

Dumazedier's attempt to develop the comparative method as a scientific method of forecasting would seem to be doomed to failure. Far too many variables are involved and, even if the necessary data were available, disentangling the effects of different variables on leisure behaviour would be virtually impossible.

Where the comparative method might be of use is in developing the scenario-writing approach already discussed. The latter suffers from its entirely hypothetical nature. Some of the scenarios drawn up could however be illustrated by reference to existing societies. This would be particularly relevant for a country like Britain which, in conventional economic terms, has become less 'developed' compared with countries such as the United States, Germany and Sweden. To be somewhat simplistic, the United States appears to exemplify a materialistic, 'success-orientated' scenario and demonstrates that, to all intents and purposes, a society can develop with no apparent limit to its ability to desire and absorb material goods and its willingness to continue to work for them. Sweden illustrates the possibilities and the problems associated with a welfare approach to the distribution of a high level of wealth (Akerman, 1979). Germany on the other hand, would seem to indicate that material wealth need not necessarily herald the demise of the work ethic (Noelle-Neumann, 1981). Thus, while taking account of differing national cultures, history and environments, it is possible to use international comparative perspectives to fill out and illustrate a scenario approach to forecasting.

A further example of the comparative approach at work takes place within one nation: the United States. America's current 'guru' of the future is John Naisbitt, whose book *Megatrends* (1982) is the 1980s version of *Future Shock*. Naisbitt bases much of his prognostication on detailed study of newspapers from all over the United States. As a result of his intense study of newspapers he claims to be able to identify the key states and communities within the United States which are leading the way in terms of life-style, values and attitudes. The visions of the future which he conjures up do not, however, appear to be characterized by an increase in or any new approaches to leisure.

Spatial Models
The pattern of a great deal of leisure behaviour outside the home is affected by the availability and spatial distribution of facilities for leisure. In fact even leisure in the home is directly affected by facilities available outside the home – if attractive facilities are not available outside the home then people are likely to spend more of their leisure time in the home, watching television or engaging in other home-based activities. The significance of this rather obvious statement for the future of leisure is that certain activities cannot grow substantially in popularity unless facilities are available in which they can be practised.

Activities which depend on specific facilities in this way might be termed *confined* activities, and those less dependent upon specific facilities *unconfined* activities. Confined activities are those like squash, ice-skating (in temperate climates), swimming (indoors) and watching professional theatre, where participation is virtually totally dependent upon the availability of specific, usually purpose-built, facilities and where facilities have a fairly clearly defined capacity. Once any spare capacity in existing facilities has been taken up, any increase in levels of participation depends on the provision of additional facilities or an increase in the capacity of existing facilities. Unconfined activities on the other hand, are those which, like trips to the countryside or jogging, while they may make some use of facilities, are nevertheless not dependent in any clear way on specific facilities and so increases in participation are not dependent on the provision of additional facilities. The notions of 'confined' and 'unconfined' lie at opposite ends of a continuum: in between are activities displaying both confined and unconfined characteristics, such as fishing or visiting museums (Veal, 1980a, p. 39).

It is, therefore, possible to think of leisure futures not simply in terms of gross 'levels of participation' in different activities, but in terms of patterns of demand arising from specific residential neighbourhoods and workplaces and being catered for by specific facilities. Forecasting then becomes a matter not of predicting total demand for a whole country or region but of predicting the spatial patterns of that demand, the origins and destinations of leisure trips, the relative impact of facilities with differing attractions, and the effect on the 'system' of the introduction of additional facilities, new transport routes, new residential neighbourhoods or new workplaces. This is what transport planners do when they consider the generation and distribution of journeys to work or shopping journeys, with the difference that in those cases workplaces and shopping centres, rather than leisure facilities, are the destinations of the trips.

Such a perspective lends itself to modelling – the mathematical representation of the leisure trip 'system'. A number of attempts have been made in the academic literature to develop such models but there have been few practical applications for recreation planning purposes.

How do such models work? Models of human behaviour can be constructed when people behave in some predictable manner. Many might object to the idea that people are assumed to behave 'predictably'; such a statement seems to deny people their individuality and freedom. But the statement is not based just on assumption but on observation. People, *en masse*, do often behave predictably. This is not to say that everybody behaves in the same way – in certain situations there is only a limited choice of courses of action which the individual can take and models are based on the observations of the proportion of the population who choose each course. Models are quite limited in what they set out to do.

An example of a situation in which modelling might be applied is the case of a town with a population of, say, 100,000 which has twenty-five major outdoor recreation areas, in and around the town, to which the population resort on fine Sunday afternoons. The number of people who actually go out on a particular Sunday afternoon will depend on such things as the weather and, for instance, whether or not the Cup Final is being broadcast on television. Who goes depends on such things as family situation and access to private or public transport. Certain proportions of these trippers will distribute themselves around the twenty-five sites according to their tastes, distances from home to site, levels of congestion, the size and attractiveness of the sites, cost of entry if any, and so on. Planners might decide to set up a model to simulate this behaviour in order to predict what would happen as population increased, or car-ownership increased, or additional sites were provided. In order to do this it would be necessary to observe what actually happens at present – to collect data on what people actually do, to observe which are the popular sites, how many users they each attract and where these users come from, which sites attract young people and which the elderly, which ones attract families, and so on. It is on the basis of this sort of information, collected by means of surveys, that the model would be established.

The fundamental observation upon which spatial recreation planning models rely is that travel distance, travel time and travel costs

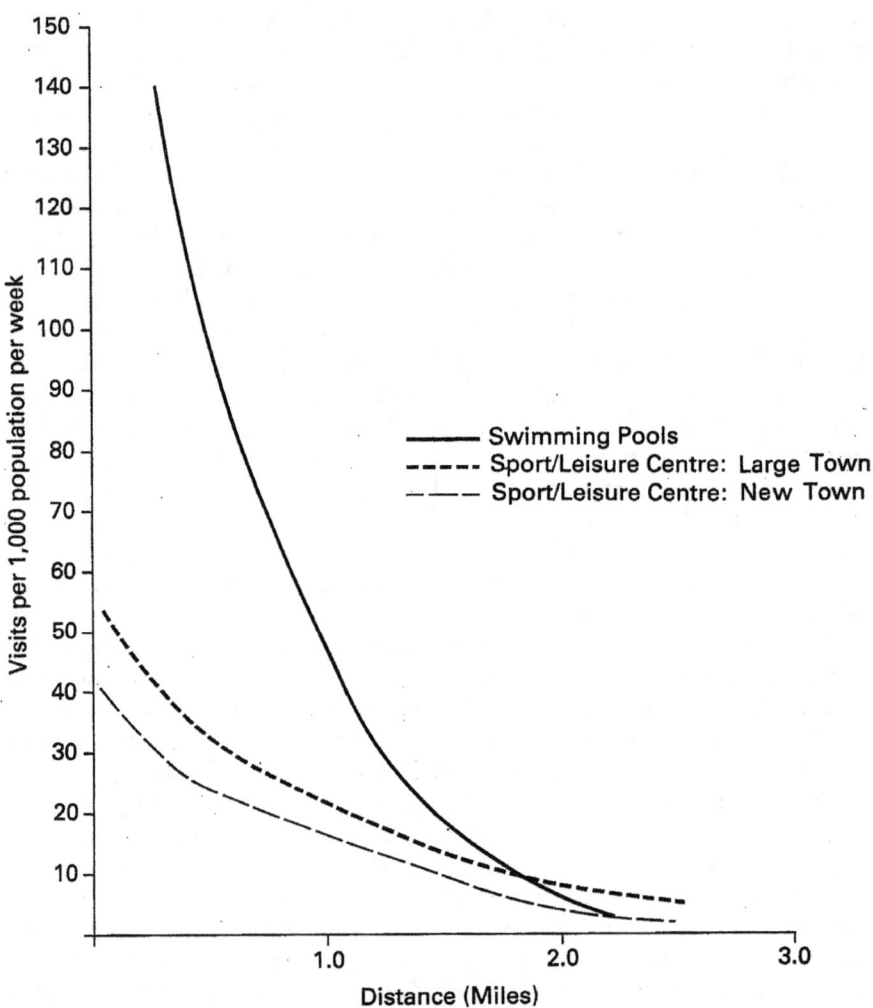

Figure 7.5 Effect of distance on participation.
Source: Veal (1979a, 1987).

affect people's use of leisure facilities. Concentrating on distance for the moment, this means that, other things being equal, the further a person has to travel to visit a leisure facility the less likely that person is to visit it. Figure 7.5 illustrates the general truth of this observation for a number of different types of leisure facility. Since the number of visits from an area will to some extent be a reflection of the number of people living in that area, the diagram shows visit *rates* at different distances from the facilities, that is, the number of visits *per 1,000 population*, in a given time period. There is generally a marked fall-off in visit rates as distance from the facilities increases. The pattern varies from facility to facility – more attractive facilities will attract larger numbers of people from greater distances than the less attractive facilities. The pattern is also affected by the type of clientele which uses the facility – for example, a swimming pool which has a large proportion of children among its users or a library which has a large proportion of elderly people among its users, will have a smaller 'catchment area' than a theatre which attracts mainly the more mobile sections of the middle class.

It is not intended to go into the mathematics of modelling here, but those readers familiar with mathematics will readily appreciate that the relationships illustrated in Figure 7.5 lend themselves to mathematical representation; those readers unfamiliar with mathematics will have to take it on trust that they do. For expositions of modelling in recreation see Burton and Veal (1971) and Gold (1973).

Early efforts at recreation modelling concentrated on single facilities rather than 'networks' and generally these were outdoor facilities such as parks. The most well-known work is that of Marion Clawson in the United States (Clawson and Knetsch, 1966). His aim was to establish a demand curve for recreation areas such as National Parks where there was no entry charge. His approach was to convert travel *distance* into travel *costs* for people travelling different distances to a recreation site and by this means to establish a relationship between demand (the number of visitors) and price (cost of getting there) – in fact, a demand curve. This could then be used to predict what would happen if a charging system were introduced. Such demand curves would also be of use in cost-benefit studies because they would enable a monetary value to be placed on the recreational experience of visitors. This methodological breakthrough led to an enormous amount of investigatory work using the 'Clawson method'. The method was however subject to some criticism and it fell under the cloud that all cost-benefit work fell under during the mid-1970s. As a result there have been few practical applications of the method (Baxter, 1979; Gratton and Taylor, 1985, p. 100).

The relationships between residential areas, recreation sites and the trips between them can also be viewed from the perspective of the 'gravity model'. Newton's law of gravity states that the force between two bodies is proportional to the product of their masses and inversely proportional to the square of the distance between them. This provides an analogy for recreational-trip-making: the recreation facility is seen as one of the 'bodies' and its size and attraction as its 'mass'; the second 'body' is the residential area from which trips are made, the 'mass' of this body being its level of population. The 'force' between the two bodies is then the number of recreational trips. The 'gravity model' then accords with observed trip-making behaviour:

(1) the greater the population of the residential area the greater the number of trips generated;
(2) the larger and more attractive the recreation facility the greater the number of trips attracted to it;
(3) the greater the distance between the residential area and the recreation facility the less will be the number of trips between them.

Again this sort of relationship lends itself to mathematical representation (Coppock and Duffield, 1975, p. 193; Duffield, 1976; Baxter, 1979; Whitaker and Rhodes, 1968).

Using the gravity model and derivations of it, models of a system of recreation sites can be developed. Such models can include not only a system of sites and the residential (and possibly business) areas from which trips are generated but also the transport routes between them (Coppock and Duffield, 1975; Milstein and Reid, 1966). Again examples of fully operational practical applications of such models are rare. They are very costly to set up because of the enormous amounts of data they require. The major exercise to attempt this in the UK, the Study of Informal Recreation in South East England (SIRSEE) failed to get much beyond the data collection stage (Davidson and Sienkiewicz, 1975; Countryside Commission, 1979).

Cross-sectional Analysis
Cross-sectional analysis is probably the most widely used technique in quantitative leisure forecasting. As its name implies, the basis of the method is the examination of leisure participation levels among a *cross-section* of the population. Levels of participation in many leisure activities are usually found to vary between different social groups such as different age groups, different income groups or those with and without access to private transport. These patterns are illustrated in Figure 7.6 for a range of activities and social characteristics. The basis of the forecasting part of the exercise is the proposition that the changing social composition of the population in the future will lead to corresponding, predictable, changes in the levels of participation in leisure activities. For instance, it can be seen in Figure 7.6 that outdoor physical recreation is engaged in by more middle class groups (professional, managerial and other non-manual workers) and car-owners than by working class and non-car-owning groups. Therefore, the cross-sectional method assumes that, if the proportion of middle class people in the population increases and if car-ownership increases, then so will participation in outdoor physical recreation. Furthermore, this

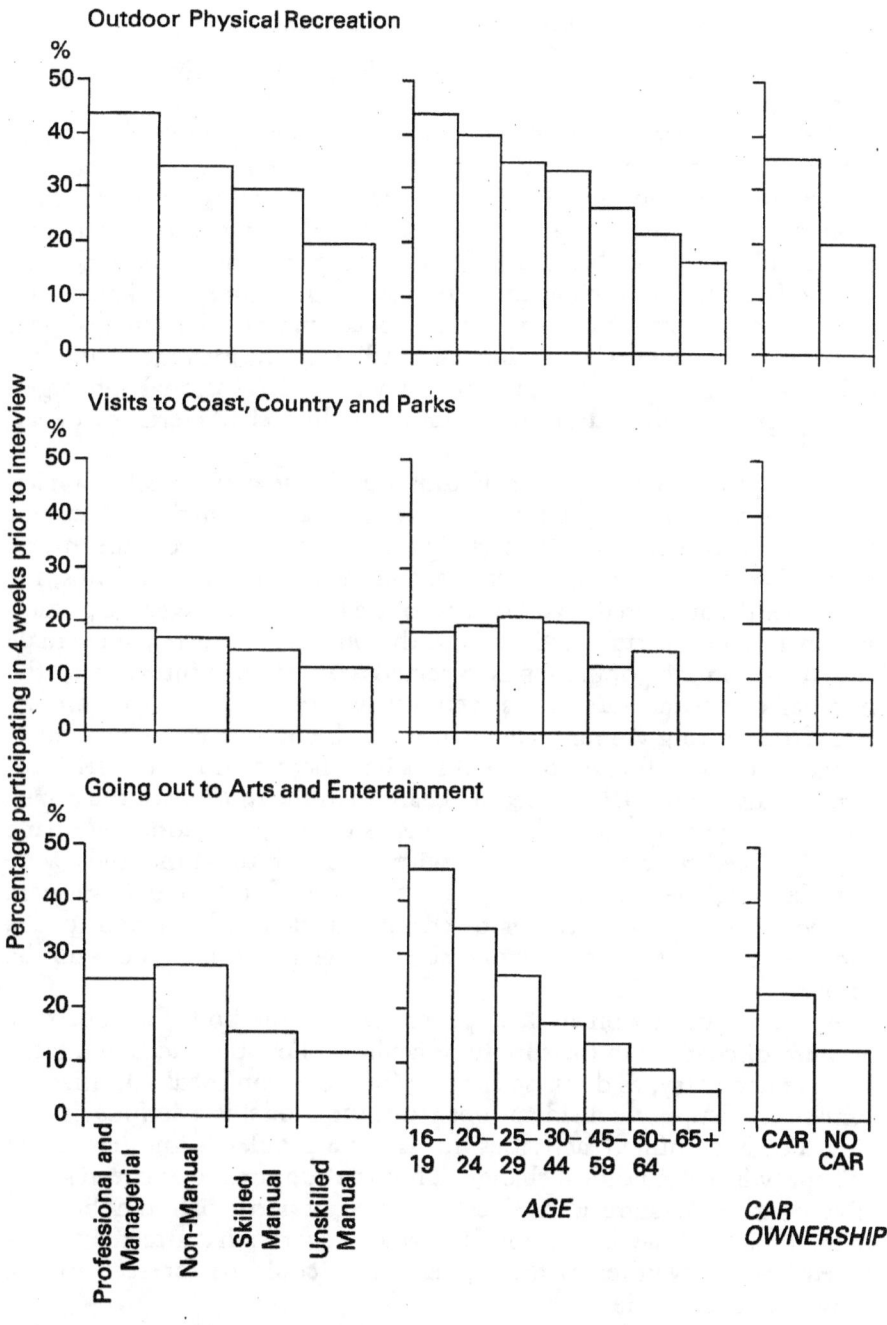

Figure 7.6 Relationships between leisure participation and socioeconomic characteristics.
Source: General Household Survey (1980): England and Wales.

can be quantified because we know the levels of participation among these groups.

The method uses the statistical technique of multiple regression (and sometimes discriminant analysis) to quantify the relationships between participation in a leisure activity and the various relevant social characteristics. As with the spatial models discussed above, the model must first of all be set up ('calibrated') using observations of existing patterns of behaviour, such as those illustrated in Figure 7.6. These data are generally drawn from substantial social surveys. The analysis can be based either on groups defined according to the average characteristics of the group (e.g. male car-owners in professional jobs aged 30–45) or on individuals and their individual characteristics (Veal, 1980a).

The approach has a number of limitations. The first, which is apparent from the description given above, is that the method does not forecast changes in levels of participation *per se* but merely the effects on participation of certain structural socioeconomic factors. Thus, for example, if young male car-owners have a higher than average participation rate in a certain activity and the number of such young male car-owners in the population is expected to increase in future, then the number of participants in that activity will be predicted to increase. But if the existing young male car-owners themselves participate more in the activity in future, this will not be reflected in the model forecasts. Thus the model is based on changes in the *structure* of the population rather than on the changing tastes of the population. We have already noted how, in the 1960s, when many of these methods were first devised, the changing size and structure of the population were indeed very important causes of changes in demand. Currently it is more likely that other factors such as changes in taste will be important.

A second limitation is that, generally, the method does not take account of changes in the supply of facilities. For some activities facilities are necessary, as discussed above; for these 'confined' activities the omission of supply considerations from the model is a serious limitation. For 'unconfined' activities this is not a problem. Another aspect of supply is technological change. Thus the appearance of cheap glass-fibre boats had a significant effect on levels of participation in boating in the 1960s and the invention of the video-recorder has affected home-based leisure. Neither of these phenomena could be foreseen by the cross-sectional model.

A third limitation is the extensive data requirements of the method. If the method is based upon the characteristics of groups rather than individuals then a worthwhile statistical exercise would need to be based upon perhaps some forty or fifty social groups. This places a strain on any sample survey in that some of these groups may contain very few subjects, calling into question their statistical reliability. Further, the more social variables included, the more difficult it is to obtain forecasts of those variables upon which to base the forecasts of leisure activity. If individuals rather than groups are used in the analysis, all sorts of problems arise because of the non-quantifiable nature of many of the variables used and the necessity to use 'dummy' variables, and also because many leisure activities are of a minority nature so that any sample divides unevenly into a small number of participants and a large number of non-participants. Although careful consideration of statistical methods can produce statistically valid results, the theoretical justification and practical application of such analyses, as for instance carried out by Settle (1977), raises problems.

The earliest forecasts using the cross-sectional approach and a substantial data base were contained in the first American Nationwide Outdoor Recreation Plan produced by the Outdoor Recreation Resources Review Commission (ORRRC) in 1962. The work was based on a 1960 survey of 4,400 persons over the age of 12 and was confined to outdoor recreation, mainly of a rural nature. The opening statement of ORRRC's Study Report 19 encapsulates the basis of the cross-sectional method: 'it was assumed that participation in a given outdoor activity is predictable from the social and economic characteristics of participants' (Ferris, 1962, p. 1). Forecasts of levels of participation were produced for the years 1976 and 2000. In a rare example of self-monitoring, the Heritage, Conservation and Recreation Service conducted a survey of participation in 1976 which enabled them to compare the 1962 forecasts with reality. The calamitous results are reproduced in Table 7.2: the level of participation in a number of activities had been underestimated by factors of two, three and even four.

What happened to produce such inaccuracies? Brown and Huston, in analysing the experience, eliminated a number of possible explanations such as sample error or the inaccurate projection of underlying variables like age structure and income levels. They concluded that what was wrong was that the model simply did not work. As we have noted, the cross-sectional model predicts changes in participation resulting from the changing composition of the population, but Brown and Huston indicated that participation levels changed substantially *within* social groups. Thus the major source of change in participation was not included in the model. Brown and Huston suggest, as do Brown and Wilkins (1975), that more localized approaches to forecasting, which include supply and spatial considerations, have more chance of success.

Cicchetti (1973) attempted to incorporate a supply factor into national forecasts based on ORRRC data, arguing that restricted

Table 7.2 *USA Outdoor Recreation 1976 – Forecasts and Reality*

Activity	Forecast by ORRRC %*	1976 Survey Results %*
Driving for pleasure	56	69
Swimming	55	70
Walking for pleasure	37	68
Sightseeing	47	62
Picnicking	57	73
Fishing	32	55
Bicycling	11	47
Outdoor sport events (spectate)	27	61
Boating	28	35
Nature walks	16	49
Hunting	14	20
Camping	8	15
Water skiing	9	17
Hiking	8	28
Outdoor concerts, plays, etc.	12	40

* Percentage participating in year prior to interview.
Source: Brown and Huston (1979).

supplies of facilities would have a generally restraining effect on participation. For instance, whereas a purely demand-based projection gave an increase in swimming participation by the year 2000 of almost 400 per cent, his model suggested that facility constraints would limit this to just 140 per cent. It is hard to believe other conclusions from the exercise, for instance, that the increase in walking for pleasure would be reduced from 260 per cent to 23 per cent or bicycling from 500 per cent to 50 per cent. Since Cicchetti worked on the year 2000 projections it will be some time before his predictions can be fully tested, but the 1976 survey evidence suggests that he was being too restrictive – possibly because many of the activities with which he was dealing are relatively unconstrained by facility considerations, or because the extensive natural and entrepreneurial resources in the USA ensure that supply does respond to consumer demand.

In the UK the earliest cross-sectional forecasts were produced by the Northern Regional Planning Committee in 1969 for the Northern region of England. Confined to sport and outdoor activities, the model used produced some curious results, with the participation rate of many activities predicted to decline, largely because of the anticipated increase in the proportion of elderly people. But the overall increase in the level of population expected at the time ensured that there were projected increases in the absolute number of participants for nearly all activities.

Later exercises were conducted in the north-west region of England (North West Sports Council, 1972; Settle, 1977) and in Scotland (Duffield and Owen, 1970, 1971; Coppock and Duffield, 1975). The most comprehensive piece of work was carried out by Young and Willmott (1973). The study was comprehensive in terms of the range of activities covered and, although the data base was from the London and south-east region it was adjusted to reflect the national population structure, so it was the first attempt at national forecasts. The social variables included in the study were age, income, occupation, age of finishing full-time education and car-ownership. Table 7.3 reproduces the key forecasts and demonstrates the range of activities covered, including not just sport and outdoor activities but arts and entertainment and home-based leisure activities as well. The measure of participation used is unique to this study, so it is difficult to monitor progress as we move towards the year 2000, nevertheless a number of trends in participation, as revealed by the General Household Survey (Veal, 1984), are moving in the opposite direction from that predicted by Young and Willmott. For instance, attendances at most spectator sports is in decline, cinema attendances have been in decline, and athletics and skating are increasing rather than being static.

The growth mentality and environment of the 1960s and early 1970s is reflected in Young and Willmott's conclusion to their exercise:

The outstanding feature of the forecasts is that almost everything is likely to increase. This is a reflection of the main finding of the survey – that richer, higher-status, more educated, car-owning people did more of almost everything. Since we assume that people will be richer, more educated, doing higher-status jobs and owning more cars, it follows that almost every activity should have more participants in 2001.

(Young and Willmott, 1973, p. 372)

My own study using the 1973 General Household Survey data for Britain, was the first national exercise using national data (Veal, 1979). The projections to 1991, which are reproduced in Table 7.4, were based on predicted demographic, income and car-ownership changes. If the General Household Surveys are continued it will eventually be possible to test these predictions. But, for all the reasons we have discussed, they are unlikely to prove at all accurate. For example, swimming in indoor pools is predicted to rise by 21 per cent between 1973 and 1991. In fact, largely because of a

Table 7.3 *Young and Willmott's 1973 Leisure Forecasts*

Activity	% Participating* 1970	2001	% Change**
Swimming	29	37	28
Sailing	3	4.5	50
Golf	7	10	43
Fishing	9	10	11
Soccer	6	7	17
Cricket	4.5	5	11
Tennis	8	10	25
Table tennis	11	13	18
Bowls	2	2	0
Ten-pin-bowling	9	10	11
Athletics	2	2	0
Badminton and squash	3	4.5	50
Rugby	—	1	250
Boating	1.5	1.5	0
Skating	1.5	1.5	0
Horse riding	1	1.5	50
All sports	44	52	18
Watching swimming	6	6.5	8
Watching golf	2.5	3	20
Watching soccer	20	22	10
Watching rugby	3.5	4.5	29
Watching cricket	10	13	30
Watching tennis	5.5	7.5	36
Watching athletics	3	3.5	17
Watching motor sports	7	8	14
Watching boxing	3	3	0
Watching wrestling	4	4	0
Watching horse racing	5.5	7	27
Watching winter sports	—	1	250
Watching showjumping	2	2.5	25
All watching sport	40	45	13
Listening to music (on radio, records)	68	70	3
Playing an instrument	9	11.5	28
Home decoration/repairs	60	66	10
Car maintenance	20.5	27	32
Car cleaning	33	50	51
Knitting/sewing	46	44	−4
Reading	67	74	10
Gardening	63	67	6
Model-building	5.5	6.5	18
Collecting (stamps, etc.)	12	13.5	13

Table 7.3 (cont.)

Activity	% Participating* 1970	2001	% Change**
Handicrafts	5	5.5	10
Technical hobbies	5	6	20
Playing cards/chess	8.5	11.5	35
Crosswords	3	4	33
Cooking	2.5	3.5	40
Painting/sculpture	3	4.5	50
Working at home	4.5	7.5	67
Going to cinema	53	58	9
Going to theatre	37	45	22
Going to museum	25	32	28
Going to art gallery	17	25	47
Going out for a meal	62	70	13
Going to pub	62	69	11
Attending church	37	41	11
Voluntary work	15	19	27
Billiards/snooker	12	12.5	4
Darts	21	22	5
Dancing	31	35	13
Going for a walk of 1 mile+	65	68	5
Going for a drive	68	78	15
Camping	7	8	14
Caravanning	10	11	10
Bingo	3.5	3	−14
Adult education	3.5	6.5	9

* Percentages of adults aged 18 and over doing the activity at least once a year.
** Young and Willmott produce a range of increases, reflecting the uncertainties in the data and method. The % changes given here are my own calculations from the data given.
— less than 0.5%
Source: Young and Willmott (1973, pp. 369–72).

70 per cent increase in the number of swimming pools in the country between 1973 and the end of the decade, indoor swimming increased by a similar 70 per cent in that period (Sports Council, 1982; Veal, 1985). Unless there is an unexpected decline, participation is likely to have at least doubled between 1973 and 1991. So it would appear that British forecasts based on the cross-sectional model are proving the same point as already demonstrated by the American work: that without a supply component they are grossly inaccurate.

Table 7.4 *1991 Leisure Forecasts (Britain)*

Activity	% increase in number of participants 1973–1991
Camping	33
Golf	33
Soccer	7
Cricket	21
Tennis	37
Bowls	17
Fishing	19
Swimming outdoors	25
All outdoor sport	23
Badminton/squash	59
Swimming indoors	21
Table tennis	29
Billiards/snooker	23
Darts	−5
All indoor sports/games	23
Watching horse racing	10
Watching motor racing	33
Watching soccer	15
Watching cricket	19
All watching sport	19
Visiting parks	6
Visiting seaside	17
Visiting countryside	21
Visiting historic buildings	25
Visiting museums	25
Visiting zoos	18
Going to cinema	18
Going to theatre	20
Amateur music/drama	25
Going out for a meal	21
Going out for a drink	15
Dancing	17
Bingo	−4

Source: Veal (1979, p. 62).

Composite Methods
Two agencies in Britain are well known for their continuous monitoring and forecasting of the leisure scene: they are Leisure Consultants, otherwise known as Martin and Mason, and the Henley Centre for Forecasting. They produce annual and quarterly monitors largely, but not entirely, devoted to trends in leisure expenditure. To produce such forecasts requires a combination of virtually all the techniques reviewed so far, plus a fair measure of common sense, experience and instinct. We have already examined Martin and Mason's approach to 'scenario writing': such an exercise provides the broad context within which more detailed work on individual products and activities can be undertaken. Such detailed work depends on extensive knowledge of market trends for individual products and services and a grasp of the total picture of consumer behaviour and expenditure patterns. For example, while future purchases of video-recorders might be predicted by means of simple extrapolation of trends in recent years, this must be set against, and if necessary modified by, knowledge of the 'product life-cycle' of such new consumer durables, 'cross-sectional' information about which groups in society are buying the machines, and the overall trends in disposable income and the share of that income available for leisure products. Monitoring of events in other countries, particularly America – the comparative method – is also part of the battery of techniques used in what might be termed the 'composite' method. As with national economic forecasts, these are not once-for-all exercises, but must be modified in the light of changing economic circumstances and government policies.

In their 1984 report on the *UK Sports Market* (Martin and Mason, 1984), Leisure Consultants identify five main influences on future sport participation:

(1) population structure,
(2) life-styles and values,
(3) economic outlook,
(4) official policies,
(5) new technology.

Examples of trends in these areas which they identify for the period 1983 to 1987 are:

(1) a sharp fall in the number of children aged 10–15,
(2) the continued effect of fashionable sports clothing and media attention on sports participation,
(3) a 3 per cent increase in leisure time and a 9 per cent increase in real personal disposable income,

(4) financial stringency in the public sector, leading to higher than average increases in charges and more co-operation with the voluntary and private sectors,
(5) growth of the use of video in sports instruction.

Their conclusions in relation to sports participation are:

(1) more rapid growth in indoor than outdoor sports,
(2) lack of growth in traditional sports where children are significant,
(3) above average growth in informal, individualistic sports,
(4) continued rise in numbers playing racket sports.

Overall this produces a predicted rise in the sports participation rate from 57 per cent of the population in 1983 to 59 per cent in 1987 and an increase in expenditure from £1.19 billion to £1.31 billion (at 1980 prices). Both participation and expenditure predictions are then subdivided into details for twenty-eight individual activities and products. In addition to a volume on sport, Leisure Consultants also produce annual volumes on Media Leisure, Hobbies and Pastimes, Entertainment and Catering and Holidays. The Henley Centre's work appears mainly in its quarterly publication *Leisure Futures* and covers similar ground to that of Leisure Consultants, with regularly updated forecasts and special features (see also Tyrell, 1982). Other organizations such as the Economist Intelligence Unit, from time to time produce leisure expenditure forecasting studies (Edwards, 1981).

Clearly all the individual forecasting methods reviewed here have their weaknesses. It is therefore no coincidence that those who earn their living from forecasting leisure tend to use what we have called the 'composite' method, which draws on a variety of techniques, compensating for the weakness of one with the strengths of another. For all the weaknesses of the methods employed there remains a demand for forecasts from those who must make investment decisions for the future. We could do worse than leave the last word on leisure forecasting to the Outdoor Recreation Resources Review Commission which said, in 1962:

> Many individuals and indeed whole groups of individuals in public and private agencies remain averse to the idea of forecasting and adamantly refuse to become involved in any project which attempts to envision the future. Certainly their position is a comfortable one, and history will never prove them wrong.
> (ORRRC, 1962, Study Report 26, p. 1)

8

Leisure Providers and their Futures

Introduction

The very title of this chapter is revealing about the way we often think about leisure in modern industrialized societies: as a product or service which someone or some organization must provide. Leisure has become increasingly 'commoditized'; not completely by any means, but there is a definite trend. For example, in an English pub it used to be the case that all that was available was alcoholic drink and a few free games such as darts and bar billiards. The essence of the pub was sociability, which is something developed out of free association between individuals. This is no longer the case in many pubs: fruit and video-game machines, commercial pool tables (electronic dart boards have been tried but have not taken off) and juke and video boxes beckon from every corner with their flashing lights, drowning out the one 'commodity' which is free and out of which the publican and brewery cannot make a percentage, namely, conversation.

In Britain, where the package holiday is so common, news reports frequently refer to a 'shortage of holidays this year' or of tour operators 'increasing the number of holidays available'. A holiday has apparently become something which is bought from an operator – a commodity – rather than a period of freedom from work. But this phenomenon is not confined to the commercial world. For example, sport was at one time an activity engaged in in the streets, on village greens and so on. Now it takes place in the local sports centre which is expensively provided by the local authority and managed by professional managers. Children used once to play in relatively safe, stimulating environments near their homes, watched over by grandparents and neighbours: now playschemes and playcentres with trained staff and expensive equipment are required. Sport and play have become commodities.

These comments are not intended to be entirely cynical or critical but aim to draw attention to a process which is fundamental to the future of leisure. Organizations and groups of people engaged in producing leisure goods and services in the commercial or public sector have an interest in seeking out new opportunities to extend their operations, whether these are described as 'new marketing opportunities' in the commercial sector or 'unmet needs' in the public sector. Furthermore, they have the resources and expertise to pursue those interests.

The purpose of these remarks is to suggest that there are at least two possible perspectives on the growth of the production of leisure goods and services. One is that as incomes and leisure time increase the need and demand for leisure goods and services increases and the providers respond to these growing demands and needs. The other view is that the providers use their professional skills and their time to find unfilled niches in the market into which they inject a new product or service which then becomes a need, for which people require money or for which taxes must be raised. Thus the skills of the professional leisure providers are used, paradoxically, to bolster the world of work and money and to keep the informal or self-service economy at bay. People have to keep working to finance their ever-increasing demands for leisure products and services. In the rest of this chapter the commercial and the public sectors are discussed in turn. From the point of view of the future of leisure, however, the differences between these two sectors may not be as great as is often thought.

The Commercial Sector

The two perspectives discussed above can be applied particularly to the commercial sector. One view is that the big corporations wield enormous power and in effect determine what is to be sold in the market place. The alternative, and more traditional, view is that the consumer is 'sovereign' and the producer, however large and powerful, can only sell what people want and are prepared to pay for. When applied to leisure this raises some serious issues. Leisure is after all supposed to be the realm of individual freedom and choice. Are people *choosing* to buy video-recorders and home computers and *choosing* to become keep-fit and health freaks, or are these trends being foisted on a gullible public by powerful corporations using Madison Avenue techniques? This is an important issue as far as the future of leisure is concerned. If all the power lies with the large corporations then *they* and *their* research, development and marketing departments will, to a large extent, decide the future of leisure.

The economist J. K. Galbraith is perhaps the most well-known exponent of the view that the large modern corporation manipulates needs and determines what will be provided:

> The direct link between production and wants is provided by the institutions of modern advertising and salesmanship ... their central function is to create desires – to bring into being wants that did not previously exist. This is accomplished by the producer of the goods or at his behest. A broad empirical relationship exists between what is spent on production of consumers' goods and what is spent synthesizing the desires for that production ... As a society becomes increasingly affluent, wants are increasingly created by the process by which they are satisfied.
> (Galbraith, 1958, pp. 133, 135)

Ralph Glasser argues that people are generally searching for a 'desirable identity', the model for which was, in the past, provided or prescribed by religious and other long-established cultural values. Now it is the commercial world which sets the pace:

> People have a basic need to attain an identity that is as close as possible to that which society and the inherited culture sets up as a standard for emulation. The desirable identity is a compound of ideas about behaviour, ethical standards, physical appearance and life-style, and achievement ... The culture of high consumption presents purely transient models for emulation in terms of the lifestyles of the new synthetic aristocracy, the folk heroes of pop-culture, sport, the business world, even the criminal world. The marketing of goods, and the persuasion process that bends consumer demand to buy them, use this emulative need to achieve their sales targets. The persuasion practitioners, by a skilful deflection of thought, lead people to behave as if the ownership of products and the life-styles these products symbolise, constitute a desirable identity. Thus consumption patterns are formed that fulfil business strategies. The practitioners of the marketing process now exercise the leadership function of the high priesthood of old.
> (Glasser, 1975, pp. 42, 43)

As long ago as 1957 Robert Bendiner wrote:

> Right now it is business that is selling the life of leisure, and the life of leisure that business can sell is necessarily a life of Aqualungs, outboard motors, Skotch Koolers, and house paint – all good in their way, no doubt, but none of them suggesting for a moment that

there was more to Greece than marathons and more to Rome than baths.

(Bendiner, 1957, p. 14)

Defenders of the modern market economy argue for the totally opposite view. Milton Friedman asks:

> What about the claim that consumers can be led by the nose by advertising? Our answer is that they can't – as numerous expensive advertising fiascos testify ... Is it not more sensible to try to appeal to the real wants or desires of consumers rather than to try to manufacture artificial wants or desires? Surely it will generally be cheaper to sell them something that meets wants they already have than to create artificial wants ... The real objection of most critics of advertising is not that advertising manipulates tastes but that the public at large has meretricious tastes – that is, tastes that do not agree with the critics.
>
> (Friedman and Friedman, 1979, p. 266)

One of the arguments of the 'critics' is, however, that in wealthy societies like the United States the average person on an average or higher than average income does not have unmet wants of a serious nature. Indeed it could be argued that the life-style of large numbers of people in the wealthy developed nations indicates a surfeit of material goods which in terms of their effects on health and well-being, is positively harmful.

One question often asked in response to the view that marketing and advertising do not create wants is: if advertising is so ineffective then why are such huge sums of money spent on it? The reply to this is that advertising is not aimed at increasing consumption or persuading people to buy something they do not want; it is primarily aimed at promoting a particular brand at the expense of competing brands. But the reply to this is to ask: if advertising is powerful enough to influence the brand people buy then why should it not be able to influence people over *what* they buy? Can it not persuade us that we *need* a video-recorder or a holiday?

The truth is, as might be expected, considerably more complicated than the bare bones of the argument above suggest. Our reasons for buying goods and services can be complex and are certainly imperfectly understood (Douglas and Isherwood, 1980). The situation is likely to vary depending on the type of product involved; so that for basics such as soap powder or toilet paper, advertising is unlikely to persuade anybody to buy more of the product, all it can do is influence choice of brand (although it may persuade us to buy a more expensive brand). But while we may argue that leisure is a basic need, leisure goods and services certainly are not. The latest leisure products are not meeting 'needs' and they are not even wants until the producers reveal them to the customers. Thus the world could survive quite happily without home video-recorders, compact disc players, theme parks or the latest coconut-flavoured liqueur. Again the purpose of these remarks is not to 'knock' the commercial world. It is to alert us to the possibility that the future of leisure is to a certain extent dependent on what commercial operators decide to develop and market. Of course the success of their business strategies depends on the whim of the consumer, but the commercial corporation has considerable resources available to study and influence those whims.

Emphasis has been placed on the 'large corporation' for good reason. It is of course true that leisure, like many other business sectors, contains large numbers of small firms. To a large extent, however, they are subject to market forces in the traditional sense. They are responding to trends in demand rather than influencing demand. If the market can be influenced by the provider then it is the large corporations, with their billions of pounds of turnover and their research, development and advertising budgets of hundreds of millions of pounds, which will do it.

We have been talking about 'new products' and 'marketing', implying that we live in an era of rapid change and development which, in a sense, is true. But in reality change is slower than we think. For example, in Chapter 1 we noted that 25 per cent of the 'leisure pound' in Britain is devoted to the purchase of alcoholic drink. The forecasters may see this creeping up by a percentage point or two or declining by a point or two over the coming decade, but it is unlikely to change dramatically. At the detailed level the forecasters predict the continuing increase in the sale of wines at the expense of beer and, within the beer market, the continuing increase in the sale of lager at the expense of traditional beer. But from the point of view of broad patterns of leisure behaviour such changes are hardly significant. New consumer durables do of course make an impact but this takes time, and their apparent impact at the time when they first arrive in the market is greater than their actual impact. Thus the high street electrical shops may fill their windows with video-recorders, colour supplements are filled with video-recorder advertisements, articles in magazines and newspapers talk of how people are 'switching on to the video age' and sales are in their hundreds of thousands. But there are 17 million households in Britain. It will take several years before video-recorders are in even half of all homes. So, depending on the movement of wages and prices, the impact of video-recorders could be making itself felt far more significantly long after the media fuss has all died down. Another example is illustrated by a fact revealed in the government report, *Pleasure, Leisure and Jobs* (Young, 1985a), that only 7 per cent of Americans possess passports. This would suggest that international tourism, as far as Americans are concerned, has hardly started. The tourism industry's 'bread and butter' will therefore continue to be catering to the same phenomenon of the 'once in a lifetime' American visitor for many years to come before that market is 'saturated'.

It is hard to conceive of changes in leisure over the next twenty-five years which could be as fundamental as those experienced by the mass of the people in Europe over the last twenty-five years. Two phenomena in particular are responsible: television and the private car. Developments over the next decades could be seen as mere elaboration and development of the changes wrought by these two commodities. Every week, on two evenings, 8 or 9 million people in Britain watch 'Coronation Street' on television, giving between 800 and 900 million viewings in a year. In a summer month in Britain some 150 million car-borne trips are taken to the coast or countryside. It seems unlikely that any completely new activity could begin to rival these two phenomena of home-based entertainment on the one hand and car-borne family trips on the other.

More television channels are expected to be provided in Britain, via cable and/or satellite, but this will not affect leisure behaviour patterns significantly; people will still be watching television, possibly for a little longer. Theme parks on Disney World lines can be expected to develop on a larger scale than hitherto in Britain, but this will merely provide one or two, albeit popular, alternatives to Blackpool Pleasure Beach or a stately home, for the family day out. We might expect large indoor seated stadia to be developed in the UK in order to drag the family away from its television set for sport or entertainment. In the USA some 300 such stadia, seating in excess of 10,000, some more than 50,000, have been built since 1945 (Grant, 1982): none have been built in the UK. But even if, say, four 20,000-seaters were built in the UK over the next ten years they would between them probably accommodate less than 20 million visits in a year – the equivalent of a normal single evening's television audience.

The Public Sector

In mixed economies the public sector, the state, is involved in leisure in three different ways: in encouraging and subsidizing certain activities, in controlling and discouraging certain other activities and in using other activities for economic or political ends. Activities such as sport and the arts are in part subsidized, promoted and provided for at the public expense. Other activities such as the drinking of alcohol and gambling are heavily controlled and heavily taxed, partly in order to discourage consumption and participation. Finally, a leisure industry such as tourism or high profile events such as the Olympic Games can be exploited by the state for economic or political purposes. So the future of these different types of activity is to a significant extent dependent on government activity. To the extent that governments reflect public opinion this may be thought to be perfectly acceptable, but leisure rarely figures in political debate, as Chapter 6 shows, so no one is exactly clear as to what public opinion is in such matters. In this chapter we consider the 'controlling' activity first, then the 'exploitation' activity and finally, at greater length, the subsidizing, promoting and providing activity.

Controlling
In the area of controls on leisure by government two opposed trends can be seen at work. First, as society becomes more complex, and possibly more anomic, the need for state involvement and regulation increases. For example, in Britain in 1985, the government has tightened the regulations covering safety at sports stadia, following a serious fire at Bradford football ground, and it has introduced additional regulations on football in an attempt to combat violence and lawlessness by spectators. Drug and solvent abuse, which for some is a leisure activity, attracts increasing government action. In these areas increasing involvement seems to be the order of the day. In other areas the trend is towards relaxation of controls. In the 1960s the law on obscene publications and stage performances was relaxed. A recent government bill to abolish the controls on Sunday trading in England and Wales was defeated in Parliament. Shopping, especially in the family atmosphere which might be possible on a Sunday, is certainly a form of leisure activity to many.

The law which, in Britain, represents one of the most widespread forms of control on people's leisure, and which could be said to amount to a significant infringement of individual liberty, is that which controls pub opening hours. Introduced during the Great War to ensure that munitions workers would be fit for work, the law has been maintained by a combination of government inaction and a small number of temperance Members of Parliament who have blocked the passage of the private members' abolition or reform bills which have from time to time been introduced in the House of Commons. The current government is rumoured to believe that the licensing laws are bad for the tourist trade and are anti-competitive, and so may be moved to change them. The report, *New Jobs from Pleasure*, produced by a committee chaired by a Tory MP and published from Conservative

Central Office (Banks, 1985), reports on the success of recent relaxation of the licensing laws in Scotland and calls for the introduction of flexible licensing laws in England and Wales 'without delay'. The government's own report, *Pleasure, Leisure and Jobs* (Young, 1985a), merely states that the government is 'considering whether to propose changes in licensing hours in England'.

Exploiting
The state exploits leisure in a variety of ways and therefore the future of some aspects of leisure will depend on governments' views on what they can get out of it. First and foremost in the catalogue of exploitation is the use of certain leisure activities to raise very high levels of taxation, and this is partly linked to the controlling of certain activities as discussed above. Leisure goods and services are of course subject to VAT (currently 15 per cent in UK) as are other goods and services. Some have suggested that this should be waived for the arts but this is not an argument to be pursued here. The interest here lies in those areas, generally leisure orientated, where high levels of duty are levied over and above VAT. This applies to alcoholic drink and gambling. Some 40 per cent of the stake in football pools is taken in duty. This, together with duty on bookmaking, bingo and gaming machines, yields hundreds of millions of pounds in income for the government. As for alcohol, more than half of the price of a bottle of spirits is duty, £1 is levied on every bottle of wine and there is a substantial duty on beer, altogether yielding billions of pounds for the Exchequer each year. The only comparable phenomenon is the duty on tobacco. In this case the justification for the high level of duty now, although this was not the case originally, is the need to discourage smoking on health grounds. Similar arguments are advanced against alcohol, although with less force since it is mainly the excessive consumption of alcohol or drinking and driving, which are injurious to health or safety. Gambling is also seen as a source of social problems if carried to excess. But of course underlying all of this is the belief that all of these activities are vices which deserve a certain amount of punishment or penance. Clearly it is within the power of governments to raise duty levels to such a level that demand begins to fall. But this might bring electoral unpopularity, it might drive the activities 'underground' and possibly into the hands of organized crime, and it would also risk a loss of income. Governments must be careful not to kill the leisure-vices which are fat geese laying golden eggs. So again we see that government has it in its power to influence very strongly what happens in future to these particular leisure activities.

Another area in which governments become involved is tourism. It is seen as an industry which creates jobs and, in its international form, brings in foreign exchange. In some Third World countries the government is the only agency with the power and access to resources necessary to develop a tourist industry: it is seen as an attractive option because very often the poorest countries are endowed with the most saleable assets such as sunshine, coastline, scenery and wildlife. In developed economies the situation is more complex but nevertheless governments become involved in marketing and developing tourism, very often on a large scale. The Young report referred to earlier states:

> The Government has a direct concern with the industry's great potential for *growth, job creation and enterprise*. As patterns in society and industry change, we need to encourage the new strong points of our economy, many of them in the service sectors. Across the UK few industries offer as great a scope for new employment as tourism and leisure.
> (Young, 1985a)

In fact the present British government is not in favour of increased state involvement in the tourist industry despite the importance it attaches to it. It believes rather that government can best help the industry by relaxing some of the regulations and restrictions under which it operates. An example of such a restriction is the licensing laws already referred to. So we have an example of one form of involvement, control, giving way to another, exploitation.

There are other examples of state exploitation of leisure which could be explored, such as the way new towns and areas seeking migrant industry develop leisure facilities, such as golf courses, not primarily for the benefit of their residents but in order to attract industrialists. Nevertheless the residents do of course benefit from the facilities provided. The Olympics have been discussed, analysed and documented sufficiently for it not to be necessary to outline here the ways in which that event is manipulated and exploited, and will continue to be manipulated and exploited by governments, for political ends (Brohm, 1978; Tomlinson and Whannel, 1984).

Providing
The state becomes involved in subsidizing, providing and promoting certain forms of leisure for a variety of reasons (Gratton, 1980). Primarily these reasons are to do with benefits which accrue to the community at large when someone engages in such leisure activities, over and above the benefits which accrue to the individual participant. For instance, the community saves money if it can save lives or reduce sickness through improved health resulting from sports participation. It can save on social and welfare services if the elderly or the handi-

capped can be kept physically and mentally active through recreation programmes. It can save in financial and non-financial terms if young people in particular can be persuaded to engage in harmless leisure activities rather than disruption, vandalism and even criminal activities. All this justifies the expenditure of public resources on what might be termed 'preventative' leisure services. Cheap leisure services can also be seen as a means of redistributing resources to the poorer sections of the community. A less 'hard-nosed' motive is the desire to promote or preserve the 'culture' or 'civilization', which is a 'collective' rather than an individual concept; such a motive gives rise to support for the arts.

These motives inspire a wide range of services such as municipal swimming pools, sports and leisure centres, parks, youth centres, centres for the elderly and for the handicapped and facilities for the arts. In Britain the scale of public leisure services is substantial with net expenditure of the order of £1.5 billion. This has grown faster than the rate of inflation over recent years and there is evidence to show that although governments of left and right have attempted to force local authorities to curtail their net expenditure in this area, this has generally been resisted (Hamilton, 1983).

National Policies
Institutionally the future of leisure seems assured. At national level there are organizations whose political influence far outweighs their financial muscle. The Sports Council and the Arts Council between them spend only some £150 million a year, but they can be a focus for a great deal of adverse publicity for the government of the day if their funding is threatened. At local level the elected politicians are beginning to realize that there are 'votes in leisure'. A new leisure pool, sports centre or arts/entertainment centre which all the family can attend (even if at different times for different purposes), can have far more impact with the electorate as a whole than services for the needy (who are nevertheless a minority) or 'invisible' services like public health, or prestige projects like new town halls. In addition, an influential lobby is rapidly emerging in the form of the recreation management profession which, like any pressure group, will ensure that the research is done and the evidence and arguments marshalled to support any case for the expansion of the service.

The aspirations of the public sector for the future are often enshrined in public documents which take the form of plans and strategies. In Britain at national level such documents are few and far between. The report enticingly entitled *Leisure Policy for the Future* (Chairmen's Policy Group, 1982), prepared for the chairmen of some twenty quangos concerned with leisure, says virtually nothing about the future: it is largely a statement of what is and what has been. If anything the report reflects a change of mood. In the period of rapid growth of the 1960s, when several of the quangos came into being, their task was to respond to 'growth', 'soaring demand', or 'pressure'. Now that the growth is no longer there the emphasis has shifted to 'needs'. In referring to the poor and the unemployed, the report says:

> They do not have 'demands' which leisure providers might meet. Rather do they have *needs* ... Leisure providers must find ways to relate to such needs, to permit people to fulfil their interests and enhance the quality of their lives ... Leisure provision has become accepted as a major element of social policy, aiming at the enhancement of the quality of life of all citizens. This calls for a change in emphasis, away from catering simply for leisure demands, to the understanding and meeting of needs ... Local authorities have, among leisure providers, a unique responsibility to the quality of life of all citizens. Recognition of this role is increasingly reflected in efforts by local authorities to understand the needs of their communities, to encourage and assist the work of all leisure providers; and to serve the needs which others do not meet.
> (Chairmen's Policy Group, 1982, pp. 60, 62, 73)

Individual quangos in the UK have more frequently committed themselves to statements about their future aspirations. The most explicit recent example is the Sports Council's plan *Sport in the Community: The Next Ten Years* published in 1982. The approach adopted in the plan illustrates precisely the point that the *providers* may be as important in determining what happens in the future as the public. The Sports Council notes that survey evidence indicates that those most favourably disposed to take more part in sport in the future are the groups in the population (male, middle class, etc.) who already take part more than other groups. They therefore conclude: 'So there will have to be a battle of the mind to induce some of the other groups to take part: a battle that has to be fought with information, marketing and leadership' (Sports Council, 1982, p. 33).

This is much closer to a commercial approach than the 'needs' perspective suggested by the Chairmen's Policy Group. The Sports Council then proceed to 'target' certain groups such as women, older people and young people in their late teens and to quantify the increases in participation in sport which they would like to see by 1991. For example, they hope to see an increase of 15 per cent in sports participation by men and no less than 70 per cent for women in indoor sport and 35 per cent in outdoor sport. This approach is of course entirely appropriate for an organization whose terms of reference are to promote participation in sport. But their powers to persuade people to do things are limited and they do not have the freedom of action of a commercial organization. They use part of their budget of £30 million a year to mount publicity campaigns and to provide grants to local authorities and voluntary organizations to establish sports facilities in pursuit of their objectives. Since such facilities are generally not commercially viable it is unlikely that they would come into being without public subsidy. Increases in participation in sport can only take place at the rate envisaged if the facilities and programmes are made available by the public sector in the form of the Sports Council and the local authorities. So while it would be an exaggeration to say that public providers *determine* the future of leisure in their respective spheres of responsibility, it is misguided to think of them as merely responding to spontaneous changes in demand: they are doing their best to influence that demand.

In the United States recreation planning and forecasting have been more fully tested than in the United Kingdom, particularly in the area of outdoor recreation. As noted in Chapter 7, the 1962 work of the Outdoor Recreation Resources Review Commission resulted in pioneering forecasts of recreation demand for the 1970s which, in the event, turned out to be largely inaccurate. The *Third Nationwide Outdoor Recreation Plan* (US Dept of the Interior, 1979) was therefore understandably cautious about forecasts and appeared to base its programme only very loosely on the demand forecasts available. Certain major assumptions about the future were made:

- The demand for recreation, especially close to home, will continue to soar during the next five years.
- The future of remaining open space in the United States, especially on the fringe of expanding urban areas, is being rapidly determined.
- Energy will continue to rise in cost and remain in short supply until major new energy sources become technologically feasible in the more distant future.
- There will be relatively fewer tax dollars to support local public services in the near future.
- The public wants to be actively involved in shaping decisions affecting tax-supported services in their communities.

(US Dept of the Interior, 1979, p. 49, Exec. Report)

The caution with which even these prognostications were expressed was clearly well advised since one of the key assumptions, concerning energy costs, has not been borne out in practice. The plan then identified ten 'new directions' for recreation planning to take. Generally these are high-flown statements about the importance of recreation, the need for ever more professional and comprehensive analysis and appraisal, more involvement with the commercial and voluntary sectors, and better training of recreation administration personnel. The 1979 'Action Program' had nine elements, concerned with:

(1) Federal land acquisition,
(2) Wild, Scenic and Recreation Rivers,
(3) National Trails and trail systems,
(4) Water resources,
(5) Energy conservation,
(6) Environmental education,
(7) The handicapped,
(8) The private sector,
(9) Research.
(US Dept of the Interior, 1979: pp. 54–5, Exec. Report)

The extent to which action on these issues will affect, or have already affected, the development of recreation since 1979, depends on the resources devoted to them and the powers taken and exercised by the government. Action taken in the area of conservation, for example, as suggested under the second item could make all the difference between a conserved environment suitable for recreation and one that is destroyed by pollution and development. Future recreation for deprived groups such as the handicapped could be substantially affected by action taken under item 7 of the plan. The Reagan government has however been committed to constraint on public sector expenditure (however unsuccessfully) so, although the situation has not been researched for this book, it is unlikely that substantial resources would have been made available. However, in the United States, Federal and State governments between them own open land, in the form of National Parks, National Forests and other reserves, which are equivalent to an area more than twice the size of the EEC, so the actions of government cannot fail to be influential in the area of outdoor recreation.

Local Policies
At local level the public sector provider is commonly the municipality or local authority. The activity of the local authority as leisure provider can be highly significant to its local community. In the UK levels of provision of leisure facilities and services vary enormously because, with the exception of libraries, there is no statutory obligation to provide for leisure. A hypothetical, but typical, inventory of public leisure facilities and their use, for a local authority area with a popu-

Table 8.1 *Hypothetical Local Authority Leisure Provision for a Community of 100,000*

Type of facility	Amount	Net running costs £'000s p.a.	No. of visits: '000s p.a.
Parks	450 (acres)	800	1,100
Indoor pool	1	200	280
'Dry' sports centre	1	110	90
Sports centre with pool	1	350	300
Libraries	4	475	220
Museum	1	90	70
Play centres	2	45	45
Community centres	3	50	45
Arts centre	1	110	120
Total		2,230	2,070

lation of 100,000, is given in Table 8.1. The facilities provided accommodate over 2 million visits a year overall. This is a great deal of leisure activity for a small community. The future programme of the authority can therefore have a significant effect on patterns of leisure behaviour in such an area. If, for example, there was unmet demand for swimming and the authority were to build another swimming pool, suitably located, to serve those areas not well served by current provision, they might bring about an increase of 50 per cent in the number of swimmers in the community, which could result in an increase of perhaps 250,000 in the number of attendances at swimming pools in a year. Of course some of this participation might be diverted from existing facilities which would then suffer a decline in use, but research suggests that if facilities are carefully planned then this effect is minimal (Veal, 1979). For the arts, because facilities are generally fewer and further between, this relationship between facility provision and level of participation is probably even more marked. If there is no theatre in a town then most of the potential audience probably stay home and watch television: the local authority, in providing such a facility or assisting others to do so, therefore directly affects leisure behaviour in the area.

The question nevertheless does arise as to whether, in the absence of these public sector providers, the facilities would be provided anyway, either by voluntary or commercial organizations. The answer must surely be 'no'. Sports clubs might provide more facilities of their own in the absence of publicly provided facilities, but it is unlikely that they could match the scale of them. Initially any withdrawal of the public sector from the field could result in a decline in club activity because many clubs depend on access to subsidized public facilities. In some countries, such as Germany, the clubs seem to be important as providers and managers, but they are very often heavily subsidized in money or kind by local authorities (Polytechnic of North London, 1980). Some additional commercial sports facilities might spring up, but, without the element of subsidy, prices to the consumer would be such as to deter demand, but by how much it is impossible to guess. In the case of arts facilities, it is unlikely that very much would be provided by the commercial sector except in the heart of large cities, and what would be provided would be closer to what is currently considered as 'entertainment' than what is considered as 'the arts' (although this distinction is a matter for some debate in its own right). Lending libraries would in all probability disappear – although it is interesting to note that certain areas of literature, such as science fiction and adult comics, and some pornography, are operated on a kind of 'hire' basis under which the purchaser can sell the publication back to the shop at a reduced price. As far as informal recreation is concerned, parks would presumably be decimated and only countryside attractions of the more commercialized variety would survive.

There are two reactions to this scenario which should be considered. The first is that it could be said that the very existence of the subsidized public service makes the above prediction almost a self-fulfilling prophecy. People have become *used* to free or subsidized facilities in certain areas, so, of course, if they suddenly had to pay the full market price, or to raise the full cost by voluntary effort, it would come as a shock. Commercial firms will not invest heavily in areas in which local authorities currently operate, not necessarily because the area is intrinsically unviable in commercial terms, but because of the fear that the local authority may undercut them with subsidized facilities, or simply because the level of prices is set by the existing local authority subsidized services. Some might suggest that once the public got over the shock of paying the full price for their sports or arts or informal recreation activity they would get used to it and a full range of services would be provided by the commercial and voluntary sector between them. Others would argue that the commercial operator would only be interested in certain profitable activities and would only cater for the relatively well-off sections of the community. The reply to this is that at the moment if anything the opposite is the case; the subsidized public facilities, especially arts and sports facilities, are used disproportionately by better-off sections of the community, whereas the working class uses the pubs, disco's and bingo halls provided by the commercial sector (Smith, 1975).

And so the debate goes on, and with far more intensity than has been seen in the past. The Banks report, referred to earlier, states:

The focus of this report is best summed up by saying that new jobs can be created by the commercial provision of pleasure and recreation to foreign tourists and Britons in their leisure time. The key is to understand the need for commercial provision. Too often, people expect their leisure to be subsidized. There are no jobs to be had there – only higher taxes. When people pay for their own pleasure they create a job for someone else.

(Banks, 1985, p. 2)

A universal change to private sector management of local authority services seems unlikely, but some see 'privatization' as very much the pattern for the future (Spiers, 1985). A chief executive of an English local authority has said that the leisure manager of the future:

will be concerned with people not buildings, because I am going to give the buildings away. There will not be a need for them to manage buildings because local government will not have any. I want a coordinator of leisure services not a provider. I see those services being provided by the private sector and volunteers. Not local government ... The real test of any profession is, in fact, its ability to manage change, not resist it.

(Gill, 1984, p. 10)

Some experiments in privatization in other areas of the public service have not been entirely successful. Even in a time of high unemployment, saving costs by reducing wages can result in the recruitment of unsatisfactory, insufficiently skilled or experienced staff. Firms have found that the sanction of public accountability is as severe as the sanction of the market place when it comes to maintenance of standards of service. Government insistence on public bodies accepting the lowest tender on offer could result in 'cowboy' firms doing considerable damage to the leisure service, and indeed to the respectable commercial firms' case for involvement. Many in the public sector are concerned that privatization is a one way street, that public bodies will not be able to reassemble skilled workforces once they have been disbanded. Once this has happened the commercial undertakers will raise their prices and the savings will disappear. On the positive side, commercial involvement in certain public leisure services may lead to the reduction of some restrictive practices, improvement of management standards and the lifting of some of the bureaucratic restrictions which prevent managers and staff from providing the best and most efficient possible service to the public.

The outcome of this debate could result in some significant changes in the public sector of leisure provision but again it is unlikely to alter the main thrust of the argument presented here, namely, that public sector agencies, particularly local authorities, will continue to have a key influence on the future of leisure, either directly or indirectly. The fact that a local authority engages a commercial management company to run its swimming pools or leases its sports halls to local clubs will not alter the fact that the local authority is involved in leisure provision. Privatization will not necessarily mean the end of subsidy. In fact, if a private company is able to cut costs and operate facilities more efficiently then for the same outgoings the local authority could reduce prices even further or increase the number of facilities provided.

A second major debate concerning public leisure services is related to the privatization debate but only indirectly. The debate is about the nature of the public service rather than its existence. In Britain the antecedents of the debate go back to the mid-1970s when certain commentators (e.g. Cherry, 1976; Rapoport and Rapoport, 1975) began to express the view that recreation planning was too concerned with facilities and not enough with people. The view led to the commissioning of a major research project by the Department of the Environment which was reported in *Leisure Provision and People's Needs*, (Dower et al., 1981). The general thrust of this report was that local authority leisure services were indeed too facility orientated, bureaucratic and inward looking; they needed to become more flexible, more concerned with people and their preoccupations and needs, and to place more emphasis on enabling and co-ordinating voluntary and even commercial activity in the community, rather than expanding their own bureaucratic empires as providers. They called for a 'new culture of leisure provision'.

This view was echoed in the United States at around the same time by Gray and Greben (1979) and in Canada by a 'think tank' report, *The Elora Prescription*, named after the resort where the think tank group of experts met (Balmer, 1979; Goodale, 1980). In the report a key-note address is reproduced from a hypothetical annual conference of a local social planning council of 1995, looking back on the previous twenty years, noting the mistakes of the 1970s and the subsequent developments which had corrected them. The main differences between 1975 and 1995, which, of course, reflected the way the think tank considered that things ought to go, are summarized in Figure 8.1.

Many of the members of the recreation management profession in Britain would probably subscribe to most of these aspirations and many of the changes are already in hand. They also accord in large part with the national aspirations expressed by the Chairmen's Policy Group in their report discussed earlier. Initiatives taken by the Sports Council and local authorities in launching 'Action Sport' programmes, 'Countryside Management' schemes promoted by the Countryside

1975	1995
Recreation Department	Department of Human Services
Narrow definitions of recreation	Broad definitions of leisure and fitness and human potential
Recreation in discretionary time	Leisure in any/all life spaces (meaningful, self-chosen activity)
Emphasis on child and youth	Equal services provided at all stages in life-cycle
Public services universal	Market segmentation to focus on groups with greatest need
Attempts to provide leisure	Focus on preconditions to leisure (time, opportunity, capacity to choose)
Beginnings of joint-use	Joint-planning, development and management of public and many private facilities
Direct public sector provision	Indirect provision – public agency co-ordinates and refers
Perception of public agencies as prime suppliers	Perception of public agencies as residual suppliers
Centralization	Decentralization
Professionals serving individuals	Community using all available human resources
Disciplinary perspectives	Interdisciplinary perspectives

Figure 8.1 Comparison of 1975 and 1995: *The Elora Prescription.*
Source: Balmer (1979, p. 22).

Commission, the encouragement of 'Community Arts' by the Arts Council, even if somewhat ambivalently, and a gradually increasing concern for the demands of different groups in the community, all reflect moves in the direction of *The Elora Prescription*.

Training
A key question is, however, whether the skills of existing staff and the training of new staff entering the profession are appropriate for the new era which seems to call for a range of skills which are 'softer' and more people orientated than those currently available in the profession. The emphasis in Britain has been on training in technical skills concerned with land and plant and business-style 'hard' management expertise. In the rest of Europe 'softer' skills are developed, with less emphasis on management, in the training of *animateurs* – an approach more akin to the training of a British youth and community worker.

Staff must however be trained for the jobs available, not for those which are mere aspirations. *The Elora Prescription* discusses the problem of the legacy of the large-scale facilities which it sees rather as dinosaurs, but which nevertheless must continue to be managed effectively and efficiently by skilled staff. There is a tendency, shared by the *Leisure and People's Needs* report, to throw these rather large babies out with the bureaucratic bath water, as if they were not providing a vital service – as if all recreational demands could be met by voluntary groups, aided and abetted by a sympathetic community worker. Clearly, if people continue to live in large cities then large-scale facilities will continue to be important, however much they need to be complemented by the smaller-scale neighbourhood facility and self-help programmes.

What perhaps is required therefore is a pluralist profession which provides 'hard-nosed' managers capable of managing a budget of millions of pounds and a staff of hundreds, as well as leaders and *animateurs* capable of working sympathetically with small client groups, with the possibility, of course, of people being able to add to their skills and experience and move between the two types of area. The latter type of training already exists for youth and community workers and it is interesting to note that the first of the 'Elora' prescriptions is the abolition of the separate recreation department in favour of a 'human services' department. There are certainly substantial overlaps between the work of leisure services, education (especially youth services and adult education) and social services which are not always recognized: in one London borough three separate departments (Leisure, Social Services and Housing) were at one time running community centres. Perhaps the future lies in the sort of amalgamation of leisure services and educational youth and community services which has begun to happen in authorities such as Birmingham and Bristol.

9
Concluding Thoughts

In Britain and a number of other Western countries there is a widespread belief that the economic recession of the 1980s is not merely a longer and more severe version of earlier recessions, but that it represents a fundamental change in the economic system requiring new attitudes and new policies. Major political parties on the whole continue to believe that either appropriate Keynesian demand management or monetarist and competitive discipline will eventually bring about an end to recession and a return to full employment, even if at a lower rate than that experienced in the 1960s. But many believe that this is extremely unlikely: that technological change is such that there is virtually no rate of economic growth which would be sufficient to create jobs faster than technology will destroy them, or indeed to make up for the loss of jobs which has already taken place.

If the traditional view of the major political parties is correct then the question of the future of leisure is a relatively simple one. There seems to be no reason, in this scenario, to suppose that in the developed economies normal weekly, annual and lifetime working hours will not continue to fall at a gradual rate as they have since the turn of the century. By the end of this century annual holiday entitlements of the full-time worker would probably be approaching six weeks compared with the current four, and the working week would probably be nearer thirty-five than forty hours. Thus leisure time would increase. The share of consumer expenditure devoted to leisure would increase as people became better off; so the leisure industries would experience a faster rate of growth than the rest of the economy. In the context of conventional economics these conclusions apply not only to the developed economies but also to many of the developing economies where the process of industrialization is proceeding at a far greater pace than that experienced by Europe and North America in the nineteenth century. While the initial stages of industrialization produce long working hours and probably a reduction in leisure time compared with agricultural economies, not to mention the suffering and disruption which usually accompanies urbanization, in later stages working hours fall as workers trade-off time for money. Altogether then, in the best of all possible conventional economic worlds, leisure takes care of itself: its future is one of growth related to the growth of the economy. In this case those concerned with the future of leisure would be primarily concerned with the forecasting techniques and sources discussed in Chapter 7.

There is, however, a major short- to medium-term problem in this scenario: namely the 3.5 million people currently unemployed in Britain, or the 12 million unemployed in the EEC, or the 20 million in the OECD countries. Even the most optimistic expansionist politician would not expect to see this eliminated in less than six or seven years, and a more realistic timespan would be ten years. During this period, and the preceding five or six years, the burden of society's inability to cure the recession falls unfairly on the unemployed, particularly the young unemployed. The question then arises as to whether direct policies should not be taken in the meantime to modify the basis upon which paid work is distributed; at least to introduce more flexibility to the system so that it can react less painfully to changing demands for labour in the economy.

If, on the other hand, in the developed economies as a whole, or in individual countries such as Britain, the effects of the introduction of new technology were to be to perpetuate high levels of unemployment regardless of the level of economic growth achieved, if it is believed that we are moving into some sort of post-industrial society as discussed in Chapter 3, then the argument in favour of policies to share paid work more equitably is surely unassailable.

We can therefore see that, either as a short-term response to currently high levels of unemployment or as a recognition of permanent change, there is a strong argument for introducing measures to share paid work more equitably and thereby reduce unemployment. The range of options is discussed in Chapter 6, the key-note of such proposals being flexibility. We are already seeing a backlash from older people against inflexible retirement ages, witness the recent ruling of the European Court of Human Rights on the question of compulsory retirement of women at the age of 60. What is required is a reform of employment law and the social security, educational support and pensions systems to enable people to reduce their working hours if they wish, to take time off to be with their families, to take time out for education and training, to share jobs and to retire when they want to. In short to facilitate what the American commentator Fred Best has called 'Flexible Life Scheduling'.

Those who believe that Western society is in the grip of a 'work ethic' would conclude that such flexibility and freedom would result in people attempting to take more paid work rather than less, so that rather than workers on average doing less hours of paid work in a lifetime they would do more, so exacerbating rather than relieving the problem of unemployment. In Chapter 5 it was suggested that the strength of the work ethic among ordinary people is open to some doubt: it appears to be more a problem of the establishment than of the average worker. One contributor to the continued belief in the strength of the work ethic is the tendency, not least among academic commentators, to juxtapose work and leisure. The impression is given that the choice facing the worker is between paid work and leisure. Clearly, it is believed, the worker will not foresake work, from which all status and income is derived, for something as trivial as leisure. But the choice is not between paid work and leisure, there are at least three other facets of life which are neither paid work nor, strictly speaking, leisure; they are education, domestic work and family life.

As Tom Stonier has argued, education, apart from being vitally important in a modern economy, is a great potential absorber of people's time and energies. Many developed countries recognize this and enable increasing numbers to enter further and higher education. Britain, with its elitist tradition, is a laggard in this respect. An example of the way the system militates against people opting for more education is the fact that it is illegal for an unemployed person supported by social security to register for a full-time education course. Thus for many unemployed people the non-work option of full-time education is denied them and they are forced to adopt a life of idleness. Similarly there are only limited opportunities for adults to take time off from paid jobs for education. And yet evidence from such sources as the Open University suggests that there is widespread demand for additional education from adults. Education is surely a 'serious', non-leisure, alternative to paid work.

Domestic work here is not meant to include day-to-day housework but major periodic tasks such as house alterations or decoration. The empirical research has not been done to confirm this, but it seems likely that a significant proportion of non-work time – which is often equated by observers with leisure – is devoted to domestic work. It is the sort of activity for which workers use some of their holiday entitlement. It is essential work, not leisure – although some may positively enjoy it as a change from their paid work. In Chapter 3 we noted that several writers have predicted the growing importance of 'own work', or the 'self-service' or 'informal' economy. Some have also suggested that this might be widened to include voluntary work in the community. Traditionally, of course, women have taken time out from paid work to cope with domestic work, particularly the demands of preschool children. Indeed, Sarah Gregory (1982) has suggested that women have been pioneers of the flexible life-styles of the future. But increasingly men are being enabled or are demanding to take time off from paid work for this purpose. Thus domestic work can be seen as another serious, non-leisure, alternative to paid work.

The third category of 'non-work', family life, is if anything, more important than work for many people. A desire for shorter or more flexible working hours is more likely to be motivated by a desire to spend time with the family than for a desire for more leisure as such, even though the researcher might classify much 'family life' as 'leisure activity'.

To equate a reduction in work time wholly with an increase in leisure time is therefore misleading. Increased leisure time is only *part* of the picture, along with increased time for education, domestic work and family life. As the Rapoports (1975) have argued, at different times of life different aspects of life assume importance: sometimes we are prepared to sacrifice time for money, or a career is important: at these times paid work may predominate. At other times domestic or leisure activity may be more important and we would be prepared to sacrifice income for more free time. What is required is a system which is responsive to these changing needs.

There is, of course, no guarantee that the mere introduction of more choice in life-scheduling for the individual worker would solve the problem of unemployment, but it would give government a wider range of tools with which to manipulate the system if they wished. All non-work options tend to cost the state, and the individual, something, either in cash or income forgone or both. The question is whether a comprehensive policy would enable government to tip the balance in favour of non-work statuses such as full-time education, part-time working, retirement and leisure for some, so that more room is made in the job market for those who are at present excluded.

Some European governments, notably the French in 1982–3, have attempted to address these issues, but generally they are ignored, or measures are introduced as piecemeal expedients. As is noted in Chapter 6, politicians who have publicly considered these issues tend to be marginal to the mainstream. Restoration of full employment involving a forty-hour week, for forty-eight weeks a year for a forty-five-year working life appears to be a virility symbol that no party or government is willing to abandon, however hopeless the task may seem. A policy for time is well overdue.

Bibliography

Adams, D. (1980), *The Restaurant at the End of the Universe* (London: Pan Books).
Adams, R. M. (ed.) (1975), *Sir Thomas More: Utopia: A New Translation, Backgrounds, Criticism* (New York: Norton).
Adler, M. J. (1970), *The Time of our Lives: The Ethics of Common Sense* (New York: Holt, Rinehart & Winston).
Akerman, N. (1979), 'Can Sweden be shrunk?', *Development Dialogue*, no. 2, pp. 71–214.
Allen, R., Bati, A. and Bragard, J. (1981), *The Shattered Dream: Employment in the Eighties* (London: Arrow Books).
Ardill, J. (1982), 'TUC drive to cut working week proves successful', *Guardian*, 30 Dec.
Aristotle (1962), *The Politics* (tr. T. A Sinclair) (Harmondsworth, Middx.: Penguin).
Aronowitz, S. (1973), *False Promises* (New York: McGraw-Hill).
Asimov, I. (1976), 'Future Fun', in *Today and Tomorrow and...* (London: Scientific Book Club), pp. 199–209.
Aznar, G. (1981), *Tous a Mi-Temps* (Paris: Editions du Seuil).
Bacon, A. W. (1972), 'The embarrassed self: some reflections upon attitudes to work and idleness in a prosperous industrial society', *Society and Leisure*, no. 4, pp. 23–39.
Bailey, A. (1982), *Futuresport* (London: Pan).
Bailey, P. (1978), *Leisure and Class in Victorian England* (London: Routledge).
Ball, C. (1984), 'Reorganising work and leisure', *Town and Country Planning*, vol. 53, no. 2, Feb., pp. 42–4.
Balmer, K. (1979), *The Elora Prescription: A Future for Recreation* (Toronto: Ministry of Culture & Recreation).
Banks, R. (1985), *New Jobs from Pleasure: A Strategy for Producing New Jobs in the Tourist Industry* (London: Conservative Central Office).
Barron, I. and Curnow, R. (1979), *The Future with Microelectronics* (Milton Keynes: Open University Press).
Basini, A. (1975), 'Education for leisure: a sociological critique', in J. T. Haworth and M. A. Smith (eds), *Work and Leisure* (London: Lepus), pp. 102–18.
Baxter, M. J. (1979), *Measuring the Benefits of Recreational Site Provision: A Review of Techniques related to the Clawson Method* (London: Sports Council/SSRC).
Bell, D. (1964), 'Twelve modes of prediction – a preliminary sorting of approaches in the social sciences', *Daedalus*, no. 93 (Summer), pp. 845–80

(also in J. Gould (ed.) *Penguin Survey of the Social Sciences* (Harmondsworth, Middx.: Penguin), pp. 96–127).
Bell, D. (1974), *The Coming of the Post-Industrial Society* (London: Heinemann).
Bellini, J. (1981), *Rule Britannia: A Progress Report for Doomesday 1986* (London: Jonathan Cape).
Bendiner, R. (1957), 'Could you stand a four-day week?' *The Reporter*, vol. 17, no. 2, 8 Aug., pp. 10–14.
Berg, I. (1975), 'They won't work: the end of the Protestant Work Ethic and all that', in *Readings in Sociology 1975/76* (Guildford, Ct: Annual Editions/Dushkin), pp. 164–71.
Best, F. (1978), 'The time of our lives: the parameters of lifetime distribution of education, work and leisure', *Society and Leisure*, vol. 1, no. 1, pp. 95–124.
Best, F. (1980), *Flexible Life Scheduling: Breaking the Education–Work–Retirement Lockstep* (New York: Praeger).
Best, F., Bosserman, P. and Stern, B. (1979), 'Income – free time trade-off preferences of US workers', *Leisure Sciences*, vol. 2, no. 2, pp. 119–42.
Billingsley, J. (1985), 'Employment sharing', *World Leisure and Recreation*, vol. 27, no. 4, May, pp. 30–6.
Blowers, A., Hamnett, C. and Sarre, P. (eds) (1974), *The Future of Cities* (London: Hutchinson).
Borrett, N. (1982), *Education for Leisure: A Guide to the Literature*, Papers in Leisure Studies no. 6 (London: Polytechnic of North London).
Bourdieu, P. (1980), 'The aristocracy of culture', *Media, Culture and Society*, vol. 2, no. 3, pp. 225–54.
Bradbury, R. (1951), 'The Veldt', in *The Illustrated Man* (New York: Doubleday), pp. 7–18.
Bramham, P. and Henry, I. (1985), 'Political ideology and leisure policy in the United Kingdom', *Leisure Studies*, vol. 4, no. 1, Jan., pp. 1–20.
British Broadcasting Corporation (1978), *The People's Activities and Use of Time* (London: BBC).
British Travel Association/University of Keele (1967), *Pilot National Recreation Survey* (Keele, Staffs.: University of Keele).
Brohm, M. (1978), *Sport: A Prison of Measured Time* (London: Ink Links).
Brown, T. L. and Huston, D. L. (1979), 'Evaluation of the 1976 ORRRC projections' in US Department of the Interior Heritage, Conservation and Recreation Service, *Third Nationwide Outdoor Recreation Plan: Appendix 2*, Survey Technical Report 4 (Washington DC: US Government Printing Office), pp. 259–76.
Brown, T. L. and Wilkins, B. T. (1975), 'Methods of improving recreation projections', *Journal of Leisure Research*, vol. 7, no. 3, pp. 225–34.
Burton, T. L. (1970), 'The shape of things to come,' in T. L. Burton (ed.), *Recreation Research and Planning* (London: Allen & Unwin), pp. 242–68.
Burton, T. L. and Veal, A. J. (1971), *Experiments in Recreation Research* (London: Allen & Unwin).
Chai, D. A. (1977), 'Future of leisure: a Delphi application', *Research Quarterly*, vol. 48, no. 3, pp. 518–24.
Chairmen's Policy Group (1982), *Leisure Policy for the Future* (London: Sports Council).

Chambers, D. and Roberts, K. (1985), 'Why shiftwork is resisted' in A. J. Veal and S. R. Parker (eds), *Work, Non-work and Leisure* (London: Leisure Studies Association), pp. 39–53.

Cherry, G. E. (1976), 'Leisure and the community: research and planning', in J. T. Haworth and A. J. Veal (eds), *Leisure and the Community* (London: Leisure Studies Association), pp. 3.1–3.6.

Cherry, G. E. and Travis, A. S. (eds) (1980), *Leisure in the 1980s – Alternative Futures*, Conference Report no. 11 (London: Leisure Studies Association).

Cicchetti, C. J. (1973), *Forecasting Recreation in the United States: An Economic Review of Methods and Applications to Plan for the Required Environmental Resources* (Lexington, Mass.: Lexington Books).

Clarke, R. (1982), *Work in Crisis* (Edinburgh: St Andrews Press).

Clawson, M. (1974), 'How much leisure now and in the future?' in D. W. Fischer, J. E. Lewis and G. B. Priddle (eds), *Land and Leisure* (Chicago: Maroufa), pp. 3–14.

Clawson, M. and Knetsch, J. L. (1966), *The Economics of Outdoor Recreation* (Baltimore: Johns Hopkins).

Clayre, A. (1974), *Work and Play* (London: Weidenfeld & Nicolson).

Clemitson, I. and Rodgers, G. (1981), *A Life to Live* (London: Junction Books).

Commission for the European Communities (1980), *Community Guidelines on Flexible Retirement*, EEC, COM(80) (Brussels: EEC Commission).

Coppock, J. T. and Duffield, B. S. (1975), *Recreation in the Countryside: A Spatial Analysis* (London: Macmillan).

Corley, J. (1982), 'Employment in the leisure industries in Britain 1960–80', *Leisure Studies*, vol. 1, no. 1, pp. 109–11.

Countryside Commission (1979), *Study of Informal Recreation in South East England* (Cheltenham: Countryside Commission).

Crosland, C. A. R. (1964), *The Future of Socialism*, revised edn (London: Jonathan Cape).

Davidson, J. M. and Sienkiewicz, J. (1975), 'Study of informal recreation in South-east England', in G. A. C. Searle (ed.), *Recreational Economics and Analysis* (London: Longman), pp. 151–59.

De Grazia, S. (1962), *Of Time, Work and Leisure* (Garden City, NY: Anchor Books/Doubleday).

De Vink, G. (1983), 'Leisure education at school', in R. Delbaere, E. Sauter, J. Swart and W. Tokarski (eds), *Leisure Today and Tomorrow: 5th European Congress on Leisure 1983* (Zurich: European Leisure and Recreation Association), pp. 49–52.

Department of Employment (1978), 'Measures to alleviate unemployment in the medium term: early retirement', *Department of Employment Gazette*, March, pp. 283–5.

Department of Environment (1975), *Sport and Recreation*, Cmnd 6200 (London: HMSO).

Douglas, M. and Isherwood, B. (1980), *The World of Goods* (Harmondsworth, Middx.: Penguin).

Dower, M. (1965), *The Fourth Wave: The Challenge of Leisure* (London: Civic Trust).

Dower, M., Rapoport, R., Strelitz. Z. and Kew, S. (1981), *Leisure Provision and People's Needs* (London: HMSO).
Dubin, R. (1956), 'Industrial workers' worlds: a study of the "central life interests" of industrial workers', *Social Problems*, vol. 3, Jan., also in E. O. Smigel (ed.) (1963), *op. cit.*, pp. 53–72.
Duffield, B. S. (1976), 'Forecasting leisure futures – an exercise in understanding and analysis', in J. T. Haworth and S. R. Parker (eds), *Forecasting Leisure Futures* (London: Leisure Studies Association), pp. 33–48.
Duffield, B. S. (1982), 'A change for the better? – conference evaluation', in Tourism and Recreation Research Unit (eds), *op. cit.*, pp. 1–10.
Duffield, B. S. and Owen, M. L. (1970), *Leisure + Countryside = A Geographical Appraisal of Countryside Recreation in Lanarkshire* (Edinburgh: Tourism and Recreation Research Unit, University of Edinburgh).
Duffield, B. S. and Owen, M. L. (1971), *Leisure + Countryside = A Geographical Appraisal of Countryside in the Edinburgh Area* (Edinburgh: Tourism and Recreation Research Unit, Edinburgh University).
Dumazedier, J. (1974), *The Sociology of Leisure* (The Hague: Elsevier).
Ecology Party (1981), *Working for a Future: An Ecological Approach to Employment* (London: Ecology Party).
Edwards, A. (1981), *Leisure Spending in the European Community: Forecasts to 1990*, Special Report 93 (London: Economist Intelligence Unit).
Encel, S., Marstrand, P. K. and Page, W. (eds) (1975), *The Art of Anticipation: Values and Methods in Forecasting* (London: Martin Robertson).
Entwistle, H. (1970), *Education, Work and Leisure* (London: Routledge & Kegan Paul).
Fache, W. (1983), 'Designing time-management policy by action research' in H. E. Olsen (ed.), *Leisure Research*, Papers of the European Leisure and Recreation Association meeting, Vaxjo, Sweden, May (Zurich: ELRA), pp. 351–62.
Faunce, W. A. (1963), 'Automation and leisure' in E. O. Smigel (ed.) *Work and Leisure* (New Haven, Conn.: College and University Press), pp. 85–96.
Ferkiss, V. (1979), 'Daniel Bell's concept of post-industrial society', *Political Science Reviewer*, vol. 9, pp. 61–102.
Ferris, A. L. (1962), *National Recreation Survey*, Study Report 19 (Washington DC: Outdoor Recreation Resources Review Commission).
Forester, T. (1977), 'Do the British sincerely want to be rich?', *New Society*, 28 April, pp. 158–61.
Forester, T. (ed.) (1980), *The Microelectronics Revolution* (Oxford: Basil Blackwell).
Friedman, M. and Friedman, R. (1979), *Free to Choose* (Harmondsworth, Middx.: Penguin).
Frith, S. (1984), *The Sociology of Youth* (Ormskirk, Lancs.: Causeway).
Gabor, D. (1964), *Inventing the Future* (New York: Knopf).
Galbraith, J. K. (1958), *The Affluent Society* (Harmondsworth, Middx.: Penguin).
Gappert, G. (1979), *Post-Affluent America: the Social Economy of the Future* (London/New York: New Viewpoints/Franklin Watts).

Gershuny, J. I. (1977), 'The self-service economy', *New Universities Quarterly*, vol. 32, no. 1, Winter, pp. 50–66.

Gershuny, J. I. (1977a), 'Post-industrial society: the myth of the service economy', *Futures*, vol. 9, no. 2, April, pp. 103–14.

Gershuny, J. I. (1978), *After Industrial Society? The Emerging Self-service Economy* (London: Macmillan).

Gershuny, J. I. (1979), 'The informal economy: its role in post-industrial society', *Futures*, vol. 11, no. 1, Feb., pp. 3–15.

Gershuny, J. I. and Pahl, R. E. (1980), 'Britain in the decade of the three economies', *New Society*, 3 June, pp. 7–9.

Gill, I. (1984), 'The future of leisure services in local government', *Leisure Management*, vol. 4, no. 7, July, pp. 10–11.

Glasser, R. (1970), *Leisure – Penalty or Prize?* (London: Macmillan).

Glasser, R. (1974), 'A case of robot's cramp', *Guardian*, 1 Feb.

Glasser, R. (1975), 'Leisure policy, identity and work', in J. T. Haworth and M. A. Smith (eds), *Work and Leisure* (London: Lepus Books), pp. 36–52.

Glyptis, S. (ed.) (1983), *Prospects for Work and Leisure* (London: Leisure Studies Association).

Gold, J. R. (1983), 'Leisure, the Modern Movement and the Future City: Comments on the Urban Imagination', Paper Presented to the International Geographical Union/Leisure Studies Association Congress on Leisure and Social Change, Edinburgh University, January (also in *Leisure Studies*, vol. 3, no. 3, 1984, pp. 101–10).

Gold, S. M. (1973), *Urban Recreation Planning* (Philadelphia: Lea and Febiger).

Goldring, P. (1973), *Multi-Purpose Man* (London: Dent).

Goldthorpe, J. H., Lockwood, D., Bechofer, F. and Taylor, P. (1968), *The Affluent Worker: Industrial Attitudes and Behaviour* (London: Cambridge University Press).

Goodale, T. (1980), *A Decade of Difficult Tasks: Municipal Recreation in the 80s* (Toronto: Ontario Ministry of Culture and Recreation).

Goodman, P. and Goodman, P. (1947), *Communitas – Means of Livelihood and Ways of Life* (New York: Vintage Books).

Gorz, A. (1980), *Farewell to the Working Class: An Essay in Post-Industrial Socialism* (London: Pluto).

Gorz, A. (1985), *Paths to Paradise: On Liberation from Work* (London: Pluto).

Goyder, C. (1977), *Sabbaticals for All* (London: NCLC Publishing Society).

Granada Television (1968), *Time off* (film) (Ipswich: Concord Films).

Grant, A. R. (1982), 'The arena industry', in *Sport and People*, Conference Report (London: Sports Council), pp. 88–103.

Gratton, C. (1980), 'Public subsidies to sport and recreation', *National Westminster Quarterly Review*, May, pp. 46–57.

Gratton, C. and Taylor, P. (1985), *Sport and Recreation: An Economic Analysis* (London: Spon).

Gray, D. E. and Greben, S. (1979), 'Future perspectives', in C. S. Van Doren, G. B. Priddle and J. E. Lewis (eds), *Land and Leisure* (London: Methuen), pp. 3–24.

Great Britain (1972), *Proposals for a Tax-Credit System*, Cmnd 5116 (London: HMSO).

Gregory, S. (1982), 'Women among others: another view', *Leisure Studies*, vol. 1, no. 1, Jan., pp. 47–52.
Griffiths, J. (1980), *Three Tomorrows: American, British and Soviet Science Fiction* (London: Macmillan).
Hamilton, W. D. (1983), *Public Expenditure and Leisure: A Study of Central–Local Government Relations*, Papers in Leisure Studies no. 8 (London: Polytechnic of North London).
Handy, C. (1984), *The Future of Work* (Oxford: Blackwell).
Hantrais, L. (1984), 'Leisure policy in France' *Leisure Studies*, vol. 3, no. 2, May, pp. 129–46.
Haworth, J. and Parker, S. (eds) (1976), *Forecasting Leisure Futures* (London: Leisure Studies Association).
Haworth, J. T. and Smith, M. A. (eds) (1975), *Work and Leisure* (London: Lepus Books).
Haworth, L. (1984), 'Leisure, work and profession', *Leisure Studies*, vol. 3, no. 3, pp. 319–34.
Hayter, D. (1978), 'When work is a clean word', *Guardian*, 1 Nov.
Hedges, B. (1983), 'Personal leisure histories' in M. F. Collins (ed.), *Leisure Research: Current Findings and Future Challenge* (London: Leisure Studies Association/Sports Council/SSRC).
Hendry, L., Raymond, M. and Stewart, C. (1984), 'Unemployment, school and leisure: an adolescent study', *Leisure Studies*, vol. 3, no. 2, May, pp. 75–188.
Henley Centre for Forecasting (1985), *Leisure Futures*, Quarterly, London.
Henry, A. (1982), 'Minister Andre Henry states free time policy', *World Leisure and Recreation Association Journal*, vol. 24, no. 4, Aug., pp. 19–20.
Hollands, R. (1985), 'Working class youth, leisure and the search for work', in A. J. Veal and S. R. Parker (eds), *Work, Non-work and Leisure*, vol. 2, *Leisure: Politics, Planning and People*, Conference Papers (London: Leisure Studies Association), pp. 3–29.
Howard, E. (1898), *Garden Cities of Tomorrow*, 1965 edn (London: Faber).
Huxley, A. (1932), *Brave New World*, 1977 edn. (London: Granada).
Huxley, J. (1959), 'The future of man', *Bulletin of the Atomic Scientists*, vol. 15, no. 10, pp. 402–4, 409.
Illich, I., McKnight, J., Zola, I., Caplan, J. and Shaiken, H. (1978), *Disabling Professions* (London: Marion Boyars).
Incomes Data Services (1982), *Cutting the Working Week* (London: IDS).
Institute of Contemporary Arts (1981), *Future Communities* (London: ICA).
Jenkins, C. and Sherman, B. (1979), *The Collapse of Work* (London: Eyre Methuen).
Jenkins, C. and Sherman, B. (1981), *The Leisure Shock* (London: Eyre Methuen).
Jennings, L. (1979), 'Future fun: tomorrow's sports and games', *The Futurist*, vol. 13, pt 6, Dec., pp. 417–31.
Joad, C. E. M. (1935), *Diogenes or the Future of Leisure* (London: Kegan Paul, Trench, Trubner).
Jones, B. (1982), *Sleepers Wake! Technology and the Future of Work* (Brighton: Wheatsheaf Books).

Jordan, B. and Drakeford, M. (1980), 'Major Douglas, money and the new technology', *New Society*, 24 Jan., pp. 167–9.

Kahn, H. and Wiener, A. J. (1967), *The Year 2000: A Framework for Speculation on the Next Thirty-Three Years* (London/New York: Macmillan).

Kahn, H., Brown, W. and Martel, L. (1977), *The Next 200 Years* (London: Abacus).

Kaplan, M. (1976), *Leisure: Theory and Policy* (London: John Wiley).

Kateb, G. (1973), 'Utopia and the good life', in F. E. Manuel (ed.), *Utopias and Utopian Thought* (London: Souvenir Press), pp. 239–58.

Kaynak, E. and Macaulay, J. A. (1984), 'The Delphi technique in the measurement of tourism market potential', *Tourism Management*, vol. 4, Dec., pp. 87–101.

Kelvin, P. (1982), 'Work, unemployment and leisure: myths, hopes and realities', in Tourism and Recreation Research Unit (eds), *op. cit.*, pp. 11–26.

Keynes, J. M. (1931), 'Economic possibilities for our grand-children', in *The Collected Writings of John Maynard Keynes*, Vol. 9, *Essays in Persuasion*, 1972 edn (London: Macmillan), pp. 321–32.

Kinser, J. (1968), 'Leisure time: a challenge for physical education', *Physical Education*, May, pp. 57–8.

Kumar, K. (1978), *Prophecy and Progress: The Sociology of Industrial and Post-Industrial Society* (Harmondsworth, Middx.: Penguin).

Lacey, I. (1966), 'Opportunity and Diversity in Planning for Leisure', Paper to the Colloquium on Planning for Leisure, Institute for Social Research, London.

Large, P. (1980), *The Micro Revolution* (London: Fontana).

Lasch, C. (1972), 'Toward a theory of post-industrial society', in M. D. Hancock and G. Sjoberg (eds), *Politics in the Post-Welfare State* (New York: Columbia University Press), pp. 36–50.

Laurie, P. (1980), *The Micro Revolution* (London: Futura).

Le Corbusier (1967), *The Radiant City* (London: Faber) (originally published in French, 1933).

Leigh, J. (1971), 'Education for leisure?' *Young People and Leisure* (London: Routledge).

Levitan, S. A. and Belous, R. S. (1977), *Shorter Hours, Shorter Weeks, Spreading the Work to Reduce Unemployment*, Policy Studies in Employment and Welfare no. 30 (London: Johns Hopkins).

Lieber, S. R. and Fesenmaier, D. R. (eds) (1983), *Recreation Planning and Management* (London: Spon).

Linder, S. B. (1970), *The Harried Leisure Class* (New York/London: Columbia University Press).

Long, J. and Wimbush, E. (1981), *Leisure and the Over 50s* (London: Sports Council/SSRC).

Maccoby, M. and Terzi, K. A. (1979), 'What happened to the work ethic?' in W. M. Hofman and T. J. Wyly (eds), *The Work Ethic in Business* (Cambridge, Mass.: Oelgeschlager, Gunn and Hain), pp. 19–58.

McCalla, J. (1981), 'Future Recreation Scenarios for Ontario', Paper to the Third Canadian Congress on Leisure Research, University of Alberta, Edmonton.

McGoldrick, A. (1982) 'Early retirement – a new leisure opportunity?' in A. J. Veal *et al.* (eds), *op. cit.*, pp. 62–74.
McGoldrick, A. and Cooper, C. L. (1978) 'Early retirement for managers in the US and the UK', *Management International Review*, Aug., pp. 35–42.
MacIntyre, A. C. (1964), 'Against utilitarianism', in T. H. B. Hollins (ed.), *Aims in Education* (Manchester: University Press), pp. 1–23.
Martin, W. H. and Mason, S. (1979), *Broad Patterns of Leisure Expenditure* (London: Sports Council/SSRC).
Martin, W. H. and Mason, S. (1981), *Leisure and Work – The Choices for 1991 and 2001* (Sudbury, Suffolk: Leisure Consultants).
Martin, W. H. and Mason, S. (1982) 'Leisure and work – the choices for 1991 and 2001' in A. J. Veal *et al.* (eds), *op. cit.*, pp. 25–40.
Martin, W. H. and Mason, S. (1984), 'The Development of a Leisure Ethic: Some Practical Issues For the Future', Paper Presented to the Leisure Studies Association Conference, Leisure: Politics, Planning and People, Sussex University, Brighton, July.
Martin, W. H. and Mason, S. (1984a), *The UK Sports Market* (Sudbury, Suffolk: Leisure Consultants).
Marx, K. (1894), *Capital*, vol. 3, 1974 edn (London: Lawrence and Wishart).
Marx, K. and Engels, F. (1846), *The German Ideology*, (Moscow: Progress Publishers), 1976 edn.
Matrix Corporate Affairs Consultants Ltd (1979), *Future for Leisure 1979–1990*, Confidential Report to Cavendish Leisure Research Ltd, 2 vols. (London: Matrix).
Maw, R. (1974), 'Assessment of demand for recreation: a modelling approach', in I. Appleton (ed.), *Leisure Research and Policy* (Edinburgh: Scottish Academic Press), pp. 79–108.
Melching, M. and Broberg, M. (1974), 'A national sabbatical system: implications for the aged', *The Gerontologist*, April, pp. 175–81.
Mercer, D. (1980), 'Alternative leisure futures', in D. Mercer and E. Hamilton-Smith (eds), *Recreation Planning and Social Change in Urban Australia* (Malvern, Melbourne: Sorrett), pp. 180–98.
Merritt, G. (1982), *World Out of Work* (London: Collins).
Miles, I., Cole, S. and Gershuny, J. (1978), 'Images of the future', in C. Freeman and M. Jahoda (eds), *World Futures: The Great Debate* (London: Martin Robertson), pp. 279–342.
Milstein, D. N. and Reid, L. M. (1966), *Michigan Outdoor Recreation Demand Study*, vol. 1, *Methods and Models*, Technical Report no. 6 (Lansing: Michigan Depts of Conservation and Commerce).
Moeller, G. H. and Shafer, E. L. (1983), 'The use and misuse of Delphi forecasting', in Lieber and Fesenmaier (eds), *op. cit.*, pp. 96–104.
More, T. (1965 edn), *Utopia* (Harmondsworth, Middx.: Penguin).
Morrel, J. (1982), *Employment in Tourism* (London: British Tourist Authority).
Morris, W. (1973 edn), *Three Works* (London: Lawrence & Wishart).
Murray, L. (1983), 'Jobs for all is not main goal' (news report), *Guardian*, 26 Aug.
Myerscough, J. (1974), 'The recent history of the use of leisure time', in

I. Appleton (ed.) *Leisure Research and Policy* (Edinburgh: Scottish Academic Press), pp. 3–16.
Naisbitt, J. (1982), *Megatrends: Ten New Directions Transforming our Lives* (New York: Warner Books).
New Society (1980), 'Towards Tom Mann's 30-hour week', vol. 53, 10 July, pp. 73–4.
Newsom, J. (1963), *Half Our Future*, Report of the Central Advisory Council for Education (London: HMSO).
Ng, D., Brown, B. and Knott, W. (1983), 'Qualified leisure services manpower requirements: a future perspective', *Recreation Research Review*, vol. 10, no. 1, July, pp. 13–19.
Noelle-Neumann, E. (1981), 'Working less and enjoying it less in Germany', *Public Opinion Quarterly*, Aug/Sept., pp. 46–50.
Nora, S. and Minc, A. (1980), *The Computerisation of Society* (Cambridge, Mass.: MIT Press).
North West Sports Council (1972), *Leisure in the North West* (Salford: NWSC).
Northern Regional Planning Committee (1969), *Outdoor Leisure Activities in the Northern Region* (Newcastle: NRPC).
Nossiter, B. D. (1978), *Britain: A Future That Works* (London: André Deutsch).
Nossiter, B. D. (1978a), 'The Leisurely British', *Sunday Times Weekly Review*, Sept. 10, pp. 33–4.
Office of Population Censuses and Surveys (1979), *The General Household Survey, 1977* (London: HMSO).
Olmsted, B. (1977), 'Job sharing – a new way to work', *Personnel Journal*, Feb., pp. 78–81.
Orzack, L. H. (1963), 'Work as a "central life interest" of professionals', in E. O. Smigel (ed.), *Work and Leisure* (New Haven, Conn.: College and University Press), pp. 73–84.
Outdoor Recreation Resources Review Commission (1962) *Outdoor Recreation for America* (Washington, DC: ORRRC).
Owen, D. (1984), *A Future that Will Work* (Harmondsworth, Middx.: Penguin).
Owen, R. (1972 edn), *A New View of Society and Other Writings* (London: Dent).
Palm, G. (1977), *The Flight from Work* (Cambridge: Cambridge University Press).
Parker, H. (1983), 'The social dividend approach', in *Alternative Policies for Income Maintenance in the Eighties*, Conference Report (London: National Council for Voluntary Organisations), pp. 2–6.
Parker, S. (1971), *The Future of Work and Leisure* (London: MacGibbon and Kee).
Parker, S. (1982), *Work and Retirement* (London: Allen & Unwin).
Parker, S. (1983), *Leisure and Work* (London: Allen & Unwin).
Peterson, A. D. C. (1975), 'Education for work or leisure?' in J. T. Haworth and M. A. Smith (eds), *Work and Leisure* (London: Lepus Books), pp. 93–101.
Pieper, J. (1965), *Leisure: the Basis of Culture* (London: Faber).

Polytechnic of North London (1980), *Free-time and Leisure in Germany and the UK* (London: Polytechnic of North London).
Poor, R. (ed.) (1972), *4 Days, 40 Hours: Reporting a Revolution in Work and Leisure* (London: Pan).
Porritt, J. (1984), *Seeing Green: The Politics of Ecology Explained* (Oxford: Basil Blackwell).
Pym, D. (1980), 'Towards the dual economy and emancipation from employment', *Futures*, vol. 12, no. 3, June, pp. 223–37.
Pym, F. (1983), 'The revolution *laissez-faire* and socialism cannot handle', *Guardian*, 10 Oct.
Pym, F. (1984), *The Politics of Consent* (London: Sphere).
Rapoport, R. and Rapoport, R. N. (1975), *Leisure and the Family Life-cycle* (London: Routledge & Kegan Paul).
Richmond, T. (1972), 'Britain and the 4-day week: with profiles of some 4-day pioneers', in Poor (ed.), *op. cit.*, pp. 161–93.
Richmond, T. (1972a), 'Profiles of some Australian 4-Day pioneers', in Poor (ed.), *op. cit.*, pp. 194–201.
Riesman, D. (1958), 'Leisure and work in post-industrial society', reprinted in J. D. Douglas (ed.) (1971), *The Technological Threat* (Englewood Cliffs, NJ: Prentice-Hall), pp. 71–91.
Ritchie-Calder, Lord (1982), 'Education for the post-industrial society', in N. Costello and M. Richardson (eds), *Continuing Education for the Post-Industrial Society* (Milton Keynes: Open University Press), pp. 11–22.
Roberts, Keith (1982), *Automation, Unemployment and the Distribution of Income* (Maastrecht, Holland: European Centre for Work and Society).
Roberts, K. (1971), *Leisure* (London: Longman).
Roberts, K. (1978), *Contemporary Society and the Growth of Leisure* (London: Longman).
Roberts, K. (1981), 'Leisure and the future', *Leisure*, 2nd edn (London: Longman), pp. 90–111.
Roberts, K., Noble, M. and Duggan, J. (1982), 'Youth unemployment: an old problem or a new life-style?', *Leisure Studies*, vol. 1, no. 2, May, pp. 171–81.
Robertson, J. (1985), *Future Work* (Aldershot, Hants.: Gower).
Rojek, C. (1984), 'Did Marx have a theory of leisure?' *Leisure Studies*, vol. 3, no. 2, May, pp. 163–74.
Rose, M. (1985), *Re-working the Work Ethic* (London: Batsford).
Rose, R. (1983), *Getting By in Three Economies: The Resources of the Official, Unofficial and Domestic Economies* (Glasgow: Centre for the Study of Public Policy, University of Glasgow).
Rostow, W. W. (1960), *The Stages of Economic Growth* (London: Cambridge University Press).
Russell, B. (1935), *In Praise of Idleness and Other Essays* (London: Allen & Unwin).
Russell, B. and Russell, D. (1923), *The Prospects of Industrial Civilization* (London: Allen & Unwin).
Samuelson, P. (1973), 'Guaranteed income today: an idea whose time has come', in F. Best (ed.), *The Future of Work* (Englewood Cliffs, NJ: Prentice-Hall), pp. 128–31.

Scarman, Lord (1982), *The Scarman Report* (Harmondsworth, Middx.: Penguin).
Seabrook, J. (1982), *Unemployment* (London: Paladin).
Settle, J. G. (1977), *Leisure in the North West: A Tool for Forecasting*, Study No. 11 (London: Sports Council).
Shafer, E. L., Moeller, G. H. and Russell, E. G. (1975), 'Future leisure environments', *Ekistics*, vol. 40, no. 236, July, pp. 68–72.
Sinfield, A. (1981), *What Unemployment Means* (Oxford: Martin Robertson).
Smigel, E. O. (ed.) (1963), *Work and Leisure: A Contemporary Social Problem* (New Haven, Conn.: College and University Press).
Smith, P. (1975), 'Comments from a commercial standpoint', in *Off the Streets: Leisure Amenities and the Prevention of Crime* (London: National Association for the Care and Resettlement of Offenders), pp. 17–19.
Spiers, L. (1985), 'Leisure: The Fashion and Fad Business', *Leisure Management*, vol. 5, no. 10, Oct., p. 29.
Sports Council (1982), *Sport in the Community: The Next Ten Years* (London: Sports Council).
Stearns, P. N. (1975), 'Is there a post-industrial society?' in *Readings in Sociology 75/76* (with a reply by D. Bell). (Guildford, Ct: Annual Editions/Dushkin), pp. 251–9.
Stebbins, R. A. (1982), 'Serious leisure: a conceptual statement', *Pacific Sociological Review*, vol. 25, no. 2, April, pp. 251–72.
Stonier, T. (1980), 'Technological change and the future', in Cherry and Travis (eds), *op. cit.*, pp. 1.1–1.14.
Stonier, T. (1983), *The Wealth of Information: A Profile of the Post-Industrial Economy* (London: Thames Methuen).
Stynes, D. J. (1983), 'Time series and structural models for forecasting recreation participation', in Lieber and Fesenmaier (eds), *op. cit.*, pp. 105–19.
Suits, B. (1978), *The Grasshopper: Games, Life and Utopia* (Toronto: University of Toronto Press).
Szalai, A. (1976), 'The future of free time', *Futures*, vol. 8, no. 3, June, pp. 279–83.
Thatcher, M. (1983), Interview in *The Director*, Sept.
Theobald, R. (1973), 'Guaranteed income tomorrow: toward post-economic motivation', in F. Best (ed.), *The Future of Work* (Englewood Cliffs, NJ: Prentice-Hall), pp. 132–8.
Tod, I. and Wheeler, M. (1978), *Utopia* (London: Orbis Publishing).
Toffler, A. (1970), *Future Shock* (London: Pan).
Toffler, A. (1981), *The Third Wave* (London: Pan).
Toffler, A. (1984), *Previews and Promises* (London: Pan).
Tomlinson, A. and Whannel, G. (eds) (1984), *Five-Ring Circus: Money, Power and Politics at the Olympic Games* (London: Pluto).
Touraine, A. (1974), *The Post-Industrial Society* (London: Wildwood House).
Tourism and Recreation Research Unit (eds) (1982), *Work and Leisure: The Implications of Technological Change*, Leisure Studies Association Conference Reports (Edinburgh: TRRU, University of Edinburgh).
Townson, M. (1985), 'Redistribution of work: a fairer way to share', *World Leisure and Recreation*, vol. 27, no. 4, Aug., pp. 8–13.

Trades Union Congress (1982), *Working Time Action Checklist* (London: TUC).
Tyrell, R. (1982), 'Work, leisure and social change', in M. F. Collins (ed.), *Leisure Research: Current Findings and Future Challenge* (London: Leisure Studies Association/Sports Council/SSRC).
United States Department of the Interior (1979), *Third Nationwide Outdoor Recreation Plan*, 10 vols, Heritage Conservation and Recreation Service (Washington DC: US Government Printing Office).
Veal, A. J. (1975), *Recreation Planning in New Communities: A Review of British Experience*, Research Memo. 46, Centre for Urban and Regional Studies (Birmingham: University of Birmingham).
Veal, A. J. (1976), 'Monitoring and forecasting trends in recreation and leisure in Britain', in Haworth and Parker (eds), *op. cit.*, pp. 49–60.
Veal, A. J. (1979), *The Future of Leisure*, Report to the Social Science Research Council, Centre for Urban and Regional Studies, University of Birmingham.
Veal, A. J. (1979a), *New Swimming Pool for Old*, Study 18 (London: Sports Council).
Veal, A. J. (1980), 'The future of leisure', *International Journal of Tourism Management*, vol. 1, no. 1, March, pp. 42–55.
Veal, A. J. (1980a), *Trends in Leisure Participation and Problems of Forecasting: The State of the Art* (London: Sports Council/SSRC).
Veal, A. J. (1984), 'Leisure in England and Wales', *Leisure Studies*, vol. 3, no. 2, pp. 221–30.
Veal, A. J. (1987), *Using Sports Centres* (London: Sports Council).
Veal, A. J., Coalter, F. and Parker, S. (eds), (1982), *Work and Leisure: Unemployment, Technology and Lifestyles in the 1980s* (London: Leisure Studies Association).
Vickerman, R. W. (1980), 'The new leisure society – an economic analysis', *Futures*, vol. 12, no. 3, June, pp. 191–200.
Vonnegut, K. (1953), *Player Piano* (London: Macmillan).
Walker, P. (1983), 'The way ahead for a better life for all', *News of the World*, 19 Nov.
Walvin, J. (1978), *Leisure and Society 1830–1950* (London: Longman).
Weber, M. (1930), *The Protestant Ethic and the Spirit of Capitalism*, 1976 edn (London: Allen & Unwin).
Wells, H. G. (1905), *A Modern Utopia*, 1967 edn (Lincoln, NE: University of Nebraska Press).
Whitaker, R. A. and Rhodes, T. (1968), 'A quantitative analysis of alternative theatre locations', *Urban Studies*, vol. 5, no. 2, pp. 121–31.
Wolfenden, J. (1962), *Sport in the Community* (London: Central Council of Physical Recreation).
Yankelovich, D. (1979), 'Work, values and the New Breed', in C. Kerr and J. M. Rosow (eds), *Work in America: The Decade Ahead* (New York: Van Nostrand Reinhold), pp. 3–26.
Young, Lord (1985), 'School leavers lack motivation to work', *Guardian*, 26 Jan.
Young, Lord (1985a), *Pleasure, Leisure and Jobs: The Business of Tourism*, Cabinet Enterprise Unit (London: HMSO).

Young, M. and Willmott, P. (1973), *The Symmetrical Family: A Study of Work and Leisure in the London Region* (London: Routledge & Kegan Paul).

Zetterburg, H. and Frankel, G. (1981), 'Working less and enjoying it more in Sweden', *Public Opinion Quarterly* Aug./Sept., pp. 41–5.

Zuzanek, J. (1974), 'Society of leisure or the harried leisure class? Leisure trends in industrial societies', *Journal of Leisure Research*, vol. 6, no. 4, pp. 293–304.

Author Index

Adams, D. 38
Adams, R. M. 28–9
Adler, M. J. 25
Akerman, N. 141
Allen, R. 9
Ardill, J. 17
Aristotle 22, 23
Aronowitz, S. 26, 122
Asimov, I. 22, 41, 130
Aznar, G. 92

Bacon, A. W. 67, 72
Bailey, A. 130
Bailey, P. 66
Ball, C. 105
Balmer, K. 173–4
Banks, R. 112, 164, 172
Barron, I. 10
Basini, A. 77–8
Bati, A. 9
Baxter, M. J. 145, 146
Bechofer, F. 26, 67–8
Bell, D. 48–50, 129
Bellini, J. 52–3
Belous, R. S. 4, 110
Bendiner, R. 159
Berg, I. 70
Best, F. 4, 85, 102, 103, 177
Billingsley, J. 90
Borrett, N. 78
Bosserman, P. 4
Bourdieu, P. 83
Bradbury, R. 38
Bragard, J. 9
Bramham, P. 111
British Broadcasting Corporation 12–15, 76
British Travel Association 132
Broberg, M. 102
Brohm, M. 165
Brown, B. 134
Brown, T. L. 149–50
Brown, W,. 48, 61
Burton, T. L. 129, 130, 132, 145

Caplan, J. 58, 59

Central Statistics Office 131
Chai, D. A. 136
Chairmen's Policy Group 3, 77, 166–7
Chambers, D. 104
Cherry, E. G. 9, 173
Cicchetti, C. J. 149
Clarke, R. 9, 26, 64
Clawson, M. 145
Clayre, A. 67
Clemitson, I. 5, 9, 26, 64, 105, 119
Coalter, F. 9
Cole, S. 138
Commission for the European Communities 95
Cooper, C. L. 95
Coppock, J. T. 133, 146, 151
Corley, J. 3, 20
Countryside Commission 146
Crosland, C. A. R. 118
Curnow, R. 10

Davidson, J. M. 146
De Grazia, S. 24
De Vink, G. 68
Department of Employment 95
Department of Environment 98, 118
Douglas, M. 160
Dower, M. 126, 173
Drakeford, M. 105
Dubin, R. 26, 67
Duffield, B. S. 69, 133, 146, 151
Duggan, J. 74
Dumazedier, J. 140

Ecology Party 1, 58, 105, 116–17
Economist Intelligence Unit 156
Edwards, A. 156
Encel, S. 129
Engels, F. 42
Entwistle, H. 78, 83–4

Faché, W. 103
Fankel, G. 71
Faunce, W. A. 93, 133
Ferkiss, V. 48, 52, 54, 57
Ferriss, A. L. 149

Forester, T. 10, 70
Friedman, M. & R. 107, 160
Frith, S. 98

Galbraith, J. K. 57–8, 66, 76, 159
Gappert, G. 54
Gershuny, J. I. 33, 55, 59, 138
Gill, I. 172
Glasser, R. 26, 159
Glyptis, S. 9
Gold, J. R. 32
Gold, S. M. 145
Goldring, P. 92
Goldthorpe, J. H. 26, 67–8
Goodale, T. 173
Goodman, P. 33
Gorz, A. 26, 42, 65, 68, 93, 105, 120–2
Goyder, C. 101
Granada Television 105
Grant, A. R. 162
Gratton, C. 145, 165
Gray, D. E. 173
Great Britain 107
Greben, S. 173
Gregory, S. 178
Griffiths, J. 38–9

Hamilton, W. D. 166
Handy, C. 9, 85, 105
Hantrais, L. 89, 111
Haworth, J. T. 67
Haworth, L. 58
Hayter, D. 27, 119
Hedges, B. 133
Hendry, L. 99
Henley Centre for Forecasting 19, 20, 156
Henry, A. 111
Henry, I. 111
Hollands, R. 100
Howard, E. 31
Howell, D. 78, 120
Huston, D. L. 149–50
Huxley, A. 39–40

Illich, I. 58, 59
Incomes Data Services 90
Institute of Contemporary Arts 34
Isherwood, B. 160

Jenkins, C. 9, 64, 89, 109, 119
Jennings, L. 130
Joad, C. E. M. 35–6

Jones, B. 9, 85, 105
Jordan, B. 105

Kahn, H. 48, 61
Kateb, C. 34–5
Kaynak, E. 136
Kelvin, P. 69, 73
Kew, S. 173
Keynes, J. M. 43–4
Kinser, J. 78
Knetsch, J. L. 145
Knott, W. 136
Kumar, K. 53–5

Lacey, I. 126
Large, P. 10
Lasch, C. 48, 50
Laurie, P. 10
Le Corbusier 32
Leigh, J. 79
Leisure Consultants 19
Levitan, S. A. 4, 110
Linder, S. B. 7
Lockwood, D. 26, 67–8
Long, J. 97

Macaulay, J. A. 136
Maccoby, M. 71
MacIntyre, A. C. 78
Marstrand, P. K. 129
Martel, L. 48, 61
Martin, W. H. 2, 9, 64, 139–40, 155
Marx, K. 22, 42
Mason, S. 2, 9, 64, 139–40, 155
Matrix Corporate Affairs Consultants Ltd 136
Maw, R. 93
McCalla, J. 137
McGoldrick, A. 95
McKnight, J. 58, 59
Melching, M. 102
Mercer, D. 1, 16
Merritt, G. 9
Miles, I. 138
Milstein, D. N. 146
Minc, A. 10
Moeller, G. H. 135, 136
More, T. 22, 28–9
Morrell, J. 3, 19, 112
Morris, W. 31
Murray, L. 120
Myerscough, J. 4

Naisbitt, J. 10, 141

AUTHOR INDEX

New Society 90
Newsom, J. 77
Ng, D. 136
Noble, M. 74
Noelle-Neumann, E. 71, 141
Nora, S. 10
North West Sports Council 132, 151
Northern Regional Planning Committee 150
Nossiter, B. D. 70

Office of Population Census and Surveys 18
Olmsted, B. 90
ORRRC – *see* Outdoor Recreation Resources Review Commission
Orwell, G. 39, 53
Orzack, L. H. 67
Outdoor Recreation Resources Review Commission 125, 131, 156
Owen, D. 99, 107, 116
Owen, M. L. 151
Owen, R. 30

Page, W. 129
Pahl, R. 59
Palm, G. 31
Parker, H. 105–6
Parker, S. 9, 67, 69, 97
Penty, A. J. 48
Peterson, A. D. C. 79
Pieper, J. 25
Polytechnic of North London 171
Poor, R. 105
Porritt, J. 1, 116
Pym, D. 58, 64
Pym, F. 115

Rapoport, R. 69, 173, 179
Raymond, M. 99
Reid, L. M. 146
Rhodes, T. 146
Richmond, T. 105
Riesman, D. 48
Ritchie-Calder, Lord 65
Roberts, Keith 105, 107, 108
Roberts, Kenneth 1, 74, 104
Robertson, J. 10, 59
Rodgers, G. 5, 9, 26, 64, 105, 119
Rojek, C. 42, 120
Rose, M. 54, 69
Rose, R. 59
Rostow, W. W. 47–8
Russell, B. 44

Russell, D. 44
Russell, E. 135
Ruthven, P. K. 16

Samuelson, P. 105
Scarman, Lord 98
Science Policy Research Unit 138
Seabrook, J. 72
Settle, J. G. 149, 151
Shafer, E. L. 135, 136
Shaiken, H. 58, 59
Sherman, B. 9, 64, 89, 109, 119
Sienkiewicz, J. 146
Sinfield, A. 72
Smigel, E. O. 67
Smith, M. 67
Smith, P. 171
Spiers, L. 172
Sports Council 153, 167
Stearns, P. N. 52, 53
Stebbins, R. A. 60
Stern, B. 4
Stewart, C. 99
Stonier, T. 9, 10, 50, 55, 99, 107, 109
Strelitz, Z. 173
Stynes, D. J. 132
Suits, B. 36

Taylor, D. 26, 67–8
Taylor, Peter 145
Terzi, K. A. 71
Thatcher, M. 6, 112
Tod, I. 27–32
Toffler, A. 37, 46–7, 54, 60, 107
Tomlinson, A. 165
Touraine, A. 48, 51
Tourism and Recreation Research Unit 9
Townson, M. 85
Trades Union Congress 17, 90
Travis, A. S. 9
Tyrell R. 156

United States Department of the Interior 168–9
University of Keele 132

Veale, A. J. ix, 9, 18, 32, 129, 132, 142, 144, 145, 148, 151–4, 170
Vonnegut, K. 38

Walker, P. 114
Walvin, J. 66
Weber, M. 65–6
Wells, H. G. 37–8

Whannell, G. 165
Wheeler, M. 27–32
Whitaker, R. A. 146
Wiener, A. J. 48
Witkins, B. T. 149
Willmott, P. 2, 151–3
Wimbush, E. 97
Wolfenden, J. 80

Yankelovich, D. 71
Young, Lord 76, 83, 112–13, 162, 164, 165
Young, M. 2, 151–3

Zetterburg, H. 71
Zola, I. 58, 59
Zuzanek 4

Subject Index

Action Sport 173
Adult Education 83
Advertising 158–60
Affluence 50
Affluent society 57
Affluent worker 67
Age and leisure demand 147
Age-structure of population 127
Agricultural production 55, 60
Alaska 108
Alcoholic drink 19, 24, 161, 164
Animateurs 174–5
Arendt, H. 35
Aristotelian view 23–4
Arts 24, 36, 61, 111, 164, 166
Arts Council 118, 166, 174
Athens without slaves 23, 114, 123
Australia 9, 16, 105

Basic income payment 105
Belgium
   time management 103
Beveridge Report 120
Billingsgate 104
Birmingham 125, 175
Birth rate 126
Black economy 59
Blackpool Pleasure Beach 162
Bradford football ground 163
Brave New World 39–41
Bristol 175
British sickness 70
British Tourist Authority 113
Brixton 98
Brzezinski, Z. 46

Cabinet Office Enterprise Unit 112
Calvin 26
Campanella 29
Canada 137
Capitalism 42, 62, 66
Career ethic 71
Carnival 33, 38
Car-ownership effect 125–7, 147
Catchment areas 145
Central life interest 67–9

Centrifugal Bubble-puppy 39–40
Children's play 111, 157
Cinema attendance 131
City decay 50
City of the Sun 29
Class
   and education 100
   idle 29
   leisure 53, 97
   New 58
   ruling 51
   structure 50
   struggle 52, 67
Classical view 23–4
Clawson method 145
Cockayne, Land of 27
Commercial provision 112, 158–62, 171
Commodification 157
Communes 122
Communist society 120
Communities 33, 80
Community arts 174
Community design 30
Comparative method 140
Composite method 155–6
Computers 135, 158
Confined activities 142, 148
Conscription 100
Conservative Party 113–15
Consumer
   expenditure 20
   sovereignty 158
Consumption maximum 7
Contemplation 24, 35–6, 38
Contribution ethic 64
Corby 112
Countryside Commission 118, 125, 173
Countryside Management 173
Craft ethic 71
Credit-based economy 50
Critical faculties 81–2
Cross-sectional analysis 146–54
Cultural capital 83
Curriculum 73–4, 78, 82

Daily Mirror 112

Delphi technique 134–6
Disneyland 112, 162
Distance decay 144
Domestic work 59, 94, 178
Douglas, Major C. H. 105
'Dries' 113
Drug abuse 163
Dual economy 58, 64
Dystopia 37

Ecology Party 117
Economic futurists 42
    growth 3–5, 6, 51, 139–40
    history, stages of 47
    output 56
    power 51, 53
    problem 43–4
Economist Intelligence Unit 156
Eden, Garden of 27
Education 51, 56, 97, 99, 102, 114, 178
    and the work ethic 73
    higher 100
    for leisure 24, 73, 77–84, 120
EEC 177
Elora Prescription 173–4
Employment
    elite 38, 49, 53
    leisure industry 19, 20, 21
    manufacturing 11
    sectors 10, 60
    service 11
English Tourist Board 112
Entrepreneurial ethic 71
Equality of opportunity 82
European Centre for Work and Society 108

Fabian Society 118
Family 77, 93, 104, 166
    life 122, 178–9
Flexible life-scheduling 103, 177
Forecasting techniques 129–56
Formal economy 116
Four days, forty hours 105
Fourier 30
Fourth wave 126
France 111, 118, 123, 179
Free choice
    in education 78–9
    in leisure 24, 79–80, 115, 158
Free Time, Ministry of 111
Freedom 24, 42, 115, 118, 121
Fun 41, 60
Future Shock 47, 141

Futures 11
Futures industry 45

Gambling 24, 28–9, 41, 164
Games 28, 36, 39, 40, 61
Garden cities 31–2
General Household Survey 18, 19, 129, 151
German workers' attitudes 121
Germany 71, 123, 141, 171
Gravity mode 145
Green perspective 7, 123, 139
Grey Panthers 95
Guaranteed income 59, 105

Hallucinogenic drugs 40
Heritage, Conservation and Recreation Service 126, 149
Hiking 41
Holidays 86–7, 89, 102, 111, 113, 157, 176
Holland 68
Home and family 68–9, 75, 77, 93
Howell, Denis 78, 120

Ideal communities 26
Identity 26, 159
Income
    average 109
    level 70
Industrial Training Board 101
Industrialization 53–4, 72, 176
Informal economy 59, 62, 116, 178
Information economy 49–50, 55, 99, 114

Japan 76, 87
Job-sharing 90–1
Joint-use 174

Keynes 117, 176
Kinnock, Neil 118, 119
Knowledge
    and post-industrial society 48–9, 51, 57
    and Utopia 36
    society 55–6

Labour movement and leisure 119
Labour Party 118
Law and leisure control 163
    and working hours 5
Le Corbusier, C. 32
Left and leisure 118
Leisure
    activity 17–19, 24, 28

SUBJECT INDEX

commercial 129, 158–62
control of 27, 163
demand 127–8, 142, 145, 167
employment 2, 19–21, 128
ethic 64
excessive 40
expenditure 2, 6, 19–20, 128
exploitation of 27, 164
and the family 19, 77, 93
industry 19–21
jobs 112
managers 174–5
markets 156, 158
measures of 128
needs 159, 161, 167
in the North West, survey 132
participation 2, 18, 128
policy 9, 166
professionals 158, 172
pure 23–4, 94
residual definition 16
services 117, 165, 169–74
skills 83, 174–5
as social service 118, 166
society 1, 28, 34, 44, 58, 60–1, 83, 116, 123
and socio-economic characteristics 147
Studies Association 9
time 1–2, 12–17, 93, 128
time-work-time trade-off 4, 86, 117
trips 143
Letchworth 31
Liberty 42
Libraries 80, 171
Licensing 67, 112, 163–4
Life
  ethic 64
  purpose 44
  time 12–15
Liverpool 98
Local government 166, 167, 169–70
London 98, 105, 151

MacDonalds 111
Manpower Services Commission 97, 112
Market
  opportunities 158
  segmentation 80, 174
Marx, K. 31, 71, 75, 120
Marxism 26, 52
Materialism 7
Matrix Corporation 136
Measuring leisure 128
Megatrends 11, 141

Micro-electronic technology 11, 86
Minister of Free Time 111
Minister for Sport and Recreation 120
Ministry of Youth, Sport and Free Time 111
Mitterrand, President 111, 118, 123
Modern movement 32
Moon parks 135
Moonlighting 75, 89–90, 93
Morality 26, 28–9
Morris, W. 117
Mosaic Law and Sabbaticals 101
Multiple regression 148
Music 24, 28

National Dividend 105
National Income Scheme 105
National Income/Tax Credit Scheme 105, 116
National Parks 126, 131, 145
National Parks Commission 118
Needs 50, 109, 158, 160–1
Negative income-tax 106–7
Neo-colonialism, in post-industrial society 51
New Class 58
Newton's Law of Gravity 145
New town blues 32
New Towns 31–4
Non-work ethic 64–5

Occupation and leisure participation 147
OECD 177
Olympic Games 37, 165
Ontario 137
Open University 102, 178
ORRRC
  see Outdoor Recreation Resources Review Commission
Outdoor Recreation Resources Review Commission 125, 149, 168
Overtime 75, 89, 90
Own work 59, 178

Part-time work 91–3
Peace Corps 100
Pensions 96, 102
Personal service society 55
Phalanx 30
Pilot National Recreation Survey 132–3
Planet earth 6
Planning 30, 32
Play 23, 34, 36
Policy Studies Institute 90

Political
  power 57
  process 62
Politics 35
Population growth 125–6
Post
  affluent society 55
  bourgeois society 54
  civilised society 54
  economic society 54
  fabricative society 54
  industrial proletariat 122
  industrial society 46–62, 70
  modern society 54
  scarcity society 54
  service society 54
Poverty 5, 50, 66, 109, 166
Poverty trap 107
Private enterprise 112, 113, 172
Privatization 113, 172
Problem solving 52
Product life-cycle 155
Productivity 4, 42, 58, 86–7, 101, 115
Professions 48, 49, 58, 166, 175
Programmed society 51
Protestant work ethic – *see* Work ethic
Pro-suming 60
Public expenditure 166
Public sector provision 19
Pubs 67, 80, 104, 157, 163–4, 171
Puritanism 65

Quangos 166, 167
Quantitative Forecasting 127
Quaternary Sector 60–1

Rand Corporation 134
Reagan, President 123
Recreational submarines 135
Religion 25–6, 61, 65, 66, 159
Resourcefulness ethic 64
Resources 6
Respondent assessment 132
Retirement 2, 86–7, 92, 94–7, 102, 120, 135, 177
Ritual 61

Sabbaticals 86–7, 100–3
Saint Monday 67
Scenario writing 136–40
School-leaving age 86–7, 120
Science fiction 37–41
Science Policy Research Unit 138
Scientific-technological revolution 46

Scotland 133
Self
  determined activity 121, 124
  development ethic 71
  service economy 33, 55, 58–60, 178
  sufficiency 7, 34
Serious leisure 60
Service class society 55
Service industry 48–50, 54, 55
Sexual activity 36, 40
Shift-working 103–4
Silkin, S. 31
SIRSEE – *see* Study of Informal Recreation in South East England
Social
  attitudes 75, 140
  control 66, 98
  credit 105
  Democratic Party 115–16
  dividend 105
  income 105
  security 105, 109
  unrest 98
  wage 30, 105–10
Socialism 114, 118
Socially useful labour 121
Space 38, 47, 52
Spatial models 142–6
Sport
  centres 157
  in the Community 167
  participation 18, 165, 167
  political considerations 111
  subsidies 24
  superstars 36
Sports Council 29, 125, 166–8, 173
Stadia 162, 163
Stonierism 114
Structural model 132
Student movement 51
Study of Informal Recreation in South East England 146
Subsidy 24, 165
Subsistence economy 33, 59, 60
Super-industrial society 37, 47
Supply of facilities 148
Sweden 71, 100, 141
Swedish workers 121
Swimming forecasts 105, 150
Switzerland 100
System break 54

Target groups 167
Tax credit 107

SUBJECT INDEX

Taxation 5, 24
Technetronic Age 46
Technological elite 38
Technology 39, 48–9, 50, 86, 89, 108, 117
Television 41, 56, 162
Thatcher, M. 107, 113
Theme Parks 162
Three-day week 88, 104
Time
  see Leisure-time, work-time
  blocks 16, 93
  management 103
Tories 113
Tourism 61, 102, 112, 164–5
  and the economy 113
  employment 112
  and Recreation Research Unit 133
  and the U.S.A. 113, 162
Tourist Boards 118, 125
Town and Country Planning Association 34
Training 101, 169, 174
Trans-national economy 50
Trend extrapolation 130

Unconfined activities 142, 148
Underemployment 58
Underwater
  recreation 41
  resorts 135
Unemployment 7, 9, 23, 65, 72, 76, 85, 87, 96, 107, 113, 115, 119, 123, 177
  and youth 74, 76, 98, 99
Utopia 27–41, 44, 46, 52–3, 58

Value Added Tax 108, 164
Values 6, 63
  in education 79, 81
Victorian values 76
Video-recorders 160–1
Visit rates 144

War 9, 35, 47, 52, 53, 67
Wealth 42
  creation 117
  of Nations 55
  of Information 55
Weber, M. 26
Welwyn Garden City 31
West Midlands 98
'Wets' 111
White Paper, *Sport and Recreation* 98, 118
Wimpys 111
Wolfenden Gap 80
Women and Leisure 2, 14–16, 23, 178
Work
  abolition of 120–1
  attitudes towards 75, 89
  based culture 72
  centrality 66–73
  compensation 83
  distribution of 75
  ethic 16, 25–6, 30, 63–77, 119, 177
  Dutch Association against 68
  force structure 10, 54
  instrumentality 67
  leisure relationships 43, 67–9, 86, 116
  preparation for 83
  time 8, 12–16, 33, 122
  voluntary 124
  and youth 74, 76
Working
  class 1, 119–20, 171
  hours 4–5, 8, 17, 28–9, 35, 40, 42, 44, 77, 85–7, 103, 110, 115, 118
  lifetime 77, 94, 115, 176
  week 86–90, 115, 135, 176
  year 89
World Cup 37
Worship 25

Youth 76, 83, 97
  training schemes 98, 99
  culture 99

For Product Safety Concerns and Information please contact our EU representative GPSR@taylorandfrancis.com
Taylor & Francis Verlag GmbH, Kaufingerstraße 24, 80331 München, Germany

www.ingramcontent.com/pod-product-compliance
Lightning Source LLC
Chambersburg PA
CBHW052116300426
44116CB00010B/1684